West Virginia Baseball

West Virginia Baseball

A History, 1865–2000

WILLIAM E. AKIN

McFarland & Company, Inc., Publishers
Jefferson, North Carolina, and London

LIBRARY OF CONGRESS CATALOGUING-IN-PUBLICATION DATA

Akin, William E.
　West Virginia baseball : a history, 1865–2000 / William E. Akin.
　　p.　　cm.
　Includes bibliographical references and index.

　ISBN-13: 978-0-7864-2570-9
　ISBN-10: 0-7864-2570-9 (softcover : 50# alkaline paper) ∞

　1. Baseball—West Virginia—History.　I. Title.
GV863.W47A35　　2006
796.35709754—dc22　　　　　　　　　　　　　　　　2006014355

British Library cataloguing data are available

©2006 William E. Akin. All rights reserved

No part of this book may be reproduced or transmitted in any form or by any means, electronic or mechanical, including photocopying or recording, or by any information storage and retrieval system, without permission in writing from the publisher.

Cover photograph: The Wheeling Nailers playing Kalamazoo, May 19, 1887 (Brown Collection, Ohio County Public Library).

Manufactured in the United States of America

McFarland & Company, Inc., Publishers
　Box 611, Jefferson, North Carolina 28640
　　www.mcfarlandpub.com

For Libby

Contents

Acknowledgments   ix
Introduction   1

1 — "A Social Game of Ball"
Statehood and Base Ball, 1865–1873   5

2 — "Wheeling's a Swell Town to Play In"
The Emergence of Professional Baseball, 1874–1895   22

3 — "A Progressive Community Must Have a Base Ball Team"
Baseball's Second Boom, 1895–1905   40

4 — "No Better Advertisement Than a Good Baseball Team"
North Central West Virginia in the Deadball Era, 1905–1920   57

5 — "Oh, Summer in Kanawha"
River Towns in the Deadball Era, 1905–1920   73

6 — "The City Is Baseball Crazy"
The Martinsburg Dynasty, 1914–1934   90

7 — "Baseball Was the Miners' Sport"
Coalfield Baseball, 1920–1941   108

8 — "Hit the Ball and Run Like Hell"
The Middle Atlantic League, 1925–1942   124

9 — "Dark and Dusty"
The Mountain State League, 1937–1942   140

10 — "Ain't Nobody Got Time for Nothing No More"
   The Post-War Years, 1945–1955   156

11 — "Folks Don't Seem to Like Baseball Like They Used To"
   The Nadir, 1955–1985   173

12 — "There's Nothing Like Baseball to Keep Your Mind Off
   Your Troubles"
   A Minor Miracle, 1985–2000   190

Notes   203
Bibliography   215
Index   221

Acknowledgments

Growing up in Alabama, I lacked a father around to do all the father-son things that most boys experienced. I did, however, have two marvelous uncles who tried to teach me to fish, hunt, swim, and ride a bike. These things did not really excite me, but when I was ten, the uncles gave me the gift of baseball. Uncle Ernest, a mathematics professor at Auburn University, took me to see the Opelika Owls (so named because they played at night) of the long-forgotten Class D Georgia-Alabama League. Uncle Davis (like Oprah, he just had one name), who worked at the coal mines north of Birmingham, took me to see the semi-pro Gorgas Mines team in action. It did not bother me that both teams played on dirt infields or that they were at the very bottom of the baseball world. I had been introduced to baseball and I was hooked forever. My uncles would be pleased to know their concern for my education eventually led to this book.

In West Virginia I discovered a new world of baseball. My octogenarian mother-in-law, Bonnie Jane Teter, remembers teams like Reppert Coal and players named Shorty Bowen and Lefty Hutchinson. I thank her for sharing her memories. On my own I discovered Sheriff Blake, Piano Legs Hickman, Muscle Shoals, and hundreds of other players, leagues, and teams.

Wherever I went, I found library staffs willing to help me in my research. None can top the efficiency of David Mill and Joan Rhodes of the Myrin Library at Ursinus College. The National Baseball Hall of Fame Library is a must stop for any baseball research. The Society for American Baseball Research (SABR) Lending Library provided me with valuable publications. The West Virginia Regional History Collection at the Charles C. Wise, Jr., Library at West Virginia University was indispensable. I wish, also, to acknowledge the following libraries: the West Virginia Archives and History Library in Charleston, Benedum Library of Salem International University,

Acknowledgments

Fairmont State University Library, Robert C. Byrd Library of Mountain State University, Clarksburg Public Library, Craft Memorial Library in Bluefield, McDowell County Public Library in Welch, Logan Area Public Library, Williamson Public Library, Raleigh County Public Library in Beckley, Berkeley County Library of Martinsburg, and the Washington County Free Library in Hagerstown, Maryland. In addition, I owe special thanks to Stuart McGhee, curator of the Eastern Regional Coal Archives, who extended himself on my behalf. I thank, also, Doug Huff, who knows more about high school sports than anyone.

Without my wife, Elizabeth Teter Akin, this book would never have been done. I celebrate life with her. Not only did she introduce me to West Virginia, she led me beyond the stereotypes of the state and its people. On a more mundane level, Libby possesses computer and editorial skills that have been of immeasurable value in this project. Finally, my children and grandchildren inspire me in ways they will never know.

Introduction

A decade ago Stefan Fatsis found in the small cities of the independent Northern League a throwback to pre-modern baseball. In those cities "communities rally around something as innocent and traditional as a baseball team." The fans understood "the word *baseball* doesn't mean only 'Major League baseball.'" There, he found, "baseball can still be fun."[1]

In these days when major league baseball is characterized by astronomical salaries, strikes, lockouts, steroids, luxury boxes, outrageous prices, and boorish behavior, the images Fatsis presents are intoxicating visions. In the baseball world below the majors we are apt to see, or imagine we see, simpler times when fathers played catch with sons, kids ran off to the sandlot to play, and the worries of the world seemed far away. I found, or thought I found, such places in the tiny ballparks of Bluefield, Princeton, Huntington, and Charleston, West Virginia.

This romantic image of baseball was one starting point for this history. West Virginia was the other. Until I married a woman from West Virginia, I subscribed to the established stereotypes of the state. I imagined its people consisted of coal miners mired in poverty and ignorance and suffering from consumption, or crazed mountain men killing each other in age-old family feuds, all of them ill-fed, ill-clothed, ill-housed, and ill-mannered. The Mountain State has long been seen as a poor, backward and dangerous place. An alternative stereotype came to overlay the first. As tourism replaced coal as the state's leading industry, it became fashionable to focus on the state's natural beauty and to describe West Virginia as a kind of American Switzerland; John Denver's "Take Me Home, Country Roads" became the state's unofficial anthem.

The problem with these images of baseball and of West Virginia is that they are wrong. I came to understand West Virginia as a land of complexities and paradoxes, a multi-varied state where stereotypes or easy generalizations appear trivial. Similarly, in the Mountain State the sentimental image of baseball as "innocent and traditional" bears no more relationship to reality than the Hatfield and McCoys do to the day-to-day reality of West Virginia. In recent years, the movies have given minor league ball a romantic quality. That should not obscure the fact that from baseball's beginnings in the Mountain State the game was associated with modernism, up-to-date mainstream American culture.

Baseball's development in West Virginia mirrors the process by which baseball became truly the National Game. In the second half of the nineteenth century, baseball reflected the cultural isolation of the state and then the region's gradual loss of its pre-industrial past. In the post–Civil War years, the game followed the railroads as they opened up the northern third of the new state to ideas and cultural forms of the Eastern Seaboard. Baseball's early promoters saw in the game the salvation of America's physical and spiritual well-being.

As coal, black diamonds as the publicists called it, and railroads brought the central and then southern coalfields into existence, baseball functioned as a symbol of the Americanization of West Virginia. By the turn of the century every crossroads, hamlet, town and city wanted a ball team. Progressive era modernizers in the first decades of the twentieth century believed that baseball would put their town's name on the national map and generate untold riches and civic pride among its citizenry. As the state gave up its folkways and, however grudgingly, adopted the cultural forms of modern America, baseball represented one of the most visible forms of modernity.

In the first half of the twentieth century, baseball also provided a powerful bond for creating a sense of community. Town, company, and professional teams provided a rallying point that cut across class, ethnic, and, sometimes, race and gender lines. Baseball gave people a feeling of belonging to something in common. At no time was this truer than in the hardscrabble economic times between the two world wars. In no place was it as true as in the isolated coal camps of southern West Virginia. Baseball not only distracted people from the economic realities; it also fostered a sense of community, optimism and pride.

In the years following World War II, the bonds of community broke apart in the coalfields and throughout the state. West Virginia experienced the end of industrialization long before the rest of the country. The strains of de-industrialization created an enormous migration out of the state as people searched for new jobs. For those who stayed, the poverty that shocked John F. Kennedy in 1960 was a reality of life. The economic realities also generated powerful internalized fear, self-hatred, and a need to escape. Baseball could hardly be expected to hold communities together in the face of all this. Towns, companies, and cities devoid of dynamism could no longer sustain baseball. The game lost much of its appeal both for boys who once played it, and for adults who were its spectators. Baseball was then left to the professional marketers. Professional teams able to offer value for the entertainment dollar survived and even prospered. Baseball in the larger sense lacked an overarching mythology to justify its special status as the National Game.

West Virginia has produced well over a hundred major league players. Few states have produced a higher ratio of major leaguers relative to their populations. Several hundred more big leaguers played in the state before or after their playing days in the majors. It is not my intention to chronicle the careers of either group. The state has also had hundreds of teams and leagues. These all had pennant races, mini-dynasties, outstanding players, and whimsy. I have attempted to capture as much of those as possible, but to do so in the context of a social history of baseball in the state.

One regret is that I do not do justice to the history of African-American baseball in the state. As I try to show, there were numerous black semipro teams throughout West Virginia, and black professional teams regularly barnstormed through the region. I have only been able to mine the surface of that history. I hope someone else will be able to dig more deeply into the memories and archives that surely are there.

Not surprisingly, little has been published about baseball in West Virginia. Until the past decade, not much had been written about baseball below the major league level. This is beginning to change. In the 1990s a number of excellent accounts chronicled the history of individual minor and independent leagues. More recently, we have seen a trickle of books on baseball in cities and states. Peter Morris' scholarly work on early baseball in Michigan is a model for such studies.[2] They begin to shed new light on the development of baseball at the local level. This history focuses on community, or more specifically, the interaction and interrelationship between baseball and the larger economic and cultural changes that have taken place since the Civil War.

1

"A Social Game of Ball"

Statehood and Base Ball, 1865–1873

On a hazy August afternoon in 1866 Jacob Hornbrook took his place next to "home base" on a baseball field he and fellow members of the Hunkidori Base Ball Club had recently laid out on the Wheeling Island commons. He signaled whether he wanted the pitch high or low. When the pitcher for the Union Club of Washington, Pennsylvania, delivered the first pitch, Hornbrook became the first West Virginian to bat in a "match game of Base Ball."[1]

Similar scenes repeated themselves in various parts of West Virginia in the years immediately following the Civil War as the newly created state caught the "base ball" fever that was sweeping much of the country. Young men from the same social stratum as Hornbrook, who would soon become a director of the First National Bank of Wheeling and of the West Virginia Insurance Company, took time off from their budding careers to participate in "a social game of ball." Coming from respectable, well-to-do families, they had every reason to be confident of their future in the post-bellum world. They were proudly conscious of the fact that by playing base ball (as they spelled it at the time), they were engaging in an activity that young men of like background and social standing in Baltimore, Washington, and New York were calling "The National Game."

Baseball historians reject the popular image of baseball's origins as a rural, pastoral, folk sport, and, instead have documented its foundation in the urban industrial cities that were transforming America from a rural, agrarian society to an industrial economy and a mass culture. Baseball had evolved into its modern form as a New York City game in the fifteen years before the Civil War. It spread from there to other northern cities, long before rural areas took up the game. The requirements of modern, as opposed to folk, sports required a social complex, which existed only in urban areas. As modern sports emerged in the third quarter of the nineteenth century they were characterized by standardized rules formulated by a national organization. Participants organized into competitive teams, with increasing numbers of spectators. This required a critical population mass, leisure time for recreation, a social ethos that encouraged recreation, and a mass communication network.[2] These prerequisites did not exist outside cities.

Baseball's early years in West Virginia conformed to the national pattern in important ways. In the more populated region of the state north of the Baltimore and Ohio Railroad's western line from Harpers Ferry on the Potomac River to Parkersburg on the Ohio River, baseball became widely played by 1868. In the north-central and northern panhandle regions—areas with cultural ties to Pittsburgh as well as to Baltimore and Washington—baseball tended to become democratized. There it moved beyond the control of the well-to-do young men and became a broad-based participation sport. In Wheeling, the state capital and West Virginia's only large city, baseball by 1868 expanded into a spectator sport with the trappings of a commercial enterprise. South of the Baltimore and Ohio line, however, baseball failed to penetrate the isolated and rural areas in the mid-state and southern regions. There boys continued to play folk games with bats and balls, but the national pastime would not be played in an organized fashion for another generation.

In other ways Mountain State baseball differed from the national pattern. After its birth and sudden growth immediately following the end of Civil War hostilities, baseball fell from popularity almost as fast as it had grown. By the early 1870s a traveler would have been hard pressed to find the National Game played anywhere in the state. Of course the game was not dead. It would return and by the end of the seventies a professional team would come into existence.

West Virginians possibly gained their first knowledge of baseball from Ohio troops stationed in the state during the Civil War. Baseball historians disagree about the impact of the war on the sport. William J. Ryczek maintains the cultural exchange of the war years spread knowledge of the game as soldiers introduced the sport to comrades and enemies alike. Soldier-players carried not only knowledge of the game's rules home from the war, but its patriotic aura as well. Recently, historian Peter Morris has challenged this view, noting that few of Michigan's post-war players were veterans. It is clear that in the northeast baseball was being called "The National Game" even before fighting broke out. At the end of the Civil War, *The Book of*

American Pastimes recorded the belief that "the game of Base Ball has now become beyond question the leading feature of outdoor sports in the United States."[3]

At the end of the war, baseball existed side by side with an older bat and ball game known as "towne ball," a genuine folk game perpetuated through oral tradition. Historians have often identified towne ball as a boy's game, but, in fact, it was an intergenerational game. Boys, young men, and old played in unorganized fashion whenever and wherever enough interested people gathered. The number of players depended on how many people wanted to play and might range from a half dozen to dozens on a side. The lack of uniform written rules permitted a wide variety of form and often generated considerable dispute. The common element in town ball games was the method of putting a player "out" by "plunking" him with a thrown ball. This led to a rough and tumble quality to the game that usually restricted participants to working class men and their sons. Boys in West Virginia certainly played towne ball and were often joined on Sundays by young men, much to the consternation of churchgoing members of the community.[4]

In the summer following Confederate General Robert E. Lee's surrender, teams appeared in the state's new capital city of Wheeling. These clubs proved short-lived and none of them actually managed to play a game. In the city's Second Ward, teenagers organized a club they named, appropriately, "Young America." After a few weeks of practicing two afternoons a week, they considered themselves ready for a game and published an open challenge for an opponent. After receiving no takers, they soon lost interest themselves and disbanded without ever playing a formal game.[5]

Young men of the city, apparently thinking the boys had a good idea, rather belatedly formed two clubs of their own. The Star Base Ball Club and the Anchor Base Ball Club both came into existence in early November 1865. Although it now seems impossibly late in the year to be playing baseball, they practiced daily until early December. Members of the Star Club took the enterprise more seriously than their Anchor counterparts. They played several intra-club practice games on the Wheeling Island Green and were anxious for a real game against the Anchor club.[6] Their counterparts, however, delayed answering the challenge until cold winter weather forced them all from the field.

The appearance of teenagers and young men playing in such organized fashion in the summer and fall of 1865 caught the attention of opinion makers of Wheeling. As the summer of 1866 approached, the *Wheeling Register* began to boost the game. In encouraging its readers to take up the sport, the paper argued that baseball had a broad social utility. According to the paper, the country's physical well being hinged on baseball's acceptability. After lamenting that "the physique of Americans had long been a vulnerable point for the satirizing criticism of foreigners who delight to decant upon the physical weakness of our race," and admitting "that hitherto we have justly merited the palpable hits which have been bestowed upon us by our outdoor sport loving cousins of England," the paper offered hope for the future. Baseball would be the answer. The game provided a means of involving city residents in healthful open-air recreation. Baseball, the paper opined, "bids fair to remove the just cause of censure."[7]

Grown men now had a justification for their play and a defense against the charge of frivolity. Whether in response to the newspaper's urging or not, many of Wheeling's best and brightest young men took up the game in the summer of 1866.

The most enthusiastic group of young men formed the Hunkidori Base Ball Club and began playing in mid-summer of 1866. Civil War veteran James M. Ewing, Jr., organized the club. A marginal player, even compared to the neophytes of the period, Ewing possessed enormous enthusiasm and an abiding interest in baseball. Ewing served as the club president with friends William G. Batelle and Clarence Irwin as vice-president and secretary.[8]

Hunkidori Club members had deep roots in the local community and would establish themselves as pillars of Wheeling society. They ranged in age from eighteen to thirty-six, but all except two were between twenty-three and thirty, with the average age being twenty-six. All had lived in Wheeling for at least fifteen years, and almost all had been born in Virginia. Unlike what Morris found in Michigan, the majority of the first West Virginia players were Civil War veterans. They were all native born, although immigrants comprised 39.1 per cent of Wheeling's 1870 population. Hugh McCord, a second generation Irish-American, came the closest to foreign birth. The Hunkidori lads had reason to believe they would do well in the coming years. Irwin later became sheriff of Ohio County, J. E. Hornbrook a bank director, clean-up hitter C. R. Hubbard went on to be president of Republic Glass Company, William and Abraham Lukins and Ewing became lawyers, and Batelle a wholesale grocer.[9]

By mid-summer, the Star and Anchor clubs reappeared to join the Hunkidoris. None of the clubs had their own playing grounds. A team would meet in late afternoons on the Wheeling Island Commons and lay out a diamond. They practiced, divided up and played a few innings of intra-club games.[10]

After a month of practice, Ewing deemed the Hunkidoris ready to take on another team, or in the parlance of the day, a "match game." He arranged for the club to become a member of the New York centered National Association of Base Ball Players (NABBP). He invited the nearest NABBP member club, the Union Base Ball Club of Washington, Pennsylvania, to play the Hunkidoris in their first game. Lying to the east of Wheeling on the B&O rail line, Washington was close enough to allow the club to make a round trip in one day. For Ewing an inter-city match lent drama to the "first-game" event.

Once the Hunkidori–Union contest started, it quickly became clear that the visitors were "much ahead of our city boys." In the rain-abbreviated game the Wheeling club lost by the resounding score of 45 to 12. In reporting the game, the *Wheeling Register* printed the first box score of a West Virginia match.

UNION	Outs	Runs	HUNKIDORI	Outs	Runs
W.A. M'Nulty	3	4	J.E. Hornbrook	1	3
T.J. Mitchell	4	5	F. Whally	1	3
S.C. Orr	1	7	C.E. Irwin	2	2
M.R. Brownlee	2	5	C.R. Hubbard	1	3
J.W. McGuire	0	6	A. Lukins	2	1
G.G. M'Conahay	3	3	W. Lukins	2	0
N.N. Patten	0	6	H. McCord	4	0
R.K. McJunkin	2	5	J.M. Ewing, Jr.	3	0
Jas. Moffatt	3	4	J.H. Briggs	2	0
	17	45		18	12

As befitted a private men's club, the match was as much a social event as it was an athletic contest. Following the game both teams gathered for refreshments, dinner prepared by "lady friends," and a "merry half hour [of] speech making, [and] toasting." Before the guests caught the train back to Pennsylvania they presented the game ball to Ewing.[11]

Before the summer of 1866 ended, the Stars easily outclassed the Hunkidoris and other Wheeling clubs on the playing field. In the first game between two West Virginia teams, the Stars handled the Hunkidoris as easily as the Washington club had done, winning 37 to 7. The Stars' dominance likely resulted from their relative youth and fitness and their broader social base. The oldest of the Stars was only twenty-six, the average age of the Hunkidoris, and at least one member was only sixteen, although most were in their early twenties. At least one player, Virgil Adams, was a laborer and several were skilled artisans (a glass blower, carpenter and cabinetmaker), but most were clerks of one kind or another. None of the Stars was a first generation immigrant but perhaps a fifth of them came from Irish immigrant parents. The third Wheeling team, the Anchors, boasted natty uniforms consisting of "white cap, white shirt, red belt, pantaloon, and canvas shoes." Unfortunately, their sartorial splendor did not help them on the field. They lost their two recorded contests to the Hunkidoris and Stars by decisive scores.

By the end of the summer of 1866, baseball clubs began to appear in other parts of the state. Downstream from Wheeling, the town of Parkersburg, where the southern fork of the Baltimore and Ohio railroad crossed Ohio River, was doubling in population from 2,500 to 5,000 in the decade of the 1860s. There, young men of the city formed two clubs, the Olympic Base Ball Club and the Blennerhassett Base Ball Club; the latter was named for an Ohio River island just south of Parkersburg.[12] Unfortunately, there is no record of either club actually playing a game against another team.

Young men in the Eastern Panhandle of the state also organized clubs in 1866. The three easternmost counties of West Virginia — Jefferson, Berkeley, and Morgan — had been grafted onto the newly created mountain state because the Union needed to control the Baltimore and Ohio Railroad, which crossed the Potomac River at Harpers Ferry and ran through these counties at the head of the Shenandoah Valley before entering the mountains. West Virginia broke off from Virginia during the Civil War because of the western region's Union ties, but the easternmost area sympathized with the South and residents retained strong loyalties to Old Virginia in the post-war period. A rich agricultural region, the east contained the old established towns of Harpers Ferry, Charles Town, and Shepherdstown and the booming railroad and manufacturing city of Martinsburg, which had a population of 4,387 in 1870.[13]

In late July 1866, David Howell, Jr., a prosperous dry goods merchant, formed the Stonewall Base Ball Club in Charles Town, the seat of Jefferson County. His club included both scions of the Old South and carpetbaggers from the Union army. None in the county could claim a more prestigious lineage than Bushrod C. Washington. Five other club members had served with Washington in the Second Virginia Infantry during the Civil War. Surprisingly, two of the Stonewall players were Union army veterans who had been mustered out at Martinsburg in 1865.[14]

Other clubs soon followed the Stonewall group. The Jefferson and Old Dominion clubs organized in Charles Town within weeks of the Stonewall Club. In mid-summer, Martinsburg residents organized three clubs, Berkeley, Star, and Virginia. The sleepy river town of Shepherdstown could boast the Potomac Club. The Stonewall Base Ball Club got the honor of playing the first game in the eastern part of the new state. As the Hunkidoris had done, Howell turned to a more advanced team from a nearby out-of-state city for the first game. The opposition, brought in from Frederick, Maryland, called themselves the Nameless Club, an appellation often adopted by informally organized teams or a collection of players from different clubs. This game also proved a disappointment for the locals, as the West Virginians came out on the short end of a close 25–21 game.[15]

Early West Virginia baseball players, like those in other parts of the country, organized their own private baseball clubs along the lines of present day golf or racquet clubs. Men paid dues to become members, drafted and approved a constitution or by-laws, and elected officers and a board of directors from among their number to manage the club's affairs. Their size varied, but a minimum of twenty members seems to have been necessary to make a club viable, because they spent most of their time playing among themselves. The Potomac club of Shepherdstown had a membership of thirty, a desirable number which allowed for the creation of a "Muffin" or second team. Most clubs had their own grounds where they played, usually property belonging to a club member or his family, although in Wheeling the Island Commons was a preferred playing site. Some clubs played daily, some only once or twice a week, normally starting at 3:00 or 4:00 PM and playing until 6 o'clock. In addition to playing, most clubs had a business or social meeting once a month.[16]

The first games had more of the characteristics of social events than of entertainment. None charged admission. Spectators included a considerable number of the players' friends, and the audience always included numerous ladies. Protocol required the host club to be gracious toward their guests, and to provide a banquet, or at least refreshments, "after the violent exercise of the afternoon." Following the Hunkidoris' first game they treated their guests to a "sumptuous repast." When the Frederick team visited Charles Town, the Stonewall club provided the "Maryland gentlemen" with "handsome entertainment prepared by that incomparable caterer Blessing." As part of the post-game festivities the hosts presented "a beautiful boquet [sic]" to the visitors. A minstrel show followed a Potomac-Virginia game the same summer.[17] Clearly, neither journalists nor players had yet distinguished between sporting events and social events.

Costs associated with playing baseball kept most working class men away from the clubs. Players had to purchase their own uniforms that consisted of billed caps, long sleeved shirts, knickers or pantaloons, socks, and canvas shoes. The shoes alone sold for $1.60, which represented one half a day's salary for a laborer.[18] In addition to the outfit, there were membership dues and costs associated with the club's social events.

On the field the game would be recognizable to today's fan, but major differences existed. The National Association of Base Ball Players had codified the rules before the Civil War and amended them annually. It would be another thirty years before the rules became fixed. The most significant difference from present day regulations was in the pitching. Pitchers threw underhanded from forty-five feet to batters who could request a pitch either below or above the waist. The pitchers' job resembled that of current slow-pitch softball. He delivered the ball to the batter to be hit. Consequently, base hits outnumbered outs and games became high scoring affairs. In one 1866 contest, the Virginia club of Martinsburg hammered the Potomacs of Shepherdstown by the score of 121 to 51.[19]

In the summer of 1867 baseball fever continued in the Eastern Panhandle. Charles Town boasted three clubs, Stonewall, Old Dominion, and Jefferson. Martinsburg, with a population twice the size of Charles Town, had only the Virginia club. The Potomacs of Shepherdstown struggled through the summer while Harpers Ferry's Valley Base Ball Club, newly organized for 1867, held its own against the other teams. On the field, Valley and Virginia stood out as the most competitive of the Eastern Panhandle teams of 1867.[20]

After two summers of enthusiasm, baseball suddenly perished in the region. In 1868 newspapers in Charles Town, Martinsburg, and Shepherdstown contained no reports of baseball. The following summer "picked nines" from Martinsburg and Charles Town squared off, but they did not represent any clubs, because, as the [Charles Town] *Virginia Free Press* moaned, "We haven't any."[21]

No one bothered to hold a post-mortem on the death of baseball in the Eastern Panhandle, and little more than speculation is possible now. Given the region's strong southern sympathies, patriotic appeals to America's National Game would be expected to fall on deaf ears. Clearly baseball failed to gain a broader base than the well-to-do young men of the initial clubs. The small population of the Panhandle did not encourage broad-based participation or the development of a spectator culture. For whatever reason the players lost interest.[22] Unlike contemporary baseball, which consists of a long season lasting from spring to fall, the players of the 1860s conceived of the match games more like today's football games; one game determined the best team. "Wait until next year" or even the next game does not seem to have been part of the mindset.

Many of the Eastern Panhandle baseball players of 1866 and 1867 turned their attention to other fads in the summer of 1868. They took to the road on velocipedes, an early French bicycle that briefly fascinated American youth at the end of the decade. Others turned to the ring tournament, a symbolic form of jousting which harkened back to antebellum southern leisure with its emphasis on horsemanship. With betting on horse racing outlawed by the new state, the ring tournament enjoyed a considerable following in the Panhandle from 1868 to 1873, in part because it allowed for ample gambling opportunities.[23] Hence, baseball's introduction in the Eastern Panhandle resulted in little more than a passing fad, adopted and then discarded by the wealthy young men of the region's towns.

While the Eastern Panhandle caught the baseball fever and then cooled toward the sport, the isolated southern part of the state experienced almost no awareness of the game before the 1880s. Excepting Charleston with 2,400 residents in 1870, no town possessed a population large enough to support even club teams. South of the B&O railroad, hunting clubs offered some leisure-time recreation in the few villages and county seats. By the 1870s, traveling circuses occasionally included Charleston and Huntington in their tours, but not in the 1860s. In the countryside, boys continued to play rounders, towne ball and other bat and ball games in an unorganized fashion, but they had only a vague familiarity with baseball. As late as the early nineties, Logan, McDowell, and Mingo counties, the center of the then-opening southern coal fields, "showed little interest in formal athletic contests." The people of Logan Court House were unresponsive to suggestions for forming a baseball team as late as the mid–1890s.[24]

As baseball declined in the east, it moved into north-central West Virginia. The more populated northern part of the state had decidedly more interest in a variety of new social, recreational, and entertainment activities than did the Eastern Panhandle or southern West Virginia. In the spring of 1868 students at Agricultural College in Morgantown, which would become West Virginia University in December of that year, formed the Woodburn Base Ball Club. The school's enrollment of 161 provided a critical mass of young men open to new cultural forms. The students played intra-club games during the spring and after a mild dispute the college administrators "reluctantly" granted the students permission to play local clubs.[25] The club could be considered the first college team in the state, but the students never claimed to represent the school and club did not identify itself as the college team.

In Fairmont, twenty miles south of Morgantown, another baseball club organized in 1868. An embryonic coal-mining center on the Baltimore and Ohio Railroad between Martinsburg and Wheeling, Fairmont received cultural vibrations from both east and west along the railroad and from Morgantown to the north. Curiously, the similar sized small cities of Grafton to the southeast and Clarksburg to the south possessed characteristics like those of Fairmont but failed to spawn teams. What Fairmont had that sister towns lacked was an energetic young man with an organizational impulse to take up the sport. At the end of the Civil War Aretus Brooke Fleming, an ambitious graduate of the University of Virginia, launched a career that would see him become a judge, one of the state's largest coal operators and its governor (1890–1893). In the summer of 1868, even though recently elected prosecuting attorney, the twenty-eight year old Fleming turned his enormous energy to baseball. He organized a club, which he named the Stars. He served as its president, field captain, and pitcher. The players outfitted themselves in "regular base ball costume, with neat belts, fancy caps, etc." and looked around for competition.[26]

On a Saturday in mid–June 1868 Fleming took his club to Morgantown to play the Woodburn boys in the first game in north-central West Virginia. Like other early games, this one was a major social event. The arrival of the Stars and their followers in carriages and wagons "created quite a stir" in Morgantown. After dining at the town's best hotel, the team members "proceeded in a carriage to the College grounds, followed by a large number of citizens, including scores of young ladies." The Woodburn boys courteously erected a tent to provide shade for the ladies while they watched the game, although, as the local newspaper reported, some preferred to protect themselves from the sun's rays with umbrellas and parasols. The game quickly made clear that Fleming's future was in coal rather than in baseball. The college boys won with ease. Teeing off on Fleming's pitches, they scored 89 runs during the three and a half hour contest. After the game the Stars dined at a hotel and headed back to Fairmont "in the best humor and spirits, cheering lustily as they started."[27]

The Star-Woodburn game generated enormous enthusiasm for baseball in the Morgantown and Fairmont areas. "Hundreds" had turned out for the match. A week later the Morgantown newspaper claimed, "Since the game was played we have heard nothing but base ball from every mouth. Dirty-faced urchins are howling 'Base Ball' on every corner. It is talked of at the tea table, in the stores and shops on the streets. The mania now rages. Old and young, large and small, talk, think and dream of little else but 'bats,' 'fly catches,' 'home runs,' etc." The excitement led town boys from Morgantown to form their own team, the Decker Base Ball Club. Another team appeared in nearby Stewartown, a few miles north of Morgantown. When the students returned in September 1868, the Decker club demonstrated its superiority over the gownies.[28]

From Fairmont baseball expanded west along the Baltimore and Ohio line to the towns of Farmington and Mannington. In Farmington, a town of less than 1,000 people seven miles west of Fairmont, M. D. Randell organized the Excelsior team. Farther to the west in Mannington, a bustling lumber center since the railroad reached there in 1852, local lads formed the

Expert club. Local elites, war veterans, merchants and clerks, rather than men employed in the post-war economic boom, made up the leadership and most of the membership of these clubs.[29]

Despite the interest in the Morgantown-Fairmont area, it became apparent before the summer of 1868 ended that the brand of baseball played in the north-central region did not compare with that played in Wheeling. Nowhere in the state did the game achieve a level of popularity comparable to that in the Wheeling area. There it had expanded rapidly as a participation sport in 1867 and 1868, and in the summer of 1868 was transformed into a spectator event. The number of clubs in Wheeling grew from three in 1866 to twenty in 1867, with three more just across the river in Ohio. This group included clubs named Fly, LaBelle, Actives, Jockey, Columbia, Bachelors, Enterprise, Avalanche, Eagle, Benedicts, National, Muscle, Buckeye, Belmont, and Champion. The best and largest were the Baltic, Resolute, and United clubs, each of which fielded a "first nine" and a "second nine."[30]

With the formation of a substantial number of clubs, baseball entered a new stage. No longer could it be confined to gentlemen's clubs. The sport now drew young men and boys from all levels of Wheeling society. The teams continued to call themselves clubs, but only because of prior usage. They eschewed the previous organizational and social formalities. The older clubs, the stately Hunkidoris, the dapper Anchor club, and even the more serious Stars, failed to make the transition to the more democratically organized game. The best and most dedicated players from the three gentlemen's clubs joined the Resolutes, but combined they were no better than the third best team in the city.[31] Baseball had ceased to be a gentleman's pastime. Wheeling newspapers no longer referred to a "social game of ball," social refinements, post game entertainment or numerous ladies in attendance.

These Wheeling teams varied enormously in their composition, abilities, and longevity. Some were, in effect, neighborhood teams. These included the Champion club of North Wheeling, the LaBelle Street club, the Nationals of Wheeling Island, and the Uniteds of South Wheeling. The Muscle club of Bellaire, the Bridgeport Buckeyes and the Belmonts of St. Clairsville functioned as town teams. Employees of the two city newspapers, the *Register* and the *Intelligence*, organized their own teams. Other teams, including Fly, Active and Jockey, were composed of teenage boys. Some of the teams proved short-lived, surviving only a few games, while others played weekly match games and daily practice games from July through October.[32] In 1867 they all remained strictly amateur, organized to allow young men to play the game for their own enjoyment.

The Baltic club emerged as a team capable of attracting a sizeable spectator following. The team collected the best players from the area regardless of social background. Nearly half the men were of Irish heritage, and one-third were laborers. They were on the Baltics because of their playing ability. In the summer of 1867, the Baltics rose to the top of the local clubs. They strengthened themselves for 1868 by recruiting several of the top players from their competitors. Among these first "free agents" were Harry List, the city's best hitter, and T. J. Mitchell, the top pitcher in the area.[33]

In 1868 the Baltics began playing games at the Fair Grounds on Wheeling Island. The availability of the enclosed fair site made possible the growth of baseball as a spectator sport. The Northwest Virginia Agricultural Society had held fairs on Wheeling Island prior to the Civil War and revived the annual event after the war. The Fair Grounds consisted of a half-mile horse track and grandstand in addition to stables and buildings to house stock exhibitions. The fair's grandstand could seat several thousand spectators. Equally important, the enclosed track and stands allowed event organizers to charge admission. This the Baltics did, setting ticket prices at twenty-five cents for adults and ten cents for children.[34]

The accessibility of the Fair Grounds, and hence the ability to pay opponents a percentage of the gate, allowed the Baltics to attract out of town clubs to Wheeling for games. As they did this, the Baltics began to attract a sizable following. Wheeling residents were eager to see teams from other towns. Because the ability of the out-of-towners was generally unknown, games between them and the Baltics offered more excitement, or at least the anticipation of excitement, than did games between local clubs. Before the end of summer 1868 teams from Cumberland, Maryland, and the Ohio cities of Steubenville, Mt. Pleasant, and Cincinnati appeared in Wheeling. In these games, the residents of Wheeling could think of the Baltics as representing their city against other cities. Local pride fostered boosterism and brought out even larger crowds. People with no previous concern for baseball could have a passionate interest when the home team played clubs from Cumberland or Cincinnati. Crowds of 500 commonly turned out for games against out of town clubs. The Red Stockings of Cincinnati, featuring Harry Wright and pitcher Asa Brainard, attracted over 1,000 fans.[35]

The Baltics also took to the road. In early September 1868 they ventured on a road trip that took them to Cumberland, Morgantown, and Fairmont. The Baltics beat the Stars of Fairmont 49 to 25. Going on to Morgantown, they embarrassed the Woodburn boys 36 to 4 and trounced Decker 63 to 13.[36]

The overwhelming defeats seem to have destroyed the enthusiasm of the players of north-central West Virginia. None of the three defeated clubs reappeared the following summer. In the summer of 1869 town boys in Morgantown did form a club with the uninspiring name of Lazy Nine. Local opponents appeared in Stewartown but after a few games these teams died a quick and quiet death. In Fairmont, Fleming lost interest in baseball but other members of his Stars formed the Eureka club, a team that beat the neighboring Mannington and Farmington teams.[37]

At the end of the summer of 1868 the Baltics and the United club of South Wheeling squared off in a proposed three game series billed as the championship of West Virginia. The Baltics had lost only two games all summer, to the Means of Steubenville and the Cincinnati Red Stockings. A string of convincing victories had taken the sting out of those losses. The Baltics closed out their season with two straight wins over the Uniteds, the second by a 50–35 score, allowing their claim to be the first champions of West Virginia.[38]

Even though the Baltics played before paying customers, they remained an amateur club in the sense that players were not paid. The team seldom fielded the same lineup, using twenty-five different players during the summer. Often, who could get away from work on the afternoon of the game determined the lineup. It mattered little because they could beat most local opponents with their second nine. The team members played for enjoyment, a joy that found expression in doggerel composed about their pitcher T.J. Mitchell by first baseman Harry List:

> Mitchell is our pitcher.
> He's the fastest on the ground
> He measures 4 feet 5 around the waist
> And weighs 200 pounds.[39]

One cannot help wondering about the team's strategy because the rotund Mitchell often batted leadoff for the Baltics.

The high point of the fledgling baseball craze in West Virginia came early in the 1869 season when the Baltics played host to the famous Cincinnati Red Stockings, baseball's first professional team. That year the Red Stockings dominated baseball as no other team before or since. When the Red Stockings toured as far east as Wheeling in 1868, many of their players were being paid but not openly. In 1869 the Red Stockings dropped all pretense of being amateur and in the process revolutionized the sport. The Red Stockings began the 1869 season with an eastern tour, playing their way through Ohio, across upstate New York to Boston, then down to New York and Brooklyn, Philadelphia, Baltimore, and Washington before heading home. Along the way they played the best teams in the country without losing a game.[40]

The last game on the Red Stockings' triumphant tour came against the Baltics in Wheeling on June 30, 1869. Wheeling newspapers exuded civic pride before the game, even daring to imagine a victory for the Baltics. On game day the crowd filled the grandstand at the Fair Grounds and the overflow spread out along the foul lines. Over 1,000 people paid their way into the grounds, the largest number of spectators to see a sporting event in the state to that date. The game itself proved to be a mismatch. While the Red Stockings had been besting the top clubs in the country, the Baltics had barely organized for the new season. In fact they had played only one game before taking on the Red Stockings. The *Register* admitted after the game that "everybody thought the Baltics would be beaten," but, of course, that was hindsight.[41]

The Red Stockings' pitcher, Asa Brainard, utterly bewildered the Baltic batters, while the professionals had no trouble clubbing Mitchell's deliveries to the far reaches of the Fair Grounds. The local newspaper reported, with tongue in cheek, that Baltic fielders "passed most of their time hunting for the ball in the neighborhood of the Seventh Ward school house, the street car stables, or among the horse stalls on the west side of the track." The visitors scored eleven times in the first inning, and fifteen in the second, and added eighteen runs in the third inning. Only two Baltics even managed to reach base during that time. Everyone seemed to agree that enough was enough and to no one's regret the game was called after three innings with the score Red Stockings 44, Baltics 0.[42]

Jack Glasscock became the first West Virginia native to reach the major leagues. He played from 1879 to 1895, and is recognized as the finest shortstop of the 1880s. Back home in 1895, he helped Wheeling to the Iron and Oil League championship, its first title. (National Baseball Hall of Fame Library, Cooperstown, N.Y.)

During the remainder of the summer the Baltics continued to book games against some of the foremost teams in the country as well as the best local teams. Games with these name clubs drew large crowds. Gate receipts for the game against the Troy (New York) Haymakers, perhaps the second best team in the country, neared those for the Red Stockings game.[43]

Despite the Baltics' financial success, by the end of the summer it had become clear the club faced a serious dilemma. Their playing ability far exceeded that of other Wheeling teams, and, as a result, games against local teams attracted little spectator or participant interest. Their claim of a second state championship generated little excitement. On the other hand, games against top notch visiting teams invariably resulted in one-sided defeats. The Baltics failed to post a single win over out-of-state teams the entire summer. If the primary motive for club members to play continued to be the enjoyment they derived from the sport, there could be little joy in overwhelming losses. The club never resolved the dilemma and when the summer of 1870 arrived the Baltics failed to reorganize. West Virginia's first champion quietly passed from existence.

The Baltics' domination of Wheeling baseball had expanded interest in the sport throughout the city, but this did not result in increased participation. In fact, it had the opposite effect. From a peak of two dozen clubs in 1867, the number of local teams declined to half that number in 1868 and 1869. By establishing a higher standard of play the Baltics made it difficult for the less skilled to actively participate in the sport.

The demise of the Baltics did not mean the complete death of baseball in Wheeling. The United club of South Wheeling and the Osceola club formed in 1869 remained active, as did a few others. The number of games played in 1870, however, declined greatly from the previous three summers. The Uniteds claimed the title of state champions in 1870. Early in the summer they defeated the Osceola club in a best of three series billed as the state championship series. In the final game of the season the Uniteds won another convincing victory over Osceola, their most serious challengers.[44]

The Uniteds got another challenge for the state title from the Olympic club of Parkersburg. The Olympics had been organized in 1869 but played few if any games. The Uniteds traveled down to Parkersburg where the teams met on the grounds "back of Prospect Hill." The Uniteds overwhelmed the Olympics by the lopsided score of 70 to 11. Following the game *The Parkersburg Daily Times* advised the Olympics "not to challenge too soon other clubs, get better organized and practice."[45] Apparently the players followed only the advice not to challenge other clubs.

Despite their success, the Uniteds never gained the public following the Baltics had in 1868 and 1869. Of course, the Uniteds lacked the ability of the Baltics. Jacob Hornbrook, an original Hunkidori who was not good enough to play for the Baltics, appeared in the United lineup. The Uniteds continued to play most of their games at their neighborhood field in South Wheeling, well removed from the center of the city's population. They also understood they were not strong enough to play top-flight teams from out of the area. When two of the top teams in the country, the New York Mutuals, a fully salaried team, and the Forest City Club of Rockford, Illinois, featuring ace pitcher Albert G. Spalding, passed through the city, unofficial area all-star teams took the field against the visitors. Even so, the results were no more encouraging for Wheeling fans than those of the Baltics had been the previous summer.[46]

Even more detrimental to the future of the sport, the commercial brand of baseball developed an association with gambling and unruly fan behavior. No doubt, wagers had been placed on games before 1870, but that summer betting became open at games played at the Fair Grounds. The revival of horse racing in Wheeling undoubtedly encouraged the spread of gambling on sporting events. In 1869 a local jockey club formed and held its own meet in September. This was in addition to races at the fair. The following year, J. Frank Reynolds constructed a driving park on Wheeling Island where he held a series of harness races. Perhaps not surprisingly, the deportment of spectators at baseball games in the summer of 1870 came to resemble that at the racetrack.[47]

After the final game of the 1870 season, the *Register* took stock of the baseball scene. It complained bitterly about the spectators. Not only did fans bet openly on games, but also now yelled at the players and umpires, a practice considered unsportsmanlike. Rowdies at games "heedlessly, thoughtlessly and needlessly insult the ladies present." The fact was, however, that few women attended games any longer. In a telling admission the writer called for the presence of policemen at future games.[48]

The *Register* article amounted to an obituary for Wheeling baseball. The complaints of the *Register* following the 1870 season contrasted sharply with the same paper's view of baseball four short years earlier and provided a clear indication of the game's transformation. Earlier, the paper had seen in baseball the promise of physical redemption for the urban population. Instead, the sport had encouraged gambling and anti-social behavior.

The 1870 season marked the demise of baseball in Wheeling for the time being. No clubs fielded teams in the summer of 1871. The Fourth of July occasioned games between squads put together for the celebration, but that appears to have been the extent of baseball in the city. Elsewhere along the Ohio River, the Eureka club of St. Mary's played a few games against Ohio teams. In Parkersburg a teenage team called the Olympic Juniors had a brief existence. The same story repeated itself in 1872 when "scarcely a respectable match [had] been played."[49] By 1873 local newspapers did not even consider the sport's absence worthy of comment.

Residents of Wheeling sought other outlets for their mass entertainment and for their desire for athletic participation. The German minority, which constituted over one-half of the immigrant population, found an outlet in the Wheeling Turnverein Society, a gymnastic club organized in 1870. Young men with the time and money could join one of the numerous boat clubs formed in 1871 on the model of the early baseball clubs. Indeed, many of the initial "baseballists" became rowers in the early seventies. For those who wanted less strenuous exercise the lawn game of croquet was the latest fad. People who desired to watch or wager on sporting events turned exclusively to horse racing, of which there was no shortage. The Island Driving Park staged both summer and fall harness racing meets, the Jockey Club sponsored a flat racing meet, and the fair had its own races.[50]

In its early years baseball in West Virginia had moved through four distinct phases in Wheeling. There it had begun as a gentleman's sport, moved to a broad-based participation game as it became democratized, then became a spectator sport and later a form of commercial entertainment. There its failure can be attributed to competitive inequality which drove local participants to become spectators, but as the sport became commercialized the excesses of the game's followers conflicted with the sport's own ideology, causing it to lose its respectable supporters.

In other areas of the state the sport either failed to plant roots at all, or failed to move beyond the club stage. The Eastern Panhandle, which clung to non-urban, agrarian, antebellum values of the Old South, seems to have found a modern sport with its emphasis on merit a socially unattractive diversion. The growing industrial, mining and commercial cities of northern West Virginia had not yet developed a thoroughly modern urban cast of mind needed to support the sport.

Baseball, of course, was not dead but only dormant. It would return to favor again by the end of the 1870s, when the creation of the National League in 1876 and the growth of independent professional teams rekindled interest in baseball. Still, in 1871 in West Virginia, the future of the sport looked bleak indeed.

2

"Wheeling's a Swell Town to Play In"

The Emergence of Professional Baseball, 1874–1895

Following the collapse of the post–Civil War baseball craze in 1871, most of the Mountain State displayed little interest in the National Game until the 1890s. Only in Wheeling, the state's largest city and its environs, did baseball gain broad acceptance, drawing participants from all social strata. In the mid–1870s, the game became a spectator sport and a commercial enterprise while continuing to be a popular participation sport. Wheeling soon boasted the first professional team in the state. The high level of participation allowed the region to contribute an impressive array of players to the early major leagues in the 1880s and 1890s. Also in the 1880s, Wheeling became home to the state's first team in an organized professional league.

Wheeling in the nineteenth century bustled with manufacturing and commerce. Its location on the Ohio River, a major north-south transportation route, and its major east-west land transportation lines—first the National Road, then the Baltimore and Ohio Railroad, which reached Wheeling in 1853—spurred economic activity. In the second and third quarter of the century, Wheeling residents imagined their city competing with Pittsburgh for economic dominance of the upper Ohio Valley and dominance in the east-west trade. Residents gained even more civic pride and hope after Wheeling became the capital of the new state. By the mid–1870s, however, reality caught up with civic boosterism. By then Pittsburgh had clearly established itself as the iron and steel center of the country. Wheeling remained an important industrial city in its own right, but it would be in the economic and cultural orbit of the Smokey City. Wheeling's civic pride suffered again in 1885 when the state capital moved to a more central geographic location in Charleston.

Despite its setbacks, Wheeling continued to be a vibrant industrial city. Its population rose from 14,000 in 1860 to 38,878 in 1890, and metro Wheeling topped 60,000 by the end of the century. Iron and steel mills belched smoke and employed the most workers. By 1890 Wheeling led the nation in the production of nails, an industry that accounted for twenty percent of the city work force. Wheeling came to be called the "Nail City." A strong tobacco industry had begun when wagoners crossing the Ohio on the trek west provided a market for cigars and chewing tobacco. Marsh Wheeling's Stogies and, after 1879, Mail Pouch Chewing Tobacco filled the pockets of men across the nation, giving the city a national notoriety. A burgeoning glass industry ranked third in importance.[1]

As in other northern cities, an immigrant population contributed to Wheeling's cultural mosaic. Although native-born residents were always the majority of the city's population, first generation immigrants accounted for nearly 40 percent of the population in 1870. Twenty percent of Wheeling's residents were German immigrants. First generation Irish accounted for another ten percent. The African-American population, however, remained small: no more than two percent of the city residents.[2]

Baseball's rebirth in Wheeling of 1874 stood in marked contrast to its beginnings the previous decade, when young men of established and respectable families formed the first baseball clubs. In the mid–1870s men of the working class planted the seeds of baseball's revival. In June 1874, workers at the Top Mill foundry of the Wheeling Iron and Nail Company and those of the Bellaire Nail Works took the lead in forming teams. Linotype operators from the city's two established newspapers soon had their own teams.[3]

By the end of the summer of 1874 a large array of baseball teams had taken the field. Some arose from the work place. Industrial workers who organized squads preferred to give their teams Indian names such as Modoc, Blackfeet, and Keokus. Others grew out of existing voluntary associations. Members of the elite Nail City Boat Club, some of them former members of the old baseball clubs, took time away from the water to join what were still termed the "baseballists." A volunteer fire company formed the Goodwill team. Some of the teams functioned as town teams. Young men from East Wheeling organized the Velocipedes. North Wheeling had the Crescents.

Martin's Ferry, across the Ohio River, boasted a team called the Olympics. Unlike the earlier club teams, these groups were informally organized without benefit of officers or social functions other than baseball. Nor did these teams take the time to go over to Wheeling Island to practice or play, preferring to stay near work or home. Instead of using established public spaces they laid out fields on mill property or vacant lots.

The newly established Standard Publishing Company, organized just the previous year, saw in the renewed interest in the National Game an opportunity to give name recognition to its newspapers, *The Evening Standard* and *Wheeling Weekly Standard*. It became the first team sponsor. Joe Junkins, son of a flourmill owner and the city's best player, got the assignment of recruiting players for the Standards. He did such a good job that by the end of the summer of 1774 the Standards became the best team in Wheeling. They beat the Nail City team 18–13 in what was billed as the city championship game. The Standards would retain that position for the next four years. After beating the local teams, the Standards traveled to Steubenville, Ohio, where they defeated that city's two finest teams.[4]

In October 1874 the baseball season concluded with Wheeling's top teams taking on out of town foes at the Fair Grounds. For one ticket price the crowd of 1,000 to 1,500 fans got to see two games. First the Standards took on Washington College (now Washington and Jefferson) of Washington, Pennsylvania. The host team suffered its only loss, 29–27. Following the Standards' game Nail City beat the boys from Bethany College, who had traveled the fourteen miles into Wheeling by carriage. The game gave Bethany rightful claim to being the first college team in West Virginia.

The Standards became more commercial in 1875. They played their home games at the Fair Grounds, charging admission. They donned "neat blue uniforms, with white trimming, including a huge 'S' on the breast of the shirt." The uniforms led locals to refer to the Standards as "the Boys in Blue." This team more than held its own against teams from Washington and New Castle, Pennsylvania, Cumberland, Maryland, and Mansfield, Ohio, but not the strong semi-pro Xantha club of Pittsburgh. The Standards did not lose to area opponents but neither did they overwhelm the local teams. They managed to beat the Bethany College boys 17–11 and the teenage Buckeyes 10–9, and played to a draw with workers from LaBelle foundry.

Before the end of the 1875 season, the Standards took measures to strengthen the team. Junkins, who pitched and played shortstop, brought in a strong pitcher in Frank Vennum. The new pitcher possessed the ability to get batters out, not merely to deliver the ball for batters to hit. Vennum's services were in demand by teams from other cities who willingly paid him to pitch in key games. An Altoona, Pennsylvania club paid him the astounding fee of $250 to pitch one weekend, if Wheeling newspapers are to be believed.

The Standards brought up the best local teenagers from the Buckeye club. Four of these boys proved to be West Virginia's best homegrown products of this era. All would make the major leagues in the next decade. Joe Moffatt, a strapping six-footer at age 16, took over at first base. Sam Barkley, a baseball-savvy seventeen year old, became the second baseman. John Wesley "Jack" Glasscock, only fifteen when he joined the Standards, was a natural shortstop. He would go on to play over 1,600 major league games at short and earn the nickname "King of the Shortstops" in the 1880s. However, Joe Junkins was not about to relinquish his position to a fifteen-year-old kid, so Glasscock played third base for the Standards. Barkley and Glasscock would also become the first West Virginia natives to manage in the big leagues. Sam Moffatt, a year older than brother Joe, claimed one of the outfield positions. He would play three years in the National League, all with teams starring his buddy Glasscock. Holdovers from 1874, Dick Robinson and Tom Wilson, joined Moffatt in the outfield. Catcher Harry Lukins rounded out the most common lineup. However, at least twenty-seven different players appeared in the lineup in 1875.

The creation of the National League and the upswing of patriotism associated with America's centennial in 1876 spurred interest in baseball in general and commercial baseball in particular. William Hulbert of Chicago, who engineered the creation of the National League of Professional Base Ball Clubs in February 1876, expected to turn baseball into a moneymaking enterprise. By attaching teams to a city, he created a local monopoly on League baseball. By ridding the game of gamblers and rowdies and playing a set schedule of games (albeit a limited number), he would create a stable, clean game which he believed would appeal to a middle class audience. The juxtaposition of the new league and the centennial year provided an occasion for the "national game" to wrap itself in the flag, a linkage baseball would exploit from then on.

In Wheeling that summer, the Standards blurred the line between amateur and professional baseball. The team generated income from admission to games at the Fair Grounds and from the occasional prize money it won. These proceeds not only paid for uniforms and travel to away games, but also allowed some of the players to get paid for their efforts. Although players had no contracts or salary, they received a portion of the gate. Pitcher Vennum was the major recipient of these payments. In late August the Standards lured pitcher Deacon Hagan away from the Allegheny Club of Pittsburgh by offering him more money to play out the season in Wheeling.

The 1876 Standards played any team that might draw fans into the Fair Grounds. Whenever possible they played on Friday and Saturday afternoons. The opponents ranged from Bethany College to the local amateur Clippers to independent professional teams, like the Pittsburgh Alleghenies, to National League teams anxious to pick up gate receipts between league games.

The Standards played competitively against the top-flight teams but were not able to beat them. They cleaned up against Bethany College and other local teams, and won most of their games against other semi-pro teams from western Pennsylvania, eastern Ohio and as far away as Covington, Kentucky, and Wilmington, Delaware. However, they never quite attained parity with strong pro teams. They lost four close games to the Alleghenies. Against the Louisville, a National League club, the Standards lost a close 8–5 game to pitcher Jim Devlin, who won 30 National League games that year.

No one kept track of individual statistics for the Standards, but Glasscock clearly established himself as the top player. Only sixteen when the season started, he became the team's clean-up hitter by mid-summer. Locals feared, with some reason, they would lose him to Pittsburgh's professional team.

In April 1877 the Standards reorganized as West Virginia's first professional team. The players wished to model the reconstructed team after the Allegheny club of Pittsburgh, which had organized that city's first professional team the year before. The team declared its independence from the publishing company and became a "salaried nine." As part of the professionalization of local baseball, Frank Vennum replaced Junkins as club manager; in modern parlance he served as a combined general manager and field manger, as well as continuing to pitch.

As professionals intent on turning a profit, the Standards needed the best possible lineup in order to compete against other professional teams on a level that would attract paying customers. That meant for the first time they brought non–Wheeling residents to town for the sole purpose of playing baseball. Not surprisingly they raided the Pittsburgh Alleghenies, signing three players. Catcher George "Cappy" Lane, first baseman Sam Wilkinson, and outfielder William Gallagher agreed to leave the Smokey City to play for the Standards in 1877.

The professional Standards did not have a set schedule of games, but managed to schedule games almost daily, except Sundays, from mid–April to mid–July, after which the season began to fade. The teenage boys had all quit their formal schooling and were no doubt happy to forgo the drudgery of low paying jobs, as were the older Wheeling players.

The 1877 Standards notched some impressive victories. They more than held their own against professional clubs, notching victories over such clubs as Erie, Pennsylvania, the Memphis Red Socks, Ludlow, Kentucky, the Quicksteps of Wilmington, Delaware, the Cincinnati Buckeyes, and Manchester, New Hampshire. The first big triumph for the Standards came on June 23 when they won a 2–1 pitching duel over the Indianapolis Dark Blues. The Standards' Hagan out-pitched Edward "The Only" Nolan, winner of an astounding 32 shutouts that season. After two more early season losses to Pittsburgh, the Standards finally beat the Alleghenies, also by a 2–1 score on June 29. In that game they beat another great pitcher, George "Pud" Galvin, who later became the first pitcher to win 300 major league games. On July 12 the Standards trounced the Tecumsehs of London, Ontario, one of the best teams in North America, by a 9–1 score. The Tecumsehs were on their way to a record of 41–26 against professional teams. They captured the title of the International Association, a loose grouping of the best professional teams outside the National League.[5]

The Standards' 1877 season went downhill after their victories over the Tecumsehs. Vennum quit as manager for unspecified reasons. Sam Wilkinson, who replaced Vennum, had trouble lining up opponents the rest of the summer. Wheeling also found out that salaries did not buy loyalties. The team's best hitters, Jack Glasscock, Joe Junkins and Cappy Lane, jumped ship for more money than the $40 per month they received from the Standards. Glasscock and Lane went to the Champion club of Springfield, Ohio, and Junkins to the Rochester (N.Y.) Live Oaks. Without the big three the losses began to pile up. The National League champion Boston Red Stockings went away from Wheeling with a 19–0 win and St. Louis of the NL swept two games. Wheeling fans began to lose interest. Only 500 paid to see the National League teams, compared to 1,000 who had turned out for games early in the summer.[6]

Nevertheless, the success of the Standards encouraged amateur teams in Wheeling. Twenty some teams took the field in 1877. These included boys from Linsly Institute, the first high school in the state to field a team. Interest in the amateur games continued even as attendance at Standards' games declined. As many spectators watched the Atlantics of central Wheeling play the Velocipedes of East Wheeling in late July as paid to see the best team in the country.[7]

Whether encouraged by the creation of the National League, the success of professional ball in Wheeling, or other reasons, baseball returned to north-central West Virginia in 1877 after a long absence. Morgantown, Fairmont, Taylortown, and Clarksburg fielded teams. Of these, the Rough and Ready club of Morgantown stood out by beating the others. After playing each other once, these teams disbanded.[8]

Wheeling's initial experience with a professional team proved short-lived. After the 1877 season the Standards disbanded. Declining attendance and the string of disheartening late season losses contributed to the decision and led to a loss of enthusiasm on the part of the Standard players. It was the decision of the West Virginia Agricultural Society to close the Fair Grounds in December 1877 that finally shut down the Standards.[9] Without access to the Fair Grounds, the team had no grandstand or enclosed park.

Baseball largely dropped from public view following the disappearance of the Standards. The *Wheeling Register* lamented in 1881, "The baseball fever has deserted us without leaving a single scar. We doubt there is a solitary organized club in the city today."[10] Actually some baseball was played between 1877 and 1882, but precious little. A couple of Wheeling area teams played in 1878. The same year in Parkersburg the Blennerhassett club reorganized and played a team from the booming oil town of Volcano, W.Va. The following year a Parkersburg team called the Stars beat a team of boys from Marietta College just across the Ohio River. In Morgantown, town and college boys played an annual game for the "city championship."[11]

While his teammates on the Standards had to content themselves playing pick-up games, Glasscock made his way to the big-time. In 1878 he caught on with an independent professional team in Cleveland called the Forest City Club. The following year, the team got a franchise in the National League and Glasscock became the first native of West Virginia to play in the major league. He would last for seventeen years in the majors, becoming the best fielding shortstop of his age. "Pebbly Jack" set major league fielding records for assists, double plays, and put outs. No slouch with the bat, he won a National League batting title and was the most difficult player of his era to strike out.[12]

In 1882 a new major league, the American Association, placed a team in Pittsburgh. This contributed to a revival of interest in baseball down river in Wheeling. W. T. English, a businessman, stepped forward to reorganize a Standards team. The revival of the Fair Grounds and the reconstruction of its grandstand that summer allowed the Standards to charge admission. Despite having an income from the gate, they remained an amateur team and played a much less demanding schedule than had the professional Standards. The team again featured Sam Barkley and the Moffatt brothers. Replacing Glasscock at third base was a strong young hitter and future major leaguer named Joe Miller. Following victories over teams from Steubenville, Ohio, and New Castle, Pennsylvania, fan interest peaked when the independent professional Pittsburgh Browns came to town for two games. After losing 6–4 on Friday, the Standards treated a huge crowd to "a Glorious Victory" on Saturday. At that game, "The grandstand was packed full, the quarter stretch was lined with a dense crowd, and the trees outside the enclosure were heavy with living fruit," reported the local newspaper. Crowd estimates ranged from 1,000 to 5,000. The Standards, however, could not beat Pittsburgh's new major league team; the Alleghenies bested the Wheeling boys 3–0.[13]

The summer of 1882 saw the appearance of the first African-Americans in West Virginia baseball. Among a dozen local amateur teams one called the Actives was identified as "colored." With fourteen-year-old Sol White playing for them, the Actives held their own against other area clubs. When the New Castle, Pennsylvania, team came to town to play the Standards, their lineup included Moses Fleetwood Walker, long thought to be the first African-American to play major league baseball, and his brother Weldy. A local scribe noted, "The colored men played nobly. Weldy is a fine thrower, and Fleet is a quick runner."[14]

The Standards nearly became West Virginia's first team in what came to be called "Organized Baseball," that is teams and leagues affiliated with the two major leagues. Pittsburgh sportswriter Benjamin Young attempted to create a Western Inter-State Association with Dayton, Youngstown, Akron, and East Liverpool, Ohio, New Castle, Pennsylvania, and Wheeling as the core. English did his best to gain a franchise, but his efforts floundered when several members of the Fair Board, identified as "old fossils" by the *Register,* objected to professional baseball. The board demanded twenty-five percent of gross admission fees as rent, a position English believed would lead to bankruptcy. So English withdrew his quest of a franchise, the league never got off the ground, and the Standards disbanded. Then a spring flood in 1884 overran Wheeling Island, sweeping away the grandstand and making a pro team out of the question for the next several years.[15]

Even without a leading team in town, Wheeling baseball continued to thrive from 1883 to 1886. Dozens of amateur teams took the field each summer. The Globes, a team that originated across the river in Bellaire, Ohio, but played its games on Wheeling Island, emerged as the top local team. Another team taking the Standards name was not far behind the Globes. Each team boasted several players who went on to professional play. The Globes roster included T. C. "Parson" Nicholson, Bob and George Westlake, George Dunn, Bill George, and Sol White. If White experienced racial slurs, they went unrecorded and he later remembered these as pleasant years. The Standards had Sammy Nichol as well as young Jesse Burkett, who showed promise as both a pitcher and hitter.[16]

The best Wheeling area players of the early eighties followed through the door Glasscock had opened. When the Toledo Blue Stockings gained a franchise in the Northwestern League in 1883, manager William Voltz came to Wheeling and left with the best available players, George Lane, Sam Moffatt, Joe Miller and Sam Barkley. He also signed Fleet Walker, formerly of New Castle, as his catcher. With Barkley, Miller and Moffatt playing leading roles, Toledo swept to the league title. Their success led the team to acquire a franchise in the American Association for 1884; the boys found themselves in a major league.[17]

Few of the West Virginia players who made the majors in the 1880s stayed long in the big leagues. Miller, Lane, and Joe Moffatt, who joined Toledo as a utility player, all batted below .240, as did Fleet Walker. Following the 1884 season Lane and Joe Moffatt returned to Wheeling. Miller had one more major league season. Sam Moffatt pitched for three seasons without distinction. Catcher Fred Haley played only two games. Bill George logged in three years as a pitcher before throwing his arm out. Only Barkley established himself as a major league regular for the decade of the eighties. In 1884, his best year, he batted .306 with a league leading 39 doubles. Barkley enjoyed a championship season with St. Louis in 1885 before being traded to Pittsburgh. His personal life, however, was an unhappy affair. He failed in business in Pittsburgh before moving to Chicago. There he married and ran a saloon. His wife divorced him in 1894 and his saloon went bankrupt a few years later. Barkley then returned to Wheeling, where he died in 1912.[18]

In the summer of 1886 the amateur Globes and Browns merged to form a semi-pro Wheeling team. With White, Nicholson, Nichol, George, Joe Moffatt, and Burkett they had success playing other semi-pro teams from the Ohio Valley. Their success spurred a number of Wheeling residents to have another try at organizing a professional team.

In August 1886 an organizing meeting gathered at the Howell House Hotel to create the Wheeling Base Ball Association. The organizers raised $2,000 capital from the sale of stock. Oscar Seeley became president, Thomas Thoner, vice-president, E. C. Mitchell, treasurer, and W. T. English, secretary and business manager. They began searching for a league. In February 1887 the newly formed Ohio State League needed two teams because Toledo and Dayton had pulled out. They offered franchises to Wheeling and Kalamazoo, Michigan. Just when it appeared Wheeling had a league team the effort again ran afoul of the Fair Association. The Fair Board demanded a $720 rental fee while English calculated the team could afford no more than $400.[19]

In 1887, unlike 1883, English was determined to have a team in Wheeling. The capital allowed him to bypass the Fair Grounds. He rented prop-

2. "Wheeling's a Swell Town to Play In" 31

West Virginia's first professional league team, the Wheeling Nailers, take on Kalamazoo at their brand new park, May 19, 1887. Note the press box to the left of the hitter and the umpire's derby (Brown Collection, Ohio County Public Library).

erty on Fink Street between South Broadway and South Front Street on Wheeling Island. Less than a block from the ferry at the foot of Twelfth Street and three blocks from the horse car lines, the site was convenient if unfamiliar to fans. In eight weeks the club managed to construct a wooden grandstand with roof and to fence the grounds. Unlike the diamond at the Fair Grounds, which had grass on the infield, the new park had a skinned infield of "sun baked clay." Wheeling had its first made-for-baseball enclosed park.[20]

The club signed John Crogan, a South Wheeling native with minor league experience, as its captain or playing manager. From the 1886 semi-pro team he kept outfielders Sammy Nichol and George Dunn, first baseman Joe "Puggy" Speidel and utility man George Westlake. Crogan also signed veteran professionals pitcher Sam Kimber, and outfielders John Shetzline and Frank Bell. In addition, he gave auditions to a number of youngsters. Of these, Jake Stenzel, a twenty-year-old catcher, would become the team's top hitter, and Sam Morrison became the club's only reliable pitcher. Notably absent was Sol White, who answered the call of an African-American team, the Keystones of Pittsburgh.

League baseball did not get off to a promising start. Crogan's mix did not gel. On the field they played uninspired, mediocre baseball. Off the field, fans complained of seeing players drunk on the streets. Attendance slumped badly in late June. Management made significant changes in early July. English dismissed Crogan and appointed Nicholson to run the club. At the urging of the new field boss, the club signed Sol White, who became available after the collapse of the Keystones.

Nicholson and White pumped new life into the team, which played exciting ball for the remainder of the season. No less than eight players batted over .300; Stenzel led the way with a resounding .390 average. White followed closely with a .381 average and a team-leading .508 slugging average. Wheeling fans responded to the energized team even though its bad start and dreadful pitching kept it out of contention for a pennant. Two days after White's debut a record 7,000 customers paid their way into the park. At season's end the club's directors could state with pride, "Wheeling turned out larger audiences ... than any town in the Ohio League."[21]

Eight players from the 1887 team reached the majors, but Sol White would not be among them. Had he been white there can be no doubt he would have been a major leaguer. Following the 1887 season, the Ohio State League took action to end integrated baseball by prohibiting teams from signing black players. Although the owners reversed their position in March 1888, White returned to the world of segregated baseball. He went on to have an amazing career playing on or managing at least fifteen teams, owning the Philadelphia Stars, and writing the first book on black baseball, entitled *Sol White's Official Base Ball Guide* (often referred to as *Sol White's History of Colored Base Ball*), in 1907. Wheeling fans appreciated White. When his Pittsburgh Keystones played an exhibition game against Wheeling in 1888, his fans presented him with a bouquet of flowers.[22]

The team and league changed significantly in 1888. The league changed its name to the Tri-State League to reflect the geography of its membership. Wheeling's team adopted a nickname, the "Nailers," appropriate for the Nail City. English gave the reins of the club to veteran minor leaguer Al Buckenberger, who had guided Kalamazoo to first place in the Ohio State League. Buckenberger brought in a raft of new players. Unlike Crogan the previous year, the new field leader had an eye for talent. Seven of the players he brought in made it to the major leagues: first baseman Milton "Buck" West, second baseman Ed Delahanty, third baseman Dick Van Zant, shortstop Billy Otterson, outfielder Steve Brodie, catcher Henry Yaik, and pitcher Frank Knauss. These were in addition to the four holdovers: Stenzel, Nichol, Nicholson and Morrison.

The most exciting Nailer was Edward "Big Ed" Delahanty. Indeed, he would be the only Hall of Fame player to ever play for a Wheeling professional team. He quickly became the most dangerous hitter in the Tri-State League. He hit a league leading .408 before a promotion to Philadelphia cut short his Wheeling season. In a sixteen year major league career, he batted over .400 three times and compiled a .346 lifetime average before a mysterious fall into the Niagara River took his life in 1902.[23] He became the first player for a West Virginia team to be enshrined in the Hall of Fame in 1945.

The Nailers finished a close second to Lima, Ohio. Delahanty and flamboyant, Shakespeare quoting outfielder Walter Scott "Steve" Brodie paced the Nailers early in the season. The team ran off fourteen consecutive wins to take the league lead by July 4. After leading most of the way they slipped in September. Buckenberger thought they would have won if Delahanty had remained in Wheeling for the whole season.[24]

The team made a tidy profit in 1888, charging 35 cents for grandstand seats, 25 cents for general admission, and 10 cents for children. A crowd of 6,000 for the July 4 doubleheader was the largest of the season. The second largest was for a post-season game against the African-American Cuban Giants, which the Nailers won. The real profits came from the sale of players. The Philadelphia Phillies paid $1,800 to 2,000 for Delahanty. Nicholson went to Detroit for $400, while Pittsburgh claimed Nichol and Yaik for $300 each, and Van Zant went to Cleveland for an unspecified amount.[25]

After such a marvelous 1888 season, Wheeling eagerly awaited 1889. English decked the Nailers out in spiffy new dark blue uniforms with white trim, red hats and red stockings. The league, however, lost its two largest cities when Columbus gained a major league franchise and Toledo shifted to the International League. With only six teams, league president W. H. McDermith of Columbus imposed a salary ceiling of $750 per team.[26]

The Nailers quickly shattered the dreams of their supporters. Sammy Nichol returned after failing to stick with Pittsburgh, and became field manager. By July, Nichol became frustrated with his team. He was the only player batting over .300 and the others played lethargically in the field and showed an utter lack of discipline on and off the diamond. He quit on July 7.

The biggest problem was the team's best pitcher, Bill "Brickyard" Kennedy. A local product, Kennedy demonstrated great potential, winning 15 games against 10 losses, but could not discipline himself to maximize his talents. A local scribe wrote, "He got the big head and the sulks." Illiterate, loud and hot-tempered, he already had a fondness for alcohol. His biographer, Jack Kavanagh, wrote: "control — of both his pitches and emotions — often got him into trouble." Kennedy eventually did make the majors and won 187 games, but in 1889 Kennedy and his buddies caused Wheeling a great deal of grief. [27]

After Nichol resigned, management made the mistake of appointing Kennedy's drinking buddy, second baseman Billy Bowman, to replace Nichol as field leader. In less than a week both were fined $25 for showing up drunk for a game. In less than two weeks they, along with shortstop Fred Miller, were fined again, and this time they were suspended. Needless to say, Bowman was relieved of his managerial duties. The new field head, third baseman George Dunn, restored a semblance of discipline but by then the Nailers had dropped into last place and stayed there for the remainder of the season.

With attendance dropping precipitously and the club facing mounting losses on the field and in the financial ledger, the club management became desperate. The solution team president W. B. Howell proposed was to play Sunday games. Howell understood Sunday was the one day all workers were free to attend a game. He also knew it violated state law and that "certain people living on the Island consider [it their] right to guard the morals of everyone else." Howell justified his action by declaring that all the Ohio cities played on Sundays, although this was not entirely true. No doubt, he hoped local officials would look the other way. On July 15 the Nailers put his logic to the test. A big crowd of 1,100 to 1,200 turned out. After one inning of play a constable walked to the plate and arrested catcher, batter, and umpire. The crowd grumbled but dispersed without serious incident. Having failed, Howell resigned the club presidency and was replaced by Meyer B. Horkheimer. The following Sunday the Nailers tried again. Visiting Mansfield refused to play, so the Nailers played local amateurs, but, again, the police acted to protect the city's morals. General manager English followed Howell's lead and resigned. That ended the Nailers' effort to play on Sundays.

The 1890 baseball season was an unhappy experience for baseball from the major leagues to Wheeling. That was the year in which most of the major league players followed their union, the Brotherhood of Baseball Players, out on baseball's first strike. Only they did not picket; they formed their own league, the Players League, to compete against the National League and American Association. In the end fans became disaffected, attendance declined and all three leagues lost money.[28]

The labor conflict at the highest level of baseball had little direct impact on the minor leagues. The Nailers opened the season without Oscar Seeley, W. T. English and W. B. Howell, the original leadership of the club. Former Wheeling Standards outfielder Tom Wilson did introduce scorecards to the park. Their new black uniforms may have been a sign of dark things to come. New field general, Bob Glenalvin, had only a $600 monthly payroll to work with, down from $750 the previous year.[29]

The Nailers challenged Mansfield for the league lead but fell short. Bill George returned home when a bad arm ended his pitching career after three major league seasons. He roamed centerfield with grace and hit .352. Outfielder Fred Osborne led the league with a .397 average, but he and Glenalvin left for the majors in mid–July, the former for Pittsburgh, and the latter for Chicago. Their departure signaled a team decision to sell players as soon as possible regardless of what it did to the Nailers' own chances. Management's priority was not lost on the fans, who began staying away in greater numbers.[30]

Other Tri-State League cities faced similar problems. Dayton and Springfield disbanded on July 10 unable to meet their payroll, thereby reducing the league to six teams. By August it was clear the league was in trouble as attendance fell off all around. Finally, on August 14, the league disbanded.[31]

Wheeling's first experience with minor league baseball came to an end after a four year run. The Nailers never recovered from the failures of 1889. The drunkenness and lackadaisical performances of players turned off fans, who often perceived professional ball players to be only slightly above rogues and vagabonds. Management made bad decisions regarding players it signed and its managerial appointments. The desperate attempt to recoup financial losses by playing on Sundays resulted in the loss of Howell and English, the driving forces behind the organization. Even though the team improved its play in 1890, the Nailers did not regain a loyal fan following.

In the Nailers' brief life, the team did contribute no less than nineteen players to the major leagues. None matched the exploits of Big Ed Delahanty. His great seventeen-year major league career led to his induction into the Baseball Hall of Fame. Other notable Nailer alumni included career

.300 hitters Jake Stenzel and Steve Brodie, and pitcher Bill Kennedy, who won 171 games for the Dodgers. The list also includes Sam Morrison, Frank Knauss, Parson Nicholson, Sammy Nichol, Milt West, Dick Van Zant, Billy Otterson, Henry Yaik, Billy Bowman, Fred Osborne, Bob Glenalvin, Henry Meyer, Edward "Pop" Lytle, and George Ziegler.

While Wheeling was without professional ball in the early nineties, amateur baseball continued to flourish. A semi-professional team, the Red Lions, played in an Ohio Valley League in 1891 against teams from smaller cities in Ohio and Pennsylvania. William W. "Will" Irwin, a druggist, captain of the Wheeling Light Infantry and baseball enthusiast, built a small, enclosed park in 1892 for the Red Cross team from the south side of Wheeling, allowing it to charge admission to its games. Company and neighborhood teams continued to play, and the recently established YMCA started a league for teenagers.[32]

As the Gay Nineties arrived baseball no longer monopolized the sporting scene. Sporting events of all kinds seemed to explode onto the Wheeling cityscape, competing for recreational participants and the sporting dollar. At first the Fair Grounds served as the center for spectator events. The reorganized West Virginia Exposition and State fair ran a season of horse races in the fall beginning in 1888. The following year a Gentleman's Driving Association began sponsoring trotting meets at the Fair track, and introduced pacing races in 1891. Also in 1888 "pedestrianism" arrived in Wheeling when professional walkers came to town in July to take on all comers in a 27-hour walk. Professional walking, although something of a hustle, had great appeal to the working classes for several years, and Wheeling remained a stop on the pro tour. The walkers expanded to include running events in 1894. Bicycles arrived in Wheeling in 1889 and remained extremely popular for over a decade. The Victor Safety Bike Company and Edward L. Rose and Company, the local retailer, consciously created a bike craze. They brought touring pros from England, Ireland and New York to town in 1898 for a 75 hour race. Local enthusiasts formed the Wheeling Wheelmen, an affiliate of the League of American Wheelmen (LAW). The LAW began to sponsor events of which the biggest was a Wheeling to Pittsburgh race that annually attracted professional riders. Soon women were joining men on bikes and the participants took to the streets and roads.[33]

Winter indoor activities came quickly on the sporting scene. Bowling arrived in 1890 with the opening of the first ten pin alleys. Two others opened in 1894 and bowling leagues began running from October through April. Gymnasiums appeared early in the decade. The downtown YMCA opened first, but the Pastime Athletic Club, organized in 1893 and located two miles east of the city limits, offered a wider range of activities. It provided boxing matches, bowling, and wrestling, and a home for the Wheeling Athletic Club. Ice skating rinks had existed shortly after the Civil War, but that activity became popular again in the 1890s.

Football would become the dominant fall sport, but it was still in its infancy. In 1893 the Wheeling Athletic Club played the Martin's Ferry YMCA. The next year football teams from West Virginia University, Bethany College and Linsly Institute began playing in Wheeling.

When professional baseball returned to Wheeling in 1895 it drove the other sports off the pages of the local newspapers. Pittsburgh sportswriter George L. Moreland had an inspiration for a new baseball league that he called the Interstate League. He lined up seven Ohio cities and Wheeling. Moreland kept the Wheeling franchise for himself, but agreed to share it with former Wheeling Nailers' manager Al Buckenberger, recently fired as Pittsburgh's field leader. When Buckenberger took the managerial reins in St. Louis, he and Moreland offered a cut to young Ed Barrow, who was managing a theater in Pittsburgh and running the concessions at the ballpark. Barrow agreed to run the Wheeling franchise as business manager.[34]

Barrow's greatest problem was finding a place for his team to play. All agreed Irwin's park was too small. Negotiations with the State Fair got nowhere. Irwin, who had become treasurer of the new club, and Buck Windsor, sports editor of the *Register*, hatched a brilliant plan. They approached local brewer Harry Schmulbach, owner of the largest brewery in the state, who also had a sizable estate on Wheeling Island near the bridge to Martin's Ferry. The trio proposed that Schmulbach build a park on his property on condition they get a license from city council to sell his beer at the park. Somehow they pulled it off. Beer would flow for the first time at a Wheeling sporting event. Schmulbach made good on his end of the bargain, spending $5,000 to build the park. The brewer obviously believed a great deal of his beer would be sold at his park.[35]

A park and beer proved no guarantee of success. Barrow appointed Will White, a Bellaire native and former major league player, as field manager. Working with a $600 monthly payroll they cobbled a team together, but the squad consisted of players who had not and would not make the majors. The inaugural season of the Inter-State League (ISL) proved to be a disaster. The Canton, Steubenville and Mansfield teams folded in late June. When Lima disbanded in early July it left the league with no choice but to fold, which it did on July 10.

Before the league shut down, one of the visiting players was future novelist Zane Grey. A student at the University of Pennsylvania, he played for

Findlay, Ohio, that summer. In his 1909 novel *The Short Stop* he left a description of Wheeling baseball. The book's hero is told by his mentor, "Wheeling's a swell town to play in. The fans here like a good game an' don't care who wins. The kids are bad, though!" Evidence of that observation came as the Findlay team left the park for their hotel. Suddenly, "a shower of stones, mud, apples, and tin cans flew from all sides."[36]

After the ISL folded, Barrow quickly found a spot for Wheeling in the Iron and Oil League, which was just about to begin the second half of a split season. Basically a group of small northwestern Pennsylvania towns, the league under President C. B. Powers gladly added Wheeling. Barrow strengthened his team for the new league. Buckenberger, having been let go by St. Louis, took the reins as on the field. They splurged on an ace pitcher in Harry Staley, who had won 137 major league games 1888–1894. Art Ball, a former major league player, took over for Will White at shortstop. The big addition was Jack Glasscock, who was back home after his long major league career was shortened by an arm injury that prevented his throwing from shortstop to first base. Barrow convinced him to play first base and bat clean-up for the Nailers.[37]

Barrow won his first of many pennants with the 1895 Nailers and Wheeling got its first taste of a champion. With Glasscock batting over .400 and Staley pitching well, the Nailers finished a close second to Warren, Pennsylvania. In the post-season playoffs, Wheeling emerged as league champion. Fifty-five years later, when Barrow wrote his autobiography, he chose to be photographed holding the 1895 pennant which A.G. Spalding donated rather than the fourteen he won as general manager of the New York Yankees or the one he captured as the Boston Red Sox manager. Over the winter of 1895–96 the actual pennant could be viewed at J. W. Grubb's Jewelry Store.[38]

Not only did Wheeling capture its first professional pennant in 1895, its native son Jesse Burkett won his first major league batting championship. Burkett had left Wheeling hoping to establish himself as a pitcher. Following two outstanding minor league seasons, he flopped with the New York Giants. After being sold to the National League Cleveland Spiders in 1891 and switched to the outfield, his career took off. The five-foot, eight inch Burkett hit a National League best .409 in 1895 with 225 hits. He followed that spectacular season with a second batting championship and .400-plus season in 1896 when he batted .410.

By the mid–1890s baseball had become firmly entrenched as the summer game across the northern half of West Virginia. After 1870 Wheeling had witnessed a remarkable growth in baseball. The sport had become democratized, widely played by boys and young men of all social classes.

Even as the growth of semi-professional, independent professional and league teams made baseball the first spectator and commercial sport in the Mountain State, amateur baseball continued to thrive. Indeed, in the 1870s and 1880s, amateur teams seemed to flourish when the area had a first-rate team to keep baseball in the public eye. By 1890, however, the amateur game had taken on a life of its own both in Wheeling and in other parts of the state.

3

"A Progressive Community Must Have a Base Ball Team"
Baseball's Second Boom, 1895–1905

In the 1890s, especially after the end of the 1893–1896 depression, baseball once again swept across segments of the Mountain State, much as it had done three decades earlier, only this time it put down deep roots. As it had in the 1860s, baseball spread from Wheeling back eastward along the Baltimore and Ohio Railroad tracks, south down the Ohio River, and up the Kanawha River. In the first years of the twentieth century, the game even reached the isolated coalfields of southern West Virginia.

Baseball's appeal varied widely in those years. For boys, and a very few girls, the sport remained a folk game, played for the joy of it and played with ever changing rules. For older boys and young men, baseball offered a chance to develop and test physical skills on organized teams as such teams proliferated throughout the state. The most skilled found a way to make money playing for semi-professional or professional teams. A handful made it all the way to the major leagues. For most participants, the game remained a form of recreation played by young and old at Fourth of July gatherings and summer picnics. Democrats played Republicans, Fats squared off against Leans, and barbers challenged linotype operators in games for bragging rights. Finally, an increasing number of West Virginians became fans who enjoyed watching skilled players and who were willing to pay for the opportunity.

The common notion that baseball was a "boys' game" gained currency around the turn of the century. Participation became broad based for kids from six to sixteen. Boys in small towns and emerging cities played sandlot ball in streets and in vacant lots, wherever they could find flat ground and whenever they could gather enough for a game. Play went on from sunup to sundown. Farmers' sons generally had other things to do from sunup to dusk, but some of these managed to find time to play as well. Balls were precious items, so boys played with them as long as they held together. Even after the seams split, boys taped them up and kept playing. Broken bats got nailed together. Lacking enough for a nine-person game, they divided up and played with however many turned up. Duke Ridgley, later sports editor of the *Huntington Advertiser*, remembered these years as the heyday of sandlot games. Hardly a boy dared not play the game.

Earlier in the nineteenth century, proponents of baseball had emphasized the patriotic aspect of the game; baseball was America's national game. Beginning in the mid-nineties, the view of baseball as a boys' game became grafted onto the earlier notion. The proliferation of baseball literature aimed at boys was, in part, responsible for spreading this new image of the game. The Frank Merriwell stories, written by Gilbert Patten under the pen name Burt L. Standish, began appearing in 1896. Soon dozens of other writers, including Zane Grey, began churning out baseball books aimed at the juvenile audience. For turn-of-the-century boys, art and life seemed to meet on the baseball field.

Older boys and young men began to form teams, repeating an earlier pattern of development. The more skilled local players formed town teams, or neighborhood teams in cities, or company teams at their place of employment. As high schools became more widespread in the first decade of the twentieth century, they too began to form teams. Less skilled players found their level in church leagues and on fraternal or YMCA teams. At whatever level, teams looked for competition against teams of a similar talent. Most important of all, they looked for ways to put on a uniform.

Town teams sprang up in villages and towns across the northern portion of West Virginia. Tiny villages such as Hinkleville, Wilsonburg, Bridgeport and Beverly sprouted teams. So did college towns like Buckhannon and Morgantown. The small cities of the North Central region along the Baltimore and Ohio Railroad — Mannington, Fairmont, Clarksburg, and Grafton — grew a variety of teams. None of these town teams had much staying power but they kept popping up year after year. In the larger cities of Parkersburg in the west and Martinsburg in the east, teams came and went at the same rate as in small towns.

Professional baseball, of course, was the apex of baseball, the level to which boys aspired. In West Virginia, pro baseball remained centered in Wheeling in the five years on either side of 1900, but other cities showed an interest in commercial baseball. None of the efforts to establish professional ball succeeded as it did in the Nail City, but a culture that prized organized baseball was building. At the center of that culture was the notion that baseball was good for the community.

College baseball was only a notch below the quality of the pros. The greatest continuity in turn-of-the-century baseball came among college teams. From 1890 onward, Bethany College and West Virginia University fielded teams each spring even though they might only play a few games. Other colleges in the state were slower to engage in intercollegiate competition. Of these other schools, only Marshall College, a state normal school in Huntington, fielded a team before the end of the century. After a fitful start, a Marshall team began in earnest in 1898. At Bethany, the oldest college in West Virginia, the students ran their own team much like other co-curricular activities, clubs, fraternities and literary societies. In Morgantown, the university boys organized the West Virginia Athletic Association in 1890 to run baseball, football, and track teams. Shortly thereafter both schools chose colors, nicknames, and mascots and developed cheers for football and baseball.[1]

The earliest college teams seldom ventured far from home, playing nearby Pennsylvania colleges such as Washington and Jefferson and Waynesburg and local town teams. Still, students invested enthusiasm in the games. Indeed, interest in the teams' exploits grew to the point that by 1892 the college teams could charge admission to games. Baseball in the spring and early summer generated as much enthusiasm as did football in the fall.

More than recreational players or even town teams, the college students quickly placed great emphasis on winning. The desire to win led the West Virginia University boys to bring in a ringer for their 1893 game against Waynesburg College. Ad Gumbert, who had won 22 games for Pittsburgh the previous season, was available because he was holding out for more money from the National League club. How much the WVU students paid Gumbert is unknown, but they got what they paid for, a victory over the Pennsylvania rivals.

Baseball at both Bethany and WVU became more ambitious in the midnineties. The first game between two West Virginia colleges occurred in 1894 when teams from those two institutions squared off. Behind the pitching of Charles "Jake" Hewitt, the university prevailed over Bethany. The following year, Bethany was the equal of the boys from Morgantown. The Bisons, as the Bethany men called their team, playing off the campus location on Buffalo Creek, played an ambitious 22 game schedule. The season high point came when the Bethany team took a swing through Ohio, playing seven colleges, including Ohio State University, whose payout covered the cost of the trip. The same year, WVU played a much more limited schedule, but a dozen years later, alumni looked upon the 1895 club as WVU's "first great team." Behind the pitching of Hewitt and hitting of football star Harry "Hurry Up" Yost, the Mountaineers compiled a 5–1 record. The only blemish on WVU's record came from an early season loss to Bethany. The Morgantown boys, however, avenged that loss with a 12–4 win in the last game of the season. Following that victory, Hewitt went directly to Pittsburgh to join the Major League team there.

The desire to win led the West Virginia University Athletic Association to hire a professional coach, T.G. "Doggie" Trenchard, beginning in 1896. Bethany looked upon such a move as professionalism, and continued the practice of having a student captain lead the team. Even so Bethany bested Trenchard's team in his first year. The new WVU coach had a stronger program by the next spring. He began by establishing the school team's first pre-arranged schedule for 1897.

The 1897 Mountaineer team featured Charles "Piano Legs" Hickman. After one impressive season at WVU he left Morgantown at the end of classes to play baseball professionally. By the end of the summer he donned the uniform of the National League Boston Beaneaters. Over the next twelve major league seasons he compiled a .301 career batting average playing for seven different teams. He would return to Morgantown following his playing career. He coached his alma mater and ran a store before World War I and later became mayor of Morgantown and sheriff of Monongalia County.

By 1900 college ball had taken on qualities of semi-professional baseball — paid coaches, admission charges, extended travel, and a heavy emphasis on winning. Despite this, neither WVU nor Bethany had more than mediocre seasons at the end of the century. Even with Charlie Hickman, the university team could do no better than split with Bethany in 1897. The following year WVU suffered a losing season, then bounced back to the plus side in 1899.

Meanwhile, Wheeling continued to boast the only truly professional baseball team in the state. There the Wheeling Nailers found a home in the newly revived Inter-State League. C. B. Powers, a sportswriter for the *Pittsburgh Ledger* and president of the Iron and Oil League, convinced the owners of teams in Toledo, Ohio, and Fort Wayne, Indiana, to bolt the Western League and join his new Inter-State League. With these large mid-western cities as a core Powers had little trouble lining up six other smaller cities, including Wheeling. His aptly named league included cities in Pennsylvania, West Virginia, Ohio, Michigan, and Indiana. The league set a 126 game schedule and a manageable $800 per month salary cap per team.[2]

Before the 1896 season started, Wheeling fans were abused by the team's co-owner, Ed Barrow, and his Pittsburgh based colleagues. Barrow, of course, had guided Wheeling to its and his first championship in 1895. Over the winter of 1895–96 he was the toast of the town in the Nail City. During the 1895 season, Barrow had been impressed by the play of two brothers who played for Warren, Pennsylvania, the team Wheeling beat out for the Iron and Oil League title. In the off-season, Barrow traveled to Carnegie, Pennsylvania, and signed both brothers to Wheeling contracts. The more experienced Al Wagner also impressed Wheeling sportswriters, but Barrow foresaw a brilliant future for the awkward young Honus Wagner. After signing the Wagners, Barrow moved quickly. He first obtained the Patterson, New Jersey, franchise in the recently formed Atlantic League. Second, as the Wheeling owner he sold Honus Wagner to Patterson. Then he sold his share of the Nailers. Wagner, of course, would go on to become the greatest shortstop of all-time. Such deals would later help Barrow establish the New York Yankees dynasty.

With a bitter taste in their mouths, Wheeling fans wished nothing more to do with absentee owners. The local streetcar company came to the rescue of professional baseball in Wheeling. W. S. Wright, general manager of the Wheeling Street Railway Company, persuaded the remaining Pittsburgh owners to sell to local interests. Wright then brokered a deal that made local attorney Louis S. Delaplaine the principal owner and William W. "Will" Irwin the largest minority partner.

The new owners faced the perennial problem of finding a place for the team to play. Schmulbach, who had build the 1895 park on his Wheeling Island farm, had torn down the grandstand and converted the field to a horse track and paddocks. The fairgrounds on Wheeling Island was the most desirable location, but the park board refused to rent to the team. The owners finally settled on the little park Irwin had built for his semi-pro team in 1892. The owners worried that the plot was too small and too wet. Wright again stepped in to solve these problems. He arranged for the team to purchase adjacent land in order to extend the plot to a full city block. Wright then convinced Wheeling City Council to build a new storm sewer to drain the grounds. It paid to have friends with Wright's political clout. A grandstand seating 2,000 spectators and bleachers on either side seating another 1,000 went up in time for opening day at a cost of $3,000. Wright's interest in the welfare of the team became clear. The new park at 47th and Jacob Streets on the far south side of the city, some thirty-five blocks from center city, was a fifteen-minute ride on Wright's trolley.

The Nailers' season opened with great enthusiasm. The *Daily Intelligencer* proclaimed: "Oh, let the rooters ralley/ From every hill and valley/ Of this our little mountain state."[3] The team finished third in the overall

Inter-State League standings of 1896. Fort Wayne and Toledo proved to be the class of the circuit. Wheeling catcher Al Shaw, described by a local writer as "brilliant and at times phenomenal," led the locals with an official but unreliable .394 batting average. He went on to play four years with Detroit. Al Wagner, who became the field manager, kept the team on an even keel and played a steady second base. Al's baseball ability did not come close to matching that of his brother, none did, but he did play in the majors. Despite a first division finish, the cost of the park assured that the 1896 team lost money.

The 1897 season produced serious problems for Wheeling baseball. At the Inter-State League annual meeting in January, the Nailers' principal owner, Louis Delplaine, clashed with league president Powers. When the owners reelected Powers over Delaplaine's sharply voiced opposition, the Wheeling owner vowed to take his team out of the league. Wright again intervened. He persuaded Delaplaine to sell the team and park to W. Claude Coyle and son Bert for $1,500. The season started in grand fashion. Carriages carried both teams, as well as the mayor and the sheriff, out to the park, the Grand Opera House band leading the way. Unfortunately, the new owners were badly undercapitalized. They hired players on the cheap. The team fell into last place in the standings, and as it did attendance dwindled.[4]

The financial crisis brought on by lack of fans soon made clear to Wheeling the reality that professional baseball had become a business. By August players had gone six weeks without being paid. Veteran minor leaguer Edward "Pop" Lytle, leader of the disgruntled players, announced the team was on strike for back pay. League President Powers acted swiftly, declaring the franchise forfeited to the league. Powers found a buyer for the distressed team in Frank Torreyson, then the player-manager of Dayton. Torreyson paid the Coyles $1,000 for the club, and gave a portion of the back pay to the players, who called off the strike. Torreyson, now in debt, sold off Wheeling's few decent players beginning with Lytle. His actions, of course, only made a bad team worse. The Nailers limped to the finish with a dismal 38–96 record.

Torreyson had not finished wrecking the Wheeling franchise. Over the winter of 1897–1898 the owner announced he would move the team to Grand Rapids, Michigan. His decision was in part an early example of an owner moving because another city offered a sweetheart deal. The traction company in Grand Rapids gave Torreyson a rent-free park, plus the company paid off his remaining Wheeling debts. Moreover, in Grand Rapids the team could play on Sundays. Torreyson, now an entrepreneur, sounded the part of a robber baron when he justified his actions. "As baseball is a business with me," he said, "I could not let sentiment keep me from doing what will make me money."[5] Indeed!

While professional baseball struggled in Wheeling, amateur ball flourished as never before. The Wheeling YMCA formed the first city league in West Virginia. It started with four teams, two neighborhood clubs, the Pike Street Sluggers and Twenty-fifth Street Stars, and two teams composed of company employees, Block Brothers, and Tobacco Chewers. The league expanded to six teams the following year, and over the next decade numerous teams entered and dropped out. Wheeling Laundry reigned superior for several years, holding off the challenge of teams named Little Havana, Elm Grove, Bridgeport, Stephens Blue Seals, and Lutz Brothers Tobacco.

Despite the thriving amateur baseball in Wheeling, the area no longer produced the number of major league players it had in the 1880s. A few from the region debuted in the big-time in the nineties, but far fewer than in the previous decade. This group included Joe Berry, Jake Hewitt, Ed McNichol and Win Mercer. Of this group, Mercer was the best but the most troubled. After nine years in the majors and an appointment as manager of Detroit, he committed suicide in 1903.[6]

In 1946, Jesse Burkett became the first player from the Mountain State to be inducted into the Baseball Hall of Fame. Hack Wilson, Bill Mazeroski, and George Brett would follow. One of the few in major league history to bat over .400, he did it twice (National Baseball Hall of Fame Library, Cooperstown, N.Y.).

Wheeling did get vicarious enjoyment out of the exploits of native son Jesse Burkett. At the beginning of the 21st Century, Wheeling would boast three members of the Baseball Hall of Fame who were born in the city, Burkett, George Brett, and Bill Mazeroski. Of the three, only Burkett grew up in Wheeling. Brett moved to California at an early age, and Maz grew up just across the Ohio River. Burkett, on the other hand, learned baseball in the Wheeling amateur and semi-pro ranks. He turned pro as a pitcher in 1888 but became a full-time outfielder with the New York Giants in 1890. His greatest seasons were with Cleveland in 1895 and 1896 when he compiled back-to-back .400 seasons. In addition to his .409 and .410 averages those years, he led the National League in 1901 with a .382 batting average for St. Louis. He retired with a resounding .338 lifetime average.

Outside the Wheeling area, promoters of professional ball had little success in the nineties. Up the Ohio River to the north of Wheeling, tiny Wellsburg had a team in a short-lived semi-pro Ohio Valley League in 1891. Efforts to found teams in the rapidly growing cities of Charleston and Huntington, in the mid-section of the state, met with failure. Both were large enough to support a team: Huntington's population had topped 10,000 in 1890 and Charleston's was on the verge of doing so. Neither city had established, well organized amateur teams, although both had teams in 1894 and 1895. Nonetheless, both cities obtained franchises in an abortive Ohio State League in 1894, but the league never opened. Organizers tried another Ohio State League in 1896. Huntington and the small Ohio River village of Sistersville obtained franchises but the needed financing failed to materialize and the franchises were returned to the league. Baseball did not return in an organized fashion until 1898 in Huntington and 1899 in Charleston.[7]

In the Eastern Panhandle, baseball returned in the early 1890s after a twenty-year absence. Amateur town teams appeared in Martinsburg, Berkeley Springs, and Shepherdstown. Martinsburg native Jack Boyd became the first player from the region to make the majors when he pitched for Washington in 1894. Martinsburg had a semi-professional team in a four-city Cumberland Valley League in July and August of 1895. This league consisted of teams from Chambersburg, Pennsylvania, and Frederick and Hagerstown, Maryland, in addition to Martinsburg. Teams played a thirty-six game schedule with matches two days a week. The league managed to complete its season, but no teams turned a profit and the league collapsed. None of the cities attempted to revive commercial baseball for another two decades.[8]

Parkersburg became the second West Virginia city to operate a professional team when a newly created Ohio–West Virginia League opened in 1897. The Ohio River city was the third largest in the state behind Wheeling and

Huntington. Local businessman Sigmund Marcus believed his city was ready to support pro ball. He gained a franchise in the newly created four-city league, which consisted of Zanesville, Marietta and Cambridge, Ohio, in addition to Parkersburg. Marcus "spent money freely on the team" and put a decent lineup on the field. Pitchers Lou Mahaffey and Charlie Hastings, shortstop Eddie Glenn, and outfielder Orville Woodruff made it from Parkersburg to the National League. In the end, however, "the people of Parkersburg ... failed to support the team," as the *Parkersburg Daily State Journal* reported in its obituary for the ball club. Marcus, who according the newspaper was losing $80.50 per game, could hardly be blamed when the "Greeks" and league folded July 6, 1897.[9]

After the abortive efforts of the nineties to spread league baseball to West Virginia cities beyond Wheeling, few promoters or civic boosters stepped forward to try again for another decade. Wheeling, however, did return to the world of professional baseball in 1899 after a one-year absence. W. B. Howell, president of the Wheeling Athletic Club, obtained a franchise in the Inter-State League. The somewhat misnamed club was located outside the Wheeling city limits in Elm Grove, five miles east of the Ohio River on the National Road. The location had become a favorite venue for boxing, wrestling, bowling, and football, and as a hangout for "sportsmen." Howell thought baseball would round out the club's activities, even though games would be played on Wheeling Island.

Howell's 1899 team, alternately called the Nailers and Stogies, finished deep in the second division. It did have some quality players. Denny Lyons, one of the true stars of thirteen major league seasons in the 1880s and 1890s, finished up his career in Wheeling. He batted .311, exceeding his .310 big league lifetime average.[10] Catcher Lou Ritter and centerfielder John Dobbs spent over five years in the majors.

After one season, Howell passed the ownership of the Wheeling club to his former field manager, Pop Lytle. In an ambitious plan for the 1900 season, the Inter-State League raised the monthly salary limit to $1,550 per month, the highest it had ever been, and increased the schedule to 154 games. Lytle, however, was determined to field a strong team. Lyons returned for another year. Future big-league outfielder Bill "Bunk" Congalton became the crowd favorite with his superb fielding and timely hitting. Two outstanding young pitchers, John Skopec and Ed Poole, stole the spotlight. Each won twenty games, the only time Wheeling ever had a pair of twenty game winners. Both would pitch in the majors, although neither matched their 1900 season totals.

Lytle, lacking solid financial backing for his ambitious payroll, once again raised the issue of Sunday baseball. Weekday attendance at Island

3. "A Progressive Community Must Have a Base Ball Team"

Park averaged about 500. The prospect of seeing 1,000 to 2,000 at Sunday games enticed Lytle. So he decided to schedule Sunday games. At the Nailers' first Sunday game, April 29, 1900, Constable Henry Stoehr served warrants sworn out by Wheeling Island residents to all the players. After doing so, he allowed the teams to complete the game. Players then paid a fine. This tableau repeated itself the next game. The club attempted a ruse: claiming the game was played for charity, the team donated $25 each to the Protestant Children's Home and the Catholic Boys and Girls Home. Judge J.R. LaRue refused to buy the argument and fined the players. At the third game, after Stoehr served his warrants, attorney Virgil McCluskey arrived with two policemen and a second warrant, this one taken out by Protestant clergy. When it became obvious that McCluskey intended to stop the game, a riot broke out. "Several hundred bleacherites" swarmed the field, physically removed McCluskey and the police from the park, and tore up the warrants. Chief of Police W.M. Clemans, apparently fearing the situation could get out of hand, let the game proceed, and it did for 18 innings.[11]

Sunday baseball received its death notice on June 3, 1900, when Judge Thayer Melvin granted an injunction preventing the team from playing on Sundays. The penalty for violating the injunction was a $2,000 fine. Lawyers for the team pegged their case on the recreational needs of working people. Those who work six days a week, they argued, "find rest and enjoyment in looking at a game of ball on the only day they can afford to be present." The court was not buying that argument.[12] It would be another two decades before Sunday baseball could become a fixture in West Virginia.

Ironically, Ed Poole would become a central character in a similar drama played out on a larger stage. Early in the 1904 season Poole was pitching for Brooklyn when he took the mound on Sunday, April 24, against Philadelphia. He was promptly arrested for violating New York's Blue Law. It was his bad luck to pitch again on Sunday, May 29, when District Attorney John Clarke arrested him. The case went to trial and became known as *The People of New York v. Poole*. The judge ruled that because an admission fee was charged, the Sunday game violated the law. The ruling governed Sunday ball in New York until 1919.[13]

Without Sunday games, Lytle quickly moved to sell the team. Again, Wright and the traction company came to the rescue. The Wheeling Street Railway Company purchased the team and put its own man, W. A. Shirley, in charge for the remainder of the 1900 season. He announced no further effort would be made to play Sunday baseball in Wheeling. The Nailers managed to complete the season with a winning record.

Wheeling's home in the Inter-State League vanished with the league in the winter following the 1900 season. When Ban Johnson's American League expanded into four eastern cities and prepared to claim major league status, it left four western cities without a home. The large western-most Inter-State League cities, Toledo, Columbus, Dayton, and Fort Wayne, wished to align themselves with the cities Johnson cut loose — Indianapolis, St. Paul, Minneapolis, and Kansas City. Indianapolis owner John T. Brush led the efforts to effect a new league. Clearly, these cities saw no place for Wheeling in their new league.[14]

Sheriff Will W. Irwin exploded at the baseball establishment. He mounted a relentless campaign to get a professional franchise back in Wheeling. In a series of letters to National League President Nick Young and Indianapolis owner John T. Brush, Irwin lambasted the magnates for destroying pro ball in the Nail City. He beseeched them to "right the wrong done Wheeling." Irwin's pleas fell on deaf ears. In fact, Brush failed in his effort to establish a league for the 1901 season. He settled for a stopgap league, called the Western Association, consisting of Louisville, Indianapolis, Columbus, Toledo and four smaller cities. Irwin's efforts finally bore fruit when one of the smaller cities, Grand Rapids, ran into problems a month into the Western Association season.

Irwin moved quickly to arrange for Wheeling to get the league franchise. He organized the sale of stock in a team and the election of B.F. Perkins as president. The duo of Irwin and Perkins would run the Stogies for over a decade. They leased the site for a park on Ohio Street on Wheeling Island, and quickly built bleachers to seat 1,200 fans. With a monthly payroll of $1,800, team management again felt the need for Sunday games to augment the budget. Irwin and Perkins arranged to play at Sisters Island Park, a small Ohio River island reachable only by water. A steamboat made hourly trips to the island park. The gambit did allow Sunday games by removing the games from local jurisdiction, but it created other problems. The short right field made the games somewhat farcical; fourteen ground ruled doubles occurred in the first game. More importantly, the games only attracted an average of 400 customers, about the same as weekday games. The Stogies finished above .500 but were well off the pace.[15]

Ed Kenna proved to be the big story of Wheeling's 1901 season. The Nailers signed Kenna the day before their first home game. The son of a United States senator from West Virginia, Kenna had been a pitching star at WVU. Kenna became a fan favorite and an effective pitcher. During his season in Wheeling, he began writing poetry. By the end of the summer, his jottings were enough to fill a book, which he published with the title

Lyrics of the Hills. Oddly enough, none of his poems contained a baseball theme. By the time Kenna reached the majors in September 1902, the press had pinned the nickname "The Pitching Poet" on him. Following his premature death from a heart attack in 1912, a posthumous book of poems, *Songs of the Open Air*, would also be published.

After the 1901 season, the largest cities of the Western Association again left Wheeling out in the cold. They implemented the plan for a new American Association. The league of Minneapolis, St. Paul, Milwaukee, Kansas City, Indianapolis, Toledo, Columbus, and Louisville remained a stable structure for the next fifty years. Wheeling would have to hunt for a new home.

Elsewhere throughout West Virginia at the dawn of the Twentieth Century, baseball enjoyed a grass-roots boom. College ball continued to flourish. West Virginia University fielded outstanding teams in the first few years of the new century. The 1900 club claimed to be the "best nine that ever represented that institution." Outfielder Lewis "Bull" Smith provided the hitting. Ed Kenna transferred to WVU from Georgetown, where he had led the Hoyas to a 14–2 record in 1899. Smith and Kenna led that WVU team to an 11–3 record. A 4–1 victory over Bethany allowed the Mountaineers to lay claim to the state title. Not content with state laurels, the team boasted it was the best in West Virginia, Ohio and Pennsylvania. The 1902 team was even stronger, becoming the first team to win over twenty games. That year the WVU team featured four future major league players. Eugene "Gene" Curtis from the town of Bethany joined Smith in the outfield and William "Buck" Washer gave Kenna relief on the mound. Kenna pitched in the majors before the summer ended. Smith played minor league ball for a decade, reaching the majors briefly. The Mountaineers dominated their games against other West Virginia colleges throughout the first decade of the century. Only a 1907 loss to West Virginia Wesleyan College marred their otherwise perfect record.[16]

Other colleges took up baseball early in the 1900s. Marshall College fielded its first team in 1896, but lacking competition, the team did not regroup the following year. Marshall returned to baseball in 1898 and seemed ready to take the sport more seriously. Morris-Harvey College in neighboring Barboursville provided strong competition for Marshall. By 1905 the *Huntington Advertiser* called Morris-Harvey "the strongest aggregation of college players in West Virginia." Of course, Morris-Harvey did not play WVU, so the claim remained unsubstantiated. West Virginia Wesleyan College joined the mix of college teams in 1903 when Ed Kenna coached the club before joining his pro team. Wesleyan, however, would not become a power until the second decade of the century.[17]

Baseball finally found its way to the coalfields of southern West Virginia. The first recorded game in the region, played in Welch, the seat of McDowell County, between a local town team and a team representing the mining town of Gary, occurred nearly forty years after the first game in West Virginia. The players were not local elites or miners. They were mine engineers who brought the game with them from Pennsylvania. In Bluefield, workers on the Norfolk and Western Railroad, who, like the Welch and Gary players, came from the north, began playing pick-up games on a field at the Tower Grounds in the west end of the city and behind the roundhouse on the north side. There the social elites also played the game. Mayor R. M. Baldwin took up the game, as did future Norfolk and Western Railroad president A. C. Needles.[18]

The midland cities of Huntington and Charleston were also discovering the sport. Huntington's economy emerged from a decade long slowdown to boom from 1903 until World War I. Charleston's growth was slower; its boom would come in the second decade of the century. Despite their size, neither city had moved past the amateur level of baseball before 1908. Marshall College's team did spur some interest in Huntington, where teams named Clippers and Acmes joined the college boys. Charleston fielded teams in 1899 known as the Superbas and Champions. Smaller towns along the Kanawha River also had teams at the turn of the century; these included Mason City, St. Albans and Montgomery. In none of these cities did the opinion makers see baseball as the harbinger of progress.[19]

The turn of the century saw baseball beginning to flourish in North Central West Virginia as well. The cities and towns along the Monongahela River and its tributaries enjoyed a booming economy based on the bituminous coal field centered in the Fairmont-Clarksburg corridor, oil west of the coal region, and the burgeoning glass industry in Clarksburg. Baseball went with the modern temper.

In Fairmont, seat of Marion County, the power elite saw value in baseball. Earl Smith, editor of the *Fairmont Times*, spoke for the city's movers and shakers. By 1902 he came to believe, "Any city with any pretense at all of calling itself a progressive community" must have a baseball team. Clearly, he believed Fairmont to be a progressive city. He called for the organization of a team to make Fairmont proud. So did coal barons Arch and Ralph Fleming, whose money came from the Consolidation Coal Company, the largest in West Virginia. The leadership of the Fairmont Traction Company quickly joined the effort. In March 1903 the Flemings took the lead in forming the Fairmont Baseball Association. The streetcar company saw great benefit in the city having a team capable of drawing spectators on its cars to the fairgrounds outside of town. The organizers had little trouble raising money to start a team.[20]

In 1903 Fairmont fielded its first semi-professional team, an outfit called the "Coalers." The team played at the fairgrounds. Although outside the city and some distance from the population center, the fairgrounds offered the only enclosed grounds in the area. The Coalers were good enough to beat West Virginia University and town teams in the region. Much like Wheeling's first experience with a commercial team, the Coalers were not competitive with traveling teams from Ohio and Pennsylvania. In 1904 the Coalers played regularly on weekends. By 1905 the team played several days a week, logging in over fifty games that summer, against clubs from as far away as Dallas, Texas. More commonly they played clubs from Uniontown, Pennsylvania, Cumberland and Frostburg, Maryland, and Piedmont, West Virginia, as well as local opponents. The Coalers held their own against all opponents.

Clarksburg took a decided backseat to Fairmont in developing a baseball culture, but, nevertheless, the game took root. Boys and occasionally teams of young men played at an East End location called Jackson Park near the B&O train depot off East Pike Street. A team composed of workers at Hazel-Atlas, the largest of the glass factories, was organized in 1902. Workers at Kobelgard, the largest wholesaler in the region, soon joined them. These teams found games against nearby town teams from Bridgeport, Lost Creek, and Wilsonburg. In what may have been the first high school game played in West Virginia, St. Josephs Academy of Clarksburg lost to Weston High School in a 1903 contest. Soon the YMCA fielded a team.

A 1903 trip through though North Central West Virginia by a "Bloomer Girl" baseball team drew attention wherever it went. The team, called the St. Louis Stars, barnstormed across the state in May 1903, working its way east along the B&O Railroad line. The Stars took on local teams in Parkersburg, Pennsboro, West Union, and Wilsonburg before arriving in Clarksburg. Some 550 spectators turned out to see the women play the Hazel-Atlas team. The women usually beat the locals, but in Clarksburg they lost a close game.

Clarksburg area baseball got a shot in the arm in 1904 when the streetcar company opened a recreation facility called Union Park east of the city. Baseball was not part of the initial plans for the park, but within a year park goers laid out a diamond. Despite this growth in Clarksburg, there was not a move to create a team to match the Fairmont Coalers.[21]

In the heart of the northern West Virginia coalfield between Fairmont and Clarksburg, teams began to crop up in mining camps. Places named Enterprise, Monongah, Gypsy, Lumberport, Worthington, Meadowbrook,

Montana Mine, and Riverside fielded teams in the first years of the new century. These grass-root teams came from the initiative of the miners themselves without assistance from the coal companies.[22]

The railroad town of Grafton seemed to have benefited from the influx of railroad workers from the east. Railroad workers formed a town team, and soon several teams were operating there. In 1904 the town team built a grandstand at Fetterman Park across the Tygart River from downtown.

West of Fairmont on the B&O railroad line, the booming oil and natural gas town of Mannington had developed a strong baseball tradition. Back in 1891 a town team from Mannington had traveled to Uniontown, Pennsylvania, to play for a $600 prize. The money provided incentive for Mannington to hire Bill Kennedy of the Wheeling Stogies to pitch for them. From 1900 until World War I Mannington fielded strong amateur, semi-pro and even professional teams. Fred Barlow, owner of a newsstand and tobacco shop, ran the town team beginning in 1903. In 1904 and 1905 the Mannington Athletics played every weekend in the summer on a field with grandstand in Hought Bottom. The Athletics held their own against the Fairmont Coalers and generally beat other teams in the region. Burt Oil Company had a team of 14 to16 year old boys. The Pittsburgh Pirates took advantage of Mannington's enthusiasm for baseball by playing exhibition games there.[23]

Amateur ball continued to flourish in and around Wheeling. No other location could boast the number of teams that Nail City had. Dozens of teams competed in such locations as the Tunnell Green, 41st Street Grounds, B&O Grounds and Island Park. Numerous company teams played neighborhood teams, and teams with names like Jacky Arthurs, Pink Garters, Jim Richards' Stars, and Modern Sluggers. In 1903 Wheeling area high schools formed the state's first inter-scholastic league. Linsly, the private prep school in the city, captured the initial title over Wheeling High School, and the Ohio schools from Bridgeport, Elliott, and Martin's Ferry.[24]

The American and National leagues ended their two-year war and competition for players in1903. The minor leagues were party to the agreement through their own new organization, the National Association of Professional Baseball Leagues. The new association established a new classification of leagues, Class A, B, C, and D. With the new agreement, the term "Organized Baseball" came into use to denote players and teams within the framework of the agreement. From then on, all others leagues would be derided as "outlaw leagues." With the new agreement, minor leagues began to flourish.

Professional ball returned to West Virginia in 1903 after a year's absence. Irwin and Parker again provided the organizational leadership. In early February they represented Wheeling at the organizational meeting of the Central League. The circuit gained a Class B ranking in Organized Baseball. Despite an injunction by "neighboring property owners ... on account of windows in their homes being broken by balls knocked over the fence," Parker and Irwin had Wheeling Island Park in playing shape for opening day.[25]

By mid-summer the Stogies put together a team capable of exciting local fans and competing with the league's best teams. Replacing Frank Kain with Edison "Ted" Price as player-manager proved a key move. Price did not make a lot of player moves and basically let the players play. Outfielder Gene Curtis became the darling of Wheeling fans. Big (6'3" and over 200 pounds), strong, fast, and local (a Bethany native and WVU graduate) he could hit, hit for power, run, and field. He batted .315 but it was his fielding and daring base running that excited the spectators. Sportswriter R.M. Archer believed Curtis to be the fastest in the Central League. Curtis used his speed to "make some of the most brilliant catches ever seen in Wheeling and we remember Brodie, Stenzel, Flick and Delahanty." Eighteen-year-old Walt Miller led the team in wins as a pitcher and batting (.325) as an outfielder. The Stogies finished in the first division and drew well enough for the club to break even financially.[26]

The Central League seemed to be a good fit for Wheeling. A team would operate there with brief interruptions until World War I. Even though the Stogies again finished fourth in 1904, the fans loved them. Price brought most of his 1903 club back and that continuity helped fans identify with the players. Infielders Charles Dieters and Bill McCombs and catcher C.P. "Pop" Shriver always hit less than .250 but they hustled, played hard and got their uniforms dirty. The addition of Bill "Brickyard" Kennedy, back home after a long career in Brooklyn, was a huge addition to the team. Kennedy had mellowed somewhat since he last played for Wheeling in the early nineties, but he remained a funloving prankster. On the mound he still had enough on his fastball to get Class B batters out. Win or lose, the Stogies gave fans a fun day at the park. At the end of the 1904 season, the club showed a profit of nearly $10,000. No West Virginia team had ever been so profitable.[27]

The Stogies won their first pennant of the Twentieth Century in 1905. Charles Cogwell, who won the Central League batting title in 1904 while playing for South Bend, replaced Curtis in the outfield. Only catcher Pat Livingstone, who compiled a .313 average, batted over .300. The pitching of Walt Miller, Bill Kennedy and Bill Robertson carried the team to the championship. In his third year with the Stogies, Miller won twenty-one games against ten losses, the best winning percentage in the league. He had only a brief fling in the major leagues, but he was the toast of Wheeling. Thirty-seven year old Kennedy won 15 games, while Fred Ehman notched 17 wins, and Robertson had 13 victories. Manager Ted Price's lads won the pennant with 5½ games to spare.

Wheeling had captured its second professional league championship ten years after Ed Barrow and Jack Glasscock led the Nailers to the city's first pennant. The 1905 Stogies not only won the flag, but also showed an $11,500 profit for the season. Clearly, baseball had reached its high point in Wheeling.

Elsewhere in northern West Virginia baseball had put down deep roots in the local communities by 1905. Participation levels on town and neighborhood teams were at a peak. It was rapidly becoming a spectator sport as well. In the larger towns and cities, voices were calling for professional teams to boost the hometown.

4

"No Better Advertisement Than a Good Baseball Team"

North Central West Virginia in the Deadball Era, 1905–1920

By the beginning of the twentieth century, Wheeling lost its monopoly on baseball just as it lost its claim to being West Virginia's most populous city. For a few more years Wheeling remained the only city with a professional team, but by the end of the first decade of the century ten other West Virginia cities had pro teams. Growing cities, anxious to shake the image of "hillbilly," took to professional baseball as a means of establishing civic identity in national terms and increasing civic pride. Not only did the professional game spread, but amateur ball also flourished so much that other parts of the state began producing more major league players than the Northern Panhandle. Indeed, measured by the number of major league players born in the state, the period from 1900 to World War I was the highwater mark for West Virginia baseball.

As the National Game exploded in popularity during the first decade of the new century, nowhere in West Virginia was the sport as popular as in North Central West Virginia. The region became the center for baseball, besides enjoying the fastest economic growth in the state. The cities and towns along the Monongahela River and its tributaries—the Tygart Valley River and West Fork River—had been established pre–Civil War towns. Grafton, Fairmont and Clarksburg benefited from the Baltimore and Ohio Railroad and the bituminous coal field centered in the Morgantown-

Clarksburg corridor. By the first years of the new century the region was industrialized, urbanized to a large degree, and economically booming. Fairmont and Clarksburg outdistanced Buckhannon, Weston, Grafton and Morgantown in population and importance. Mannington was close behind Fairmont and Clarksburg, until 1910 when its population began a decline that would reduce its size over fifty percent by 1920.

Clarksburg, seat of Harrison County on the West Fork of the Monongahela River, experienced its greatest boom in the first two decades of the century. Between 1900 and 1910 its population more than doubled from 4,000 to 9,000, and in the next decade its population shot past that of Fairmont to nearly 28,000. Clarksburg's economic base moved beyond coal, as it became the industrial center of the region. Glass manufacturing boomed as national companies including Republic Glass, Hazel-Atlas, and Owens established large plants there. Specialty firms including McNicol China and Akro-Agate Marble, the world's largest producer of marbles, prospered and grew. National Carbon, the forerunner of Union Carbide, began with a chemical plant there in 1904. Tin Plate Mill opened in 1905 and quickly became the largest manufacturing enterprise in Central West Virginia. Although coal production in Harrison County did not peak until 1915, by 1910 Clarksburg ceased being known as a coal town, and had developed an urban cast of mind.[1]

Fairmont, twenty-five miles north and down river from Clarksburg, continued to see itself as the cultural and economic center of the region. Its location at the center of the east-west axis on the Baltimore and Ohio Railroad between Grafton and Mannington, and the north-south axis between Morgantown and Clarksburg, gave Fairmont a centrality in the region. Consolidation Coal Company, headquartered there, was the largest in the state. Few Fairmont residents noticed as Clarksburg passed it in most economic indices. Like Clarksburg, but to a lesser extent, Fairmont experienced a growth of glass and other small manufacturing industries. Its population grew over 70 percent between 1900 and 1910 and by 84 percent in the second decade of the century. Its power elite and much of its economy, however, remained tied to coal.

By 1906 an elaborate interurban rail transportation system connected the towns of North Central West Virginia. If, as has been said, major league baseball grew up with the rumble of trains, then minor league baseball at the beginning of the century lived to the clang, clang, clang of trolley cars. The streetcar companies injected new life into baseball by constructing enclosed ballparks with grandstands that had the ability to charge admission. Most were built some distance from center city. Of course the traction companies expected their streetcar lines would carry fans to the games.

Clarksburg's locally owned traction company sold out early in the century to a group headquartered in Fairmont that then operated as the Fairmont and Clarksburg Traction Company. Interurban lines soon linked Clarksburg, Weston, Mannington, and Fairmont. Grafton had its own car lines.

The newly consolidated traction company built ballparks in Clarksburg and Fairmont, but they were far from identical. At Union Park, four miles outside Clarksburg, the company erected a traditional wooden park with covered grandstand enclosed by plank fence. The Fairmont based company pulled out all the stops in its home city. In 1906 Thomas S. Haymond, an energetic and wealthy coal operator and Fairmont civic booster in his midthirties, became vice president and, in effect, operator of the Fairmont Baseball Association. He wanted a franchise in organized baseball for the Coalers. He felt he needed a new park close to the center of the city's population. The Coalers' home at the fairgrounds he judged inadequate. When the Fleming family of Consolidation Coal Company made available a portion of their farm on the South Side of Fairmont, the traction company built a state-of-the-art park on the site. When completed, the 2,500-seat

The Fairmont and Clarksburg Traction Company built baseball parks in both cities. Union Park, seen in 1907, located four miles from Clarksburg, was reachable only by the streetcar line (West Virginia Archives and History Library, Charleston, W.Va.).

steel, concrete and stone park was reputed to be the finest minor league park in the entire country. The new park, located on Twelfth Street, was known variously as South Side Park and Traction Park. Portions of the park, including the stone entrance, continue to exist one hundred years later incorporated into East-West Football Stadium.[2]

Haymond's 1906 Coalers played serious baseball. They drew good crowds charging a 25-cent admission, and played over 60 games. The team's schedule included games against teams from the professional Pennsylvania-Ohio-Maryland League, which gave fans a taste of Organized Baseball. Haymond flirted with a "Coal Town League" to include Fairmont and Piedmont, West Virginia and Frostburg and Cumberland, Maryland, but he decided such a league had little chance of success. Although he had little baseball experience, Haymond understood he needed a better team if the Coalers were to move into a professional league. To underline the team's limitations, the Coalers lost to the Mannington Athletics in a game billed as for the championship of West Virginia. The Mannington team then easily beat a town team from Clarksburg to further its championship claim.

With the new park as bait, Haymond went searching for a league to join in 1907. *The Fairmont Times* endorsed his efforts, explaining "there is no better advertisement a town can get than a good baseball team." Haymond found teams from Pennsylvania, Ohio and Maryland reluctant to make the trip to Fairmont, but they conceded that if another nearby city joined Fairmont, such a trip would become more economically viable. Haymond then began to negotiate for a team in Clarksburg as well as Fairmont. He did not bother to ask anyone in Clarksburg for permission. Haymond found spots for the Coalers and for Clarksburg in the new Western Pennsylvania League. Alex "Al" Lawson, a Philadelphia promoter, and Charles B. Powers, *Pittsburgh Dispatch* sports writer, put together a league with six towns from Western Pennsylvania and they were happy to include the two West Virginia cities.

Clarksburg had a park but no infrastructure to support a team. No readymade organization existed to support a team, let alone a team ready to make the leap to pro ball. Haymond convinced Frank J. "Buggy" Welch, proprietor of Welch's Pharmacy in Clarksburg, to take the organizational lead. Welch had some baseball experience, having operated an amateur team in town for several previous years. Somehow he fielded a team for the start of the 1907 season.[3]

In the first year of professional baseball in North Central West Virginia, Fairmont dominated the league both on the field, at the box office and in the leadership of the organization. Haymond decked his team out in spiffy pearl gray uniforms with green stripes and blue socks with a white band. He brought Joseph "Reddy" Mack, a former major league second baseman, to town to direct the Coalers. Contrary to popular opinion, the Fairmont manager was not related to Philadelphia Athletics' owner Connie Mack, but Reddy seemed happy to let people believe what they would. The 1907 Coalers ran away from the rest of the Western Pennsylvania League, winning ten more games than their nearest rival. Catcher Walt Snodgrass, who hit .366, and outfielder Elmer "Doggy" Haught were all-stars. First baseman Louis "Steve" Evans was good enough to be sold to the New York Giants; he stayed in the big leagues eight years. Pitcher Buck Jackson won 19 games while losing only once.[4]

Haymond's Fairmont team made money in 1907. They were, however, the only team in the league to finish in the black. The league's $1,800 monthly salary limit was ambitious for a Class D league. The young league faced trouble as early as the third week of the season when the Pennsylvania cities of Beaver Falls, Greensburg and Latrobe experienced financial difficulties. Haymond urged moving the Beaver Falls franchise to Morgantown, but the Beaver Falls team disbanded before the move could be arranged. Latrobe threw in the towel in late May. President Lawson, who had played fast and loose with league funds, did likewise. In fact, the National Association banned Lawson from baseball for financial irregularities. Powers became acting league president and transferred the Latrobe team to Cumberland, Maryland. That move did not work; Cumberland folded on June 27. Powers then gave up, resigning as league president. Haymond took over as the league's third president in a month.

Haymond transferred the beleaguered Cumberland franchise to the tiny industrial village of Piedmont, West Virginia, on June 27, 1907. The site of a West Virginia Pulp and Paper Company mill since 1888, Piedmont's population of under 3,000 clung to a hillside upstream from Cumberland between the Potomac River and Baldy Mountain. A sulfur smell from the mill often permeated the town, but residents quipped, "It smells like money." Although virtually inaccessible from the rest of West Virginia by road, its location on the B&O railroad between Grafton and Cumberland made the town accessible to league teams. Despite the inhospitable location, Piedmont already had a baseball tradition. A mill team began playing there in 1903 and by 1904 it was recruiting out of town lads to play in Piedmont. One such recruit was Bill Louden, who came there from his native Pittsburgh in 1904 and resided there for the rest of his life. In 1906 he left town with a barnstorming team from Dallas, Texas. He jumped from there to the majors. Piedmont had played Haymond's Fairmont Coalers in 1906, and a Pennsylvania-Ohio-Maryland (POM) League team briefly operated there the same year.

Piedmont's stay in the Western Pennsylvania League proved short-lived. The team that came to Piedmont was in last place and going nowhere in the standings. After only ten days in the league Piedmont faced a crisis. Players went on strike for back pay. On July 11 the league gave up on Piedmont and again moved the franchise, this time to Somerset, Pennsylvania. In the team's brief stay in Piedmont it had a record of four wins and six losses. Only catcher Archie Frankenberry showed much promise.[5]

Clarksburg's first experience with pro ball was better than Piedmont's, but far from as good as Fairmont enjoyed. The season began with Union Park in need of work; drainage presented a problem, no screen stood in front of the grandstand, and grass had not yet covered the outfield. Between the lines, the team struggled. Firing manager Tom Huling did little good. New manager Elmer Essler led the club into last place. The local newspapers turned on the team. In one of the most vitriolic attacks launched against the hometown team, the *Telegram* wrote, "When the Clarksburg players took the field it was noticed that they had ruffles on their panties and rouge on their cheeks." A few days later, it referred to the team as "the Old Maid's Knitting club." Little wonder that only 74 spectators attended the next home game.[6]

After appointing Lewis "Bull" Smith as manager in early July, Clarksburg did make a quick turnaround on the field. The former WVU star had played briefly in the majors with Pittsburgh in 1904 and Cincinnati in 1906. The aura of a major leaguer brought Smith respect from his players. Veteran minor league pitcher Johnny Lower threw a no-hitter against Scottdale to ignite the team. Smith brought in a pitcher named Bill "Doc" Wilson to bolster the staff. By the end of the season Smith had the Mountaineers playing with confidence. They managed a fourth place finish.

Clarksburg's most consistent play came from their eighteen-year-old first baseman, who played under the name of Bobby Hollister. He batted a strong .293. Not until the following summer when the Cincinnati Reds wished to acquire him did his Clarksburg fans find out that Hollister's real name was Dick Hoblitzel. For the 1908 season Clarksburg lent him to Wheeling but retained his contract. When the Reds tried to purchase him from the Stogies, Clarksburg management appealed to the National Association. In the end Clarksburg received $1,000 for Hoblitzel. Before his playing career ended he established himself as the best West Virginia born first baseman. After over six years with Cincinnati, he went to the Boston Red Sox for five seasons. There he held down first base on the 1915 and 1916 World Champion teams.[7]

The example of professional baseball touched off a wave of amateur ball in the region. The Mannington Athletics stood out as the strongest of the area teams. The Athletics even beat Western Pennsylvania League champion Fairmont Coalers 7–3 in a July game at Traction Park. As they had done in 1906, Mannington proclaimed themselves champions of West Virginia. Mannington had its own enclosed field, Blackshere Park, where the team charged admission for games. Several youth teams sponsored by local merchants served as feeders for the Athletics. Those same merchants provided jobs for Athletics players from out of town.[8]

In Clarksburg neighborhood teams in Adamston, Northview and Stealey popped up. The independent Clarksburg Americans and Hazel-Atlas Glassworkers were the strongest of the local clubs. Clarksburg High School fielded its first team in the spring of 1907. Along the West Fork River between Clarksburg and Fairmont, amateur teams in the coal and market towns formed a Central Valley League consisting of Shinnston, Lumberport, Gypsy, Enterprise, Glen Falls, and Monongah. Buckhannon, Wilsonburg, Rosemont, and Lost Creek had town teams. In Fairmont, the East End Victors were the top of the class. Grafton, the seat of Taylor County, had a town team, plus the Grafton Elks fielded a team, as did Grafton High School.

After the 1907 season, Haymond began searching for a new league for his Coalers. The Pennsylvania-Ohio-Maryland (POM) League was anxious to include Fairmont, but Haymond passed on that opportunity because the league did not want Clarksburg. Haymond then decided to put his own league together. He corralled the Connellsville and Scottdale clubs that had finished the 1907 Western Pennsylvania season. Then he found two additional Pennsylvania towns, Uniontown and Charleroi. With Fairmont and Clarksburg he had a six-team circuit that he named the Pennsylvania-West Virginia League, or "Pawva" for short. A $1,000 per month salary cap made it easier for teams to avoid red ink on their financial ledgers. After putting the league together Haymond turned its administration over to young James Groninger, who had captained the WVU team in 1906 and stayed in Morgantown to coach the Mountaineers.[9]

Clarksburg enjoyed a much better 1908 season than did Fairmont. In April the original owners, Frank Welch and his partner Lucis Hague, owner of Home Furniture Store, sold the team to the newly created Clarksburg Baseball Association, a stock company. William Harrington and Louis Carr headed the new organization. The team signed Fred and John Dawson from Mannington. Fred led the Pawva League in runs and stolen bases. It was the pitching of John Lower, Doc Wilson, and Joe Miller that carried the team to the most wins in the league. Lower and Wilson were all-stars. Unfortunately for Clarksburg, Uniontown played fewer games and finished with a higher winning percentage. A three game playoff was arranged to resolve the disputed crown. After losing in Uniontown, Wilson pitched

Clarksburg to victory in the second game played at Fairmont. Then the hometown boys wrapped up the series at Union Park with an 8–3 victory. The Dawson boys and all-star first baseman Bobby Conoway led the way. Clarksburg had its first championship.[10]

After winning the league championship, Clarksburg played several exhibition games at Union Park, including one against the Cincinnati Reds. John Lower shut the Reds out for six innings before being removed. As if on cue, Dick Hoblitzel, a native of Waverly between Clarksburg and Parkersburg, clubbed a home run to give the major leaguers the 5–4 win.[11] Exhibitions like this against touring major league teams were huge draws and often made the difference between teams finishing in the black or the red.

The Fairmont team, known as the "Prohibs" because a local prohibition preceded the passage of statewide prohibition, finished well down in the standings. Ironically, part of the Prohibs' problems stemmed from "demon rum." Manager Reddy Mack quit in frustration following a July 4 double-header loss to Clarksburg. Several of his players appeared "in no condition to play"; whether drunk or hung-over was not clear. Haymond released the worst culprits and appointed catcher Walt Snodgrass as manager. The team held its own for the rest of the season. The high point of the summer for Fairmont came after the regular season. The Fairmont pros finally beat Mannington's semi-pro outfit. Then they beat the Brooklyn Dodgers 4–3 before the largest crowd of the year. Pawva All-Star Elmer Haught homered for the home team.

A third North Central city got its first taste of organized baseball when the league transferred the Scottdale franchise to the Grafton Traction Company on July 31, 1908. That streetcar company, following the examples of Fairmont and Clarksburg, had recently constructed Fetterman Ball Park. The park, however, still needed work, and visiting clubs groused about "bad grounds," its "poor shape." The team known as the "Railroaders" occupied the league's cellar when it came to Grafton and finished in the same place. Before the season ended John T. McGraw, Grafton's wealthiest citizen, had to rescue the team from bankruptcy.[12]

The Pawva League managed to start the 1909 season with the same six teams that finished in 1908. The decision to raise the monthly salary cap from $1,000 to $1,500 made it more difficult to turn a profit. In hopes of generating more interest late in the season the league went to a split season format with a playoff at the end. By the end of the season, however, the league was reduced to four clubs.

Fairmont, called the "Hunters" after popular manager Lou Hunt, raced out to capture the first half. Hard-hitting catcher Waldo Jackey, a Cameron, West Virginia, native, won the league batting title with a .326 average. Ralph

Carlisle, working his third season at Fairmont, was the pitching ace. The team faded after selling outfielder Chester King, the only other .300 hitter, to Dallas after the first half. The Hunters then lost the playoffs to Uniontown four games to three. Uniontown featured all-around star Joe "Hooker" Phillips, who had won the league batting title in 1908 and led pitchers in 1909 with 29 victories.

Grafton finished with a .500 record but they featured some outstanding players. Del Gainer from Montrose, West Virginia, south of Grafton, stood out as the Engineers' brightest star. He batted .316 and showed speed, leading the league in runs and stolen bases. At the conclusion of the season, Grafton sold Gainer to Detroit, where he played two games before the Tigers' season ended. He stayed in the majors for ten years. Shortstop John "Red" Hinton batted .343 but lacked the requisite number of at-bats to qualify for the batting title. Outfielder Guy "Gunner" Zinn from Clarksburg hit .294. He would be with the New York Giants in 1911, the first of five major league seasons.

Clarksburg experienced a terrible baseball summer in 1909. Even though the team returned four 1908 all-stars — outfielder Fred Dawson, shortstop James McGinty, catcher John Gribben, and pitcher Doc Wilson — the team started poorly. Fans accustomed to a winning team stayed away from rickety Union Park. By July the club could not meet its payroll. The players threatened to strike but decided to wait until after July 4 in the hope of a big holiday crowd to recoup revenues. It was not enough. Finally, on July 8 the players struck for back pay. Two days later the club management announced the team was disbanded.

A second team, Charleroi, exited the league, providing an opportunity for Parkersburg to return to Organized Baseball. The city on the Ohio River had grown to over 15,000 people by 1909, making it the largest city in the league. This was Parkersburg's second attempt at supporting a professional team. The city's first pro team in 1897 disbanded for lack of support. Amateur or semi-pro ball had not taken hold there, although Curt Bernard came off the city's sandlots to make the New York Giants in 1900. By 1909 the city had a four team Fraternal League and a semi-pro club, the "Profs." The team that came to Parkersburg from Charleroi possessed neither talent nor pep. The new club lasted just over a week before it folded on July 10. The league struggled along with four teams following the departure of Clarksburg and Parkersburg.

At the conclusion of the 1909 season, Pawva president James Gronninger urged expansion to an eight-team league by including Huntington and Charleston. Haymond, keenly aware of the problems that beset the 1909 league, scaled back his aspirations in 1910. He bypassed Groninger and formed a four team West Virginia League. Mannington, with its strong semi-pro tradition, joined Fairmont, Clarksburg and Grafton. A booming oil and natural gas town, Mannington had grown to 8,050 by 1910. It had two enclosed baseball parks with grandstands, one at the fairground, a short walk from downtown, and the other at the village of Blackshere east of town toward Fairmont. Teams from the other three cities could easily reach Mannington by either the B&O Railroad or interurban trolley via Fairmont.[13]

Lou Hunt's Fairmont club took the lead and stayed there until the end of the 1910 season. The Hunters finished with five more wins than the Mannington Drillers. Catcher Waldo Jackey again led the league in batting with a .345 average. Outfielder Orlando Keller also batted over .300. Hunt, a Fairmont resident, became extremely popular with fans around the league.

Hunt had a defensive whiz at shortstop in seventeen-year-old Everett "Deacon" Scott. At five foot, eight inches tall and 145 pounds, he looked very much the kid he was. The youngster fielded his position better than West Virginia had seen since Jack Glasscock's days in the 1880s. Scott hit a respectable .282 for Fairmont. When Scott reached the majors with the Boston Red Sox in 1914, he joined Dick Hoblitzer and Del Gainer, not to mention young George Herman Ruth, on the world champion 1915 Red Sox team. Between 1916 and 1925 Scott broke Steve Brodie's major league record for playing in the most consecutive games. Scott's record would in turn be broken by Lou Gehrig.[14]

Mannington made a successful transition to pro ball. Many of the players from the semi-pro Athletics proved they could play pro ball. Unlike other clubs that had legally become stock companies, the Drillers continued to be sponsored by local businessman Fred Bartlet. Mannington stayed close to Fairmont in the 1910 pennant race thanks to the pitching of Doc Wilson, picked up from Clarksburg, and Bill Chambers, a Cameron, West Virginia, native. Following the season, the Drillers sold Chambers to Wheeling and from there he went to the St. Louis Cardinals by the end of the 1911 season.

Financial problems in Clarksburg and Grafton brought the league down. Neither team kept a nucleus from their 1909 clubs. Grafton had two holdovers, Clarksburg none. Both teams signed players they could get cheaply, and that scheme did not pan out. Clarksburg, called the "Moguls," did bring Bull Smith back as manager, but he had too few skilled players to move the team out of the league basement. The Clarksburg newspapers gave far less coverage to the team than in previous summers. The team limped along until July and then disbanded. Grafton followed with its own announcement that it could not continue.

After the West Virginia League folded, amateur and semi-pro ball flourished in the area. Several Mannington players, including infielders Charles "Biggie" Reeder, Bob Prysock, and Billy McCombs, remained in town playing for the semi-pro Drillers. The team drew as many paying customers as it had as a pro team. Lou Hunt helped organize a six team Fairmont City League following the demise of pro ball. Hunt assumed the reins of the Fairmont Mining Machinery team, leading it to the title. Several of Hunt's former pros joined one or another team in the City League. A strong African-American team, the Meade Wonders, played at South Side Park against teams from Wheeling, Grafton, Morgantown, and from nearby Pennsylvania towns.[15]

Tom Haymond attempted to resurrect the small league of West Virginia cities in 1911. He proposed changing the league name to Virginia Valley League, but the cosmetics did not work. Clarksburg withdrew before the season started. The proposed league fell by the wayside.

Bull Smith put together a strong semi-pro team in Clarksburg. The club played on Sundays at Union Park against amateur and semi-pro teams from the region. They won most of their games in May, June and July, including victories over Mannington, Grafton, Elkins, Buckhannon, Monongah, and an all-star team from the Fairmont City League. Their only loss came to the Pittsburgh Collegians. When pitching ace Earl Danley jumped to another team in late July, Smith's club fell on hard times. By the end of the summer, Biggie Reeder's Mannington team and the Monongah town team, with former pro pitcher Vic Toothman, emerged as the strongest in the area.[16]

In the winter of 1911–12, Haymond finally gave up on Clarksburg. For the first time since 1906 he attempted to gain Fairmont a place in a league without a partner in Clarksburg. The Ohio-Pennsylvania League showed interest in Fairmont but decided the trip into West Virginia would be too long and costly for its Ohio members. A disappointed Haymond passed the leadership of the Fairmont Baseball Association to Lou Hunt. When Hunt died suddenly, Elmer H. Smith took over as club president and maintained a readiness as the 1912 season started.

When the 1912 Ohio-Pennsylvania League ran into trouble, as so often happened with early minor leagues, it provided an opening for Fairmont. Two teams dropped from the league in mid–June. In mid–July it reorganized. The league adopted a split season format with Salem, Ohio, the first half winner. Salem then shifted to Fairmont on July 9, 1912. Second place Steubenville moved to tiny Follansbee, West Virginia. Those shifts allowed the league to limp along as a four-team circuit for the remainder of the season.[17]

The new Fairmont Fairies were actually atop the league when the team shifted to Fairmont. Manager Elmer Daily proved popular with local fans. A former Bethany College athlete, Daily quickly made friends in the city and integrated himself into the town. In an effort to help local rooters identify with the new team, the Fairies signed several local players. Biggie Reeder and Fred and Otto Schmitt came from Mannington, and pitcher Earl Danley moved up from Clarksburg. Fairmont, however, went on a losing streak that cost them first place and paying customers. Despite a record crowd for another exhibition game against the Brooklyn Dodgers, the Fairmont team lost money for the first time. Still, Fairmont could claim its third professional championship when the second-half winner, the Follansbee Bees, failed to show for the playoffs.

Follansbee's only experience with professional baseball proved disappointing. Why the Steubenville franchise chose to shift to the Northern Panhandle town of Follansbee remains unclear. The West Virginia town sits just across the Ohio River from Steubenville, so simple proximity may have been the reason. The team that played as the Follansbee Bees, beginning July 16, performed reasonably well, despite a roster of non-descript players. By season's end players and management were glad to cut their losses.

The national reform movement of the early twentieth century known as the Progressive movement energized Protestants with a moral agenda. Two of the reformers' goals, abolishing the use of alcohol and the enforcement or passage of Sunday blue laws, cut deeply into the welfare of baseball. West Virginia adopted prohibition before the rest of the country, first as county option and then as a statewide prohibition. Fairmont and Clarksburg had reputations of being good Sunday towns for baseball. The amateur and semi-pro teams all played on Sundays as well. In 1913 the prosecuting attorney of Marion County announced that baseball had been 'tolerated' on Sundays before, but he would now stop it in the county.

In part because of the ban on Sunday games and in part because Tom Haymond decided it was time for him to get out of baseball, Fairmont and all of the North Central region went without professional ball in 1913. In Clarksburg, a four team City League consisting of the Elks, Goff Building, Scholastics, and Bowlers absorbed the players from Bull Smith's semi-pro teams of 1911–12. By July, the best players were again playing on a Clarksburg town team, but this team played fewer games than Smith's previous town teams had played. Fairmont's six team City League continued, as did a Sunday School League.

A new Pennsylvania–West Virginia League came into being for 1914. The circuit was another four-city league with Fairmont and Clarksburg

4. "No Better Advertisement Than a Good Baseball Team"

teaming with the Pennsylvania cities of Connellsville and Uniontown. Opening day for the Clarksburg Colts, as the team was called, proved memorable because it was the first time the opening day parade proceeded from downtown to Union Park in automobiles. Helped by local businesses closing at noon, a crowd of 2,000 attended the first game.

Despite the city's official ban on Sunday games, Clarksburg was determined to play on the Protestant Sabbath. Manager Hugh Shannon believed the revenue from large Sunday crowds stood between profit and bankruptcy. At the first Sunday game, Sheriff Ross F. Stout tried to stop the game but the umpire ejected the law officer from the park. At the second Sunday game, Stout returned, backed by the Harrison County prosecuting attorney and a police escort. Despite a loud protest from the crowd, the officers handcuffed the umpire, manager Shannon, and one of the players. The other players fled. Shannon, needless to say, was outraged. He protested, "They have taken from the laboring man his only chance of getting out into the open air." Shannon singled out at Prosecuting Attorney A. Judson Findley as "one of those narrow-minded men who should have been living during witchcraft days." Of course, Prichard's outcry missed the point of the reformers, who stood their ground. Citing losses of $500 to $1,000 for each Sunday game, the Colts disbanded. The league had little choice but to fold as well.[18]

With the passing of the Pawva in 1914, professional baseball came to an end in North Central West Virginia for over a decade. West Virginia was not alone because as World War I broke out in Europe, baseball declined sharply across the country. The number of leagues dropped by over fifty percent between 1914 and 1916. In the region's first experience with pro ball, Fairmont had enjoyed the most successful run both on the field and at the box office. Fairmont teams won pennants in 1907, 1909, 1910, and 1912. The club turned a profit every year except one. This success came from the leadership of Tom Haymond, the solid backing of the local newspaper, and the finest ballpark in the state, easily accessible from the population center. In Fairmont, baseball became a community enterprise. By 1914, however, pro ball in the Monongahela Valley awaited a loosening of attitudes and the opportunity to play again on Sundays.

As professional ball faded, college baseball reached the peak of its popularity in West Virginia. In the 1890s only Bethany College and West Virginia University had fielded teams. In 1903 West Virginia Wesleyan College started to play. Marshall College and Morris Harvey College in the Huntington area had fitful starts and stops in the first decade of the century, but both developed stable programs in the teens. Normal colleges at Fairmont, Glenville and West Liberty started the sport between 1909 and 1913. Salem

College joined in 1916. Baseball stood on a par with football at all the colleges until World War I. After that football reigned supreme.

West Virginia University, not surprisingly, fielded the strongest college team more often than not, but the smaller schools were quite capable of taking the measure of the university teams into the twenties. At Bethany College, baseball remained the top sport until 1913 with football second. The Bisons challenged WVU's supremacy between 1910 and 1913. The university team, with Lawrence "Larry" McClure as coach and occasional player, prevailed in 1910. When the season ended, McClure, a diminutive outfielder weighing only 130 pounds, left the campus to play professionally in Huntington, and then went on to join the New York Highlanders by the end of summer. Bethany, led by Bill Batsch, who played briefly for the Pittsburgh Pirates, claimed to be the strongest in the state in 1911 and 1912.[19]

Interest in college baseball was so high that games between major rivals were transferred from the campuses to professional baseball parks, first to South Side Park in Fairmont and then to League Park in Wheeling. In the teens, the college games had all the color and atmosphere of football games. Fans packed the stands with as many spectators as attended football games in the fall. Bands played and fans waved pennants and responded to their cheerleaders. College baseball games usually outdrew the local professional team.

Between 1912 and 1918, West Virginia Wesleyan College, Marshall College, and WVU engaged in a struggle for supremacy that captured the imagination of the state. In these years, Wesleyan featured the school's greatest athlete, legendary Earle "Greasy" Neale. He was followed by future major league pitchers Harry Shriver and Fred "Sheriff" Blake. The university team, coached by alum Charles Hickman, had Ira "Rat" Rodgers, the Mountaineers' first football All-American, and its own future major league pitcher, Frank Barron. Marshall boasted several future big league players as well.

The West Virginia Wesleyan Bobcats fielded its strongest teams in the teen years. Wesleyan and WVU split two games in 1913, so neither could claim to be state champion. In 1914, former Fairmont professional star Elmer Daily took over as coach at Wesleyan. That year the schools played three games. They split the first two games. The rubber match was played at Fairmont. Wesleyan left little doubt which was the better team, clobbering WVU 12–0. Centerfielder Neale was the batting and fielding star for WVWC. He had somehow managed to play professionally in London, Ontario, while enrolled in college and hit college pitching with seeming ease. Following the 1914 college season, he played professionally for Wheeling, batting .373 in the Central League.[20]

Marshall College challenged WVWC and WVU for preeminence in 1915 and 1916. The university boys bested Wesleyan three times in 1915. Frank Barron pitched three consecutive shutouts for WVU in 1915 as he closed out his three-year college career with a 25–10 record. Marshall, however, claimed the state title by surprising WVU in a game played at Wheeling. The Marshall team got a huge boost when Arch Reilly transferred from Ohio State University to play third base for the Herd. Marshall's lineup also included future big leaguer Wilber Fisher. The university returned to the top of the college heap in 1916. The Wheeling *Intelligencer* offered a silver cup to the state champion and sponsored a five game series between West Virginia University and Marshall to determine which team would carry the cup home. The teams split the first four games. In the deciding fifth game, WVU's freshman pitcher Kester June bested Marshall 4–2 in a twelve-inning game.

Wesleyan and WVU contended for the top rung in the state for the remainder of the decade. In 1917 Rodgers had his best year in baseball, batting .431. Despite Rodgers' efforts, Wesleyan regained the top rung in 1917. Pitchers John Frederick "Sheriff" Blake of Ansted and Harry Shriver from Wadestown led the way. In the championship game Shriver and Kester June locked up in a pitching duel. Earlier in the year, June had pitched WVU's first non-hit game. WVWC managed only four hits off June, but tall (6'4") and lanky (180 pounds) Shriver pitched a three hit shutout to beat WVU 3–0. Shriver made it to Brooklyn in 1922, but lasted only the one season; Blake spent ten years in the majors beginning in 1920. In 1918 West Virginia University dropped Wesleyan from its schedule in both baseball and football for four years. That decision effectively ended the rivalry. Kemper Shelton took over as coach at WVU in 1918 and had strong teams in 1918 (13–4) and 1919 (14-3-1), probably the best in the state. In those years, the Mountaineers had little trouble beating Marshall, but, of course, did not test themselves against Wesleyan. WVU had a down year in 1920; the Mountaineers experienced their first losing season of the twentieth century, losing even to Bethany. With future big leaguer Ken Ash on the mound, WVWC could lay claim to being the strongest college club in 1920.[21]

Amateur and semi-pro teams continued to play following the demise of professional baseball, but fewer and fewer teams took the field each year. Town teams came and went much as they had at the beginning of the century. City leagues and church leagues provided a venue for amateurs who loved to play the game with buddies on other church teams and service club teams. In Fairmont, the city's industrial league lasted until 1917. A few company teams—Hazel-Atlas in Clarksburg, Consolidation Coal in Fairmont, and Consumer Fuel in Mannington being the most prominent—continued to field teams through the World War I years. Consolidation's roster included a number of former Fairmont professional players. The Mannington team managed to bring in the best players. Outfielder Lee King from Hundred, West Virginia, and pitchers Harry Shriver and Jesse Winters played in Mannington before they made it to the majors. Al "Three-Finger" Braithwood pitched for Consumer Fuel after his big league days ended.[22]

By 1918, World War I and the influenza epidemic kept players from the sandlots. Union Park outside Clarksburg became the site of a housing development. In Grafton the traction company allowed the grandstand at Fetterman Park to fall into ruin. Blackshere Park at Consumer Fuel mine outside Mannington fell into disrepair. The jewel of West Virginia ballparks, South Side Park in Fairmont, became the favorite site for local high school football teams to play. Except for Ken Ash, who grew up a stone's throw from Union Park, and Clarksburg's Babe Barna, no player from the region would make it to the majors between the wars.

5

"Oh, Summer in Kanawha"
River Towns in the Deadball Era, 1905–1920

In the first decade of the Twentieth Century, North Central West Virginia outdistanced the rest of the state in adopting baseball and its cultural forms. Along with the North Central cities, Wheeling in the northern panhandle was closer than other parts of the state to the cultural vibration of urban America emanating from Pittsburgh, Baltimore, and Washington. The North Central cities achieved an urban cast of mind sooner than the middle or southern parts of the state. As part of that "progressive" mindset, members of the North Central power structure and opinion makers saw baseball as a tool to advertise the city and make it modern. In their reasoning they were mirroring the attitudes seen in Wheeling a decade earlier.

The second decade of the century, however, belonged to the towns and cities along the Ohio and Kanawha rivers. Wheeling remained the largest city in the state, but Huntington grew to 50,000 people by 1920, almost as many as Wheeling. Charleston's population increased from 1910 to 1920 by almost fourfold to 40,000. Professional baseball spread from Wheeling south to the bourgeoning city of Parkersburg to the village of Point Pleasant at the confluence of the Ohio and Kanawha rivers, and on to Huntington. Along the Kanawha, teams came into existence at Point Pleasant, Charleston and on to Montgomery. Even Williamson on the Tug River across from Kentucky briefly hosted a team in a professional league. The smaller cities, however, fell by the wayside and before World War I broke out the three largest cities in West Virginia — Wheeling, Huntington and Charleston — proved to be the only cities on the western rivers capable of sustaining professional ball.

Members of the 1898 West Virginia University team clearly enjoyed themselves. Front row, left to right: Scott Lowe, p and captain; Jim Pratt, c; bat boy; unknown. Middle: George Anderson, 1b; Fred Mitchell, rf; Sam Dent, 2b and p; Charles Middleburg, cf. Back row, left to right: Lee Llewellyn, lf; Charles McWhorter, 3b; Laughead, sub; Dwight Miller, ss; Ed Shelby, c (why is he holding an umbrella?). Watching (left to right) are: Ed Naret, student; unknown; Dr. Robert W. Douthat, professor of Latin; unknown law student (West Virginia and Regional History Collection, West Virginia Libraries).

If the number of native-born West Virginians who made the major leagues is any measure of an area's interest in baseball, the first two decades of the century, 1900–1920, represented the peak of West Virginia baseball. Over forty percent of West Virginia born major league players made their big league debut in those two decades. From sandlot to pros West Virginians were playing baseball. Of that group of deadball players, nearly three-quarters of them came from the flatlands along the Ohio and Kanawha rivers. Admittedly, none of those players made the Hall of Fame, although Earle "Greasy" Neale was inducted into the football Hall for his coaching after his baseball career. Wilbur Cooper of Bearsville was the best of the group. The best left-handed pitcher ever from West Virginia, Cooper pitched a Pirate record 263 complete games, won over 200 games, and compiled a 2.89 earned run average over fifteen years. In 1969 Cooper was selected the best pitcher in Pittsburgh Pirate history.

This pattern suggests a broad based participation in baseball and enhanced opportunities for turning professional. Duke Ridgley, sports editor of the *Huntington Advertiser,* reflecting back on his youth remembered the pre-war years as the heyday of sandlot baseball. Games on vacant lots or in the streets were a constant from sunup to sundown in the summer. Balls were precious items, so boys played with them as long as they held together; even after the seams split boys taped them up and kept playing. Broken bats got nailed together. Hardly a boy dared not play the game.

Although Fairmont emerged as the brightest light in West Virginia's baseball firmament between 1905 and 1915, Wheeling continued to field professional teams as well as strong amateur clubs. Between 1905 and 1910 the fortunes of the Wheeling Stogies went down and up like a yo-yo. From first place in 1905 the team plummeted into the Central League second division in 1906. The next year the Stogies rebounded to a second place finish without the aid of even one .300 hitter. The era was not called the deadball era for nothing. Pitching dominated and the Stogies had two of the league's best. Former major leaguer Bill Friel won 20 games, Bill Robertson notched 17 victories, and Nick Maddox had 13 wins. Friel's victories included a no-hitter, and Maddox boasted two no-hit games. The Stogies might have captured the league crown had they not sold Maddox to Pittsburgh in early August. Once in Pittsburgh, on September 20, 1907, he pitched his third no-hitter of the season, the first in Pirate history. The next season Maddox won 23 games for the Pirates plus a World Series game.[1]

In 1908 the Stogies went down again, plunging from second place all the way to the league's cellar. The club was not just last; it was 25 games worse than the seventh place team. Dick Hoblitzel, Clarksburg's star of 1907 who batted .356, over 100 points higher than anyone else on the team, was the only bright spot. He donned a Cincinnati Reds uniform before season's end.

That year, the Central League toyed with a proposal to travel by interurban trolleys. Under the plan, each team would own its own trolley for sixteen players. Theoretically possible, it would be cheaper than train travel. The thought of going from South Bend, Indiana, to Wheeling on streetcars failed to excite enough teams. The league did raise the monthly salary limit to $2,500. Owners agreed to use turnstiles to count attendance.[2] Wheeling's did not click very often.

After the disastrous 1908 season, team president B.F. Perkins and secretary Will Irwin cleaned house. They brought in Bill "Whoa Bill" Phillips to manage and pitch. Under Phillips' guidance, the team made a remarkable transformation, going from last to first in 1909. The Stogies won with great pitching and solid fielding. Even though he was six years removed from the majors, Central League batters hit only .201 against Phillips, making him the hardest pitcher in the league to hit. Mound mate Johnny Fisher compiled the league's most wins with a 24-9 record, and was the second most difficult for opposing batters. Rufe "Spitter" Nolley won 18 games and Phillips compiled a 12-3 record. The Stogies lacked a .300 hitter, but they had a "stonewall infield that outclassed many in the higher leagues." Third baseman Bill McKechnie led the team with a .275 average and topped the circuit in stolen bases. McKechnie wore a Pittsburgh uniform the next eleven seasons. His later Hall of Fame selection came from his managerial ability rather than his playing skills. In 1909 he was just the sparkplug that fired Wheeling's third pennant in 15 years.[3] It would be another 20 years until the city tasted another pennant.

By 1910 professional baseball was on the verge of reaching its peak in West Virginia. Wheeling ceased being the sole city with pro ball when the North Central cities of Fairmont, Clarksburg, Mannington, and Grafton fielded teams. Piedmont, Follansbee and Parkersburg briefly entered pro leagues, but lacked staying power. Martinsburg would gain a pro franchise in 1915. The expansion of pro ball into the river cities and towns of the West Virginia's Midland brought baseball to a whole new part of the state. Between 1910 and 1915 teams would play in Huntington, Charleston, Point Pleasant, Montgomery, Parkersburg, and Williamson. At no other time would West Virginia have so many professional teams.

Both major midland cities, Charleston and Huntington, experienced boom years after 1900. Although the capital city grew by leaps and bounds, the real growth was occurring outside the city, across the Kanawha River. In South Charleston the chemical industry, which began in 1913, was the basis for that city's exponential growth through World War I. The glass industry, just up river in Kanawha City, began about the same time. The federal government's high explosive plant started up in Nitro a few miles down the Kanawha, creating an industrial sprawl along the south side of the river.

Amateur baseball was hopping in the Capital City area by 1910. A new venue named Ruffner Park, located at Virginia and Elizabeth Streets near the capitol building, was reachable from almost anywhere in the city by the Virginia streetcar line that ran parallel to the river. It was the newest and best but not the only place to play. The YMCA had grounds in the west end of the city. Wherle Park on the Southside was home to the South Side Smokies and other local teams. One of the first, if not the first, African-American teams, the Charleston Clippers, also played at Wherle Park.[4]

5. "Oh, Summer in Kanawha"

With Ruffner Park came a new team, the Charleston Collegians. Whether all the players attended college is doubtful, but the organizer and pitcher, Ed Kenna, had starred at West Virginia University. Kenna, thirty-two years old and seven years from his "cup of coffee" with the Philadelphia Athletics, was capable of besting local players. He arranged games for the Collegians against town teams from Montgomery and Scarbro, easy train rides to the east, and with Huntington.[5]

Huntington's youth had taken to baseball even faster than those in Charleston. The city, built on the large floodplain of the Ohio River, possessed more flat land on which to play than any other West Virginia city. An organization called the Mountain State Athletic Association fielded a team in 1908. It played at Camden Park, a recreation and amusement park between Huntington and Ceredo. This team angered local Protestant churches by playing ball on Sundays. The Huntington team played town teams from Wayne, Kenova and Williamson, West Virginia, and from Ashland, Kentucky. Students at Marshall College also fielded a team, as did those of Morris-Harvey College in nearby Barboursville. By 1910 Huntington had a Twilight League that provided playing opportunity for teams from fraternal organizations and businesses. The Elks, Red Men, Woodsmen, Knights of Pythias and Eagles sponsored teams.[6]

In 1910, John H. Spinney of Cincinnati and John C. Bond, a rising Republican politician from Charleston, set out to form a professional league of teams on either side of the Ohio River. Since an Ohio Valley League already existed, they called their league the Virginia Valley League. The organizers invited interested parties to a meeting in Charleston set for early April. John Wherle, not Kenna, represented the capital city. Wherle, a rotund, mustached, middle-aged man, owned the park bearing his name. W. L. Hager attended from Huntington. He did not bother to tell the group that Mayor William Siebert had already obtained a franchise for Huntington in the Ohio Valley League. It would take more than a month until Hager and Spinney sorted out the issues to give the Huntington territory to the Virginia Valley League. Ashland and Catlettsburg, Kentucky, joined forces for an opportunity at professional ball. From up the river in Parkersburg, Huston G. Young and his designated manager, Frank Locke, attended the meeting. Parkersburg had already failed to support a pro team, but it was the fourth largest city in the state so the organizers wanted the city in the league.[7]

Finding two more cities to make a six-team circuit proved difficult. In the end, they settled on the towns of Point Pleasant and Montgomery. Point Pleasant had the advantage of being centrally located at the confluence of the Kanawha and Ohio Rivers. Although the town numbered just 2,000 residents, Gallipolis, Ohio, across the river had a like number. The town had dry docks and some ship manufacturing, but was best known as the site of a pre–Revolutionary War battle between white settlers and Native Americans. Montgomery, on the other hand, was a coal town of under 2,000 some thirty miles up river from Charleston in the heart of the Kanawha coalfield. It was reachable by the Chesapeake and Ohio Railroad. Both Point Pleasant and Montgomery had town teams in 1909.

The league's organizers left only one month from the league's founding until the season started on May 5, 1910. The group obtained approval to operate as a Class D league in Organized Baseball. Somehow the founders put their organizations, parks and teams together by the scheduled start of the season. Most of the clubs organized as joint stock companies. Respected local citizens usually served as team officers. The initial prime movers in establishing the league became business managers, essentially general managers in later terminology.

All the league cities except Point Pleasant had parks suitable for professional baseball. That is, they had some grandstand seats in an enclosed park and could charge admission. Wherle Park in South Charleston was the best. It had a skinned infield "as smooth as a ballroom floor." Huntington played weekday games at new League Park, a 4,500 seat facility centrally located on Ohio Street at Eighth in the downtown area right on the banks of the Ohio River. Sunday games were played outside Huntington's city limits at Camden Park. Parkersburg settled on Shattuck Park but it was small and needed lots of improvements, most of which were not made. Only Point Pleasant failed to have a park ready by Opening Day. The Pointers had to play on the road for the first two weeks of the season.[8]

In the first year of play the river city teams in the Virginia Valley League were surprisingly evenly balanced. Last place Montgomery trailed first place Huntington by just fourteen games. Second place Charleston actually won one more game than Huntington, but lost several more. It was, as the *Sporting Life* reporter noted, a "remarkably successful season."[9]

Huntington's Blue Sox boasted two outstanding pitchers and two fine outfielders. George Baumgardner, a teenager from nearby Barboursville, established himself as a dominating workhorse on the mound.[10] Lefty Frank Nicholson was just a notch below Baumgardner in ability. Both pitchers would be in the majors in 1912. Two former West Virginia University players, outfielders Larry McClure and Andrew Kemper Shelton looked like they belonged in higher leagues. The diminutive McClure, only 5'6" tall and weighing just 130 pounds, moved up to the majors during the season, but he would not stay for long. On July 26, 1910, he appeared in one game for the New York Highlanders. That cameo appearance was his only time in the majors. Huntington native "Skeeter" Shelton had to wait until 1915 to get into the Yankee lineup. In the summer of 1910, however, McClure and Shelton wreaked havoc on the other league teams.

Parkersburg boasted the best and most enigmatic player in the league in mercurial Benjamin "Benny" Kauff. Statistics for the league's first year of operation were unreliable at best. All reports credit Kauff with winning the league batting championship and with leading the league in stolen bases. The numbers, however, vary widely. His batting average may have been as high as .417 or as low as .336. In his obituary *The Sporting News* credited him with 87 stolen bases, but the *Minor League Encyclopedia* lists only 36 steals. Throughout his career, Kauff, whose moral development seemed to lag behind the norms of his day, had a different image of his ability on the field and of his actions off the field than did contemporary observers. It is likely that the inflated numbers derived from Kauff's habit of embellishing his accomplishments. One biographer even credits him with a 14–4 pitching record, a statistic that certainly did not derive from the box scores. Although small, only 5'8" and 155 pounds, Kauff was a hardnosed, tough, strong young man. He had quit school at age eleven to work in the coal mines around Pomeroy, Ohio. Such experience made him hard and tough and gave him an overwhelming desire to get ahead however he could. He played baseball in the image of Ty Cobb. His greatest season came in 1914 while playing in the Federal League. Dubbed "the Ty Cobb of the Federal League," he led the loop in batting average, hits, runs, and stolen bases. Overall he compiled a .311 lifetime average in the major leagues. His baseball career ended with a lifetime suspension from the game for his involvement with his brother in an automobile theft racket.[11]

League cities had a widely varied experience in the 1910 season. Huntington won the pennant and turned a profit. The Charleston Statesmen also finished in the black and could point to a winning record on the field. At Point Pleasant, Pointers manager Joe "Reddy" Mack had a 17 game winner in left-handed Lee Dasher, who would pitch for Cleveland in two years. The Montgomery Mountbacks struggled in the field and at the gate. The local newspaper concluded that the season "was not a financial 'howling success.'" On the other had, the team made the town proud and "did much to advertise the town ... carrying the name of Montgomery to all parts of the United States."[12] That was enough to bring the team back for 1911. The same was not true in Parkersburg.

Despite being large enough to support a professional team, Parkersburg just did not seem to be a good baseball town. The best player in the league did not put paying customers in the stands. Nor did one of the league's top pitchers, Howard "Muck" McGraner, who was good enough to have a "cup of coffee" in the majors in 1913. Part of the club's problem stemmed from the limited coverage it received from the Parkersburg *State Journal*, which devoted much less space to its home team than other league newspapers.

The young league made organizational changes for the 1911 season. At the winter meeting in February 1911, Ironton, Ohio, replaced Parkersburg. The circuit changed its name to the Mountain States League and Lon H. Barringer of Charleston replaced John Bond as league president. The league kept its original $1,000 monthly salary cap. In the hope of sustaining fan interest late in the season, it adopted a split season format. This decision would play havoc at the end of the season.[13]

Huntington, sporting natty blue uniforms, captured the first-half flag with ease. Baumgardner matured into a dominant pitcher. His 24–9 record gave him the most wins and the best winning percentage (.727) in the league. He also struck out 292 batters, the most of any minor league pitcher except several in the long season Pacific Coast League. Nicholson again backed Baumgardner with 16 wins. The St. Louis Browns grabbed Baumgardner after the season, and the Philadelphia Athletics purchased Nicholson. Kemper Shelton batted .331, but the rest of the team contributed little and the team faded in the second half of the season.

The second half champion was not decided as easily as the first half. At the end of the first half, Point Pleasant, called the Indians in 1911, was in last place and drawing few fans to the park. With local prohibition beginning on July 1, team president H. H. Howard and business manager Hebar H. Henry feared even worse attendance ahead. They decided to transfer the team to Middleport-Pomeroy, Ohio. Miracle of miracles, the team caught fire, and trailed Montgomery, now called the Miners, by only one game when the season ended. Pitcher Howard Cochran, who matched Baumgardner with 24 wins, had led the Miners. As Montgomery prepared for the post-season playoff against Huntington, a protested game between Charleston and Montgomery came to light. President Barringer, a Charleston resident, refused to decide the merits of the case. With the title in dispute, the playoffs were cancelled. The argument was not settled until the National Association of Professional Baseball Leagues met in December and awarded the game to Charleston. That gave the second-half pennant to Middleport-Pomeroy with a winning percentage of .625 against Montgomery's .620. Montgomery even posted the best overall record but had no official championship to show for it.[14]

With no post-season playoffs, Huntington manager "Dutch" Nazel put together an all-star team to barnstorm through southern West Virginia. His team traveled east on the Norfolk and Western Railroad playing town teams in Williamson, Gary, Welch, Bluefield and Hot Springs, then it worked its way back east on the Chesapeake and Ohio Railroad playing in Glen Jean, Hinton, Thurmond and Charleston.[15]

The fiasco at the end of the 1911 season left a sour taste in the mouths of many team leaders. By the winter meeting it was a foregone conclusion that league president Lon Barringer would not pass a vote of confidence. Huntington president William Seiber supported Ceredo resident Samuel J. Wright for president. Charleston backed favorite son Ed Kenna. Wright was selected for the presidency. Kenna became vice-president.

Kenna, who after his playing career had gone on to become editor of the *Charleston Gazette,* did not live to assume office. He suffered a fatal heart attack while vacationing in Florida before the season started. One of his last poems was "Oh Summer in Kanawha," which included the lines "Oh Roses of Kanawha, when my body lies cold, your petals may around me fall."

The 1912 season was no more successful than 1911's. In an effort to help the smaller cities, the league reduced the maximum monthly salary limit from $1,000 to $800. Williamson replaced Montgomery, giving the seat of Mingo County its first professional team. Businessman W. B. Blottman, who had operated Williamson's town teams since 1908, named his team the "Billionaires," but his club did not play like its name. The team stank. It finished 43 games behind the league leader. Montgomery briefly regained a franchise when Middleport-Pomeroy transferred there in mid–June. Tiny Montgomery could not support a team any better than it did in 1911; the team disbanded in less than two weeks. Charleston also experienced serious problems, following Montgomery into bankruptcy. Only Huntington had a winning team, but the league collapsed on July 10.[16]

Despite the league's woes, Bluefield was anxious to join. Bluefield knew baseball, having had amateur and semi-professional teams. Businessman W. L. Otley had a semi-pro team in 1906. In 1908 baseball men in Bluefield had discussed a league with Bluefield, Bramwell, Welch and Gary, but it failed to materialize. In 1912, Ray Prince had what he thought was a strong enough team to play in a pro league. Mountain States League members, however, already strapped for money, saw only added transportation costs if Bluefield were admitted.[17]

The disastrous 1912 season wrote the obituary for the Mountain States League. In fact, it appeared that professional baseball might be dead throughout the state. In North Central West Virginia, where pro ball had such a promising beginning a few years earlier, league ball was a thing of the past. Clarksburg, Grafton, Mannington, and even Fairmont were without teams. In the eastern part of the state the professional game had failed to take hold yet, except briefly in the company town of Piedmont. Even the Wheeling Stogies were in trouble. Following the 1912 season, the Central League revoked the Wheeling franchise after the club ran into serious financial difficulty.

Wheeling had not done well, either on the field or in the financial ledger, since winning the 1909 Central League pennant. Following their championship season the 1910 Stogies plunged all the way to the bottom of the league, as if they fell off a cliff. Manager Bill Phillips, hailed as a miracle worker the year before when he led a last place team to the title, could do nothing to prevent the free fall. It did not help that Phillips lost his two best pitchers and field general Bill McKechnie, or that his own pitching arm went dead. The club not only finished last but also lost over $6,000. Team owner B. F. Perkins let it be known he was willing to sell; however, no one offered to match his $12,000 asking price.[18]

Perkins' 1911 Stogies moved out of the league cellar but were never in contention for the title. A. L. "Bull" Durham led the Central League with 11 homers and batted .311, making him Wheeling's first .300 hitter in three years. The team boasted an excellent pitching prospect in Bill Doak. The previous year, Doak lost 20 games for the Stogies, but in 1911 he won fifteen games with an impressive 1.90 ERA. Two years later he won 20 National League games and compiled a league leading 1.72 earned run average.

In 1912 the Central League made the mistake of going to a twelve-team circuit and raising the salary limit from $1,800 to $2,100 per month. Only four of the twelve teams managed a profit under the new arrangement. Perkins, again, was among those who finished in the red. On the field, the Stogies finished sixth under manager John "Goat" Anderson. The team claimed to have the fastest player in the league in centerfielder Everitt Booe. He flew around the bases in 14 seconds, if the club could be believed. He also was the team's only .300 hitter. In two big league seasons, his speed did little good, as he batted a weak .219. The Stogies had little else to brag about.

Not only did Wheeling lose money in 1912, it lost its team. In a move to solve the financial problems of its member clubs, the Central League cut loose half its members. By divesting itself of the six easternmost teams, the league became a geographically tighter circuit, thus reducing transportations costs.[19]

Despite the dark clouds hovering over baseball in West Virginia, before the start of the 1913 baseball season the three largest cities in the state found homes in new leagues. The six ousted cities from the Central League formed a Class D group called the Interstate League. Meanwhile, the Ohio State League, which had lost teams after the 1912 season, invited Huntington and Charleston to join that Class D organization.

The Interstate League proved not to be a good answer for what ailed Wheeling baseball. Problems surfaced even before the season. Spring floods had damaged Island Park, requiring $2,000 in repairs. Ray Ryan, a veteran catcher and manager in the Virginia League, came in to manage the Stogies. He had no more success than Anderson had the previous year. After winning six of their first seven games, Wheeling's season turned sour. The Stogies limped along through the first half of the 1913 season. At that point, four Ohio based clubs disbanded, leaving the league with only four teams. The remaining four, Erie, Akron, Youngstown and Wheeling, attempted to continue. After a week in which the Stogies lost their four games, Perkins came to the end of the line. He lacked the money to pay his players. On July 21, 1913, Wheeling and the league decided to disband.[20]

After the collapse of the Interstate League, Wheeling had nowhere to go. Team owner B. F. Perkins lamented, "I have been losing [money] steadily for 13 years." Still, he was not ready to give in. "I guess," he said, "I would rather lose some more than quit the game permanently." Despite his desire to continue, Perkins could not find a league for his team.[21] So, in 1914, for only the second time in the past twenty years, Wheeling was without a professional baseball team.

Wheeling and its surrounding area continued to have flourishing amateur baseball. An Elks League had four member teams. A Trolley League had three teams on the West Virginia side of the Ohio River and three on the west side. A dozen or more teams, neighborhood and company teams, also played.[22] Huntington and Charleston were delighted to join the Ohio State League for the 1913 season. Joe Carr, the secretary-treasurer, undertook to reorganize the league after it faced serious problems in the 1912 season. Carr was a sports entrepreneur. He owned a professional football team, the Columbus Panhandlers, and would later become president of the National Football League (1921–1939) and president of the short-lived American Basketball Association in 1925. Despite the league's name, he pulled in two cities from Kentucky, Lexington and Maysville, along with the two from West Virginia.

In Charleston everything was new and the excitement over the team had never been higher. Roy R. Pennywitt took over as club president, bringing new energy to the club leadership. He moved the team into a new park, Exhibition Park, on the west side of Virginia Avenue. The team also had a new nickname. Gone were the Statesmen. In came the Senators. Pennywitt found a new manager in Henry "Buzz" Wetzel. It was Wetzel's first managerial job but not his last; he managed in the minors until 1928. What he lacked in experience he made up for in enthusiasm. The Senators opened the season with new uniforms. The white, three-quarter length sleeves sported a "C" on each sleeve. Black socks and a white cap with a black bill topped off the uniform. Pennywitt used all the allowed $1,200 in monthly salaries to build a strong team.[23]

Huntington did not undergo the transformation that was seen in Charleston. A new manager, Sam Wright, took over, but otherwise things remained the same. The Blue Sox, as they had done each year since their inception, found a great pitcher to lead them, but lack of hitting doomed the team to a .500 season. Albert Mamaux was the league's best prospect. Rail thin at 6'0" and 165 pounds, the nineteen-year-old right-hander from Pittsburgh was just beginning a pro career. From the start, the former Duquesne University player proved to be a workhorse. He won 18 games while losing 16. Late in the season, on August 14, 1913, he pitched a perfect game against Maysville. Following Huntington's season he returned to Pittsburgh to pitch for his hometown Pirates. Mamaux would pitch twelve years in the majors, winning 21 games in both 1915 and 1916.

Charleston's Senators fared better than Huntington. They opened to great excitement. The team paraded to the park for the opening game in automobiles for the first time. A crowd of 4,000, the largest in Charleston to that date, came out for the first game at the new park. The fans displayed new enthusiasm that *The Charleston Gazette* captured with doggerel: "Here are the fans who helped with the day/In their loud shouting, boisterous way/They bawl out like cattle/The pitcher they rattle."[24]

No doubt Charleston had the league's most rabid fans. Even statewide prohibition failed to dull the fans' enthusiasm.

Had there been an Ohio State League Most Valuable Player Award it would have gone of Charleston outfielder Carl "Dolly" Gray. All he did was lead the league in batting with a .366 average, home runs with 33, and total bases with 325. All were Charleston records. Locals mistakenly thought his 33 homers to be a record for professional baseball. It was, in fact, more than any major league player had hit, but other minor league players had hit more.

Charleston experienced the most exciting finish in its history. In a scenario reminiscent of Montgomery's 1911 season-ending fiasco, the Senators won, but then lost the 1913 pennant. Going into the last day of the season, Charleston and Chillicothe battled nose-to-nose, neck-to-neck for the crown. The fact that Chillicothe had played fewer games complicated matters, but if the Senators swept their double-header at home against Maysville they would be assured of the pennant. The Maysville manager, anxious to catch a train home, requested the games be played as seven-inning matches. The Senators did their part, winning both ends of the double-header. Charleston celebrated its first championship with an outpouring of civic pride. *The Charleston Gazette* ran banner headlines on page one that screamed: "Ohio State Flag Will Wave Over Exhibition Park." Ecstatic backers feted the team at a banquet at the Hotel Kanawha. After recognizing all the players, Pennywitt presented manager Buzz Wetzel with a diamond ring to commemorate the pennant.[25]

Charleston's celebration was a tad too soon. Chillicothe protested, arguing that league rules specified games must be nine innings unless called for rain or darkness. Since the Charleston-Maysville games were seven innings, they should not count. The Ohio State League ruled in favor of the Ohio city. That left the Senators with a record of 84–50, a win more than Chillicothe, but the latter's 83–49 record gave them the better winning percentage and the championship. Charleston appealed the decision to the National Board, but in November it too ruled against the Senators. So, the 1913 championship won on the playing field was lost on a technicality. The flag would not fly over Exhibition Park.[26]

In 1914 Charleston made another run at a championship but Huntington's season came to an early, bitter, and unhappy end. The difference between the two cities was reflected in the attitudes of their respective newspapers. In Charleston, the *Gazette* proclaimed, "A ball club is one of the biggest boost[s] a growing city can have."[27] Huntington was clearly a growing city, but the *Huntington Advertiser* failed to connect baseball and city growth. It gave scant attention to its team. The lack of media support contributed to Huntington's low attendance. The Blue Sox also were a weak, second division team. After a run of pitching stars—George Baumgardner, Frank Nicholson, and Albert Mamaux—the Blue Sox failed to find even a strong arm in 1914. Huntington withdrew from the league on July 21.

Charleston started slowly in 1914 but came on strong in the second half of the season. At the mid-point of the campaign, the Senators were playing sub–500 ball. They replaced Wetzel as manager with Biddy Beers. After Huntington disbanded, the Senators picked up hard-hitting outfielder Ernie "Crazy Snake" Calbert, who had been the Blue Sox's best player. The compact, 5'10", 190 pound Calbert went on a tear, ending up the league leader with 17 home runs. Shortstop Harry "Jake" Daubert, who would play for Pittsburgh the next season, played nearly flawless ball. Pitcher Able Applegate won a league-high 22 games. The Senators nosed out Portsmouth to win the second half championship by one game, and "capture the coveted gonfalon." There was no playoff.[28]

In southern West Virginia an attempt to create another professional league for 1914 died before it could be born. Ray Prince, manager of a town team in Bluefield, tried in vain to put together a league of towns along the Norfolk and Western Railroad. He elicited interest in Princeton, seat of

Mercer County, and coal towns of Pocahontas and Gary. Gary raised $3,000, which allowed that town to expand its park into the baseball showplace of southern West Virginia. No other towns evidenced interest and Prince had to drop the plan.[29]

Despite the early collapse of the 1914 Ohio State League, Joe Carr was able to put the Ohio State League back together for 1915. This was not easy because hard times for minor leagues across the country coincided with the outbreak of war in Europe. The number of leagues declined from forty-four in 1914 to thirty-two in 1915, and would continue to drop again to twenty-six in 1916. In Carr's six-team league there was a place for Charleston but not for Huntington.

The Charleston Senators of 1915 gave their fans little to cheer about. Charleston's season was symbolized by a game against Lexington on June 27. The two teams played twenty innings before the Senators lost 5–2. It was the longest game in West Virginia to that point and would remain the record for over seventy years. The struggling Senators never got untracked. The team remained mired in the second division the entire season. No one knew it at the time but Charleston baseball got a long-term benefit that season when an outfielder named Walter "Watt" Powell joined the team. He batted a weak .240 but it began a connection with Charleston baseball that would last until his death in 1948, and beyond in the stadium that bore his name until 2005.

Huntington rejoined the Ohio State League in 1916 after a year without a team. In Huntington, John Dearmond organized the Huntington Boosters Association as a stock company to obtain the franchise. The investors gave their own name, "Boosters," to the team. Unfortunately the group was undercapitalized and money became a concern even before the season started. Ezra "Salt Rock" Midkiff returned home to manage the Huntington club and to play third base. The veteran of three major league seasons was the only Booster to hit over .300. Except for pitcher Clarence Fisher, Midkiff got little support. Fisher, a seventeen year old from Letart, West Virginia, would make it to the Washington Senators in 1919 and 1920. The Boosters were mired in the second division from the start of the season and never improved.[30]

In Charleston, Powell took over as manager of the 1916 club. Before the season started, Powell and business manager Clarence Barrett were delighted to have a new park. F. M. Staunton, president of the streetcar company, was the prime mover in building the park. The $8,000 facility, christened Kanawha Park, was located across the river from Charleston in Kanawha City at the end of the new streetcar bridge. Staunton bragged that it was just an eight-minute ride from downtown Charleston. Things started well for Powell's club. Opening Day saw a packed house. The grandstand spilled over, forcing some 300 customers to stand along the outfield fence.[31]

Powell's initial enthusiasm proved short-lived. Despite the pitching of Paul Carpenter, who led the league in strikeouts, and shortstop Harry "Jake" Daubert, who led the team with a .349 batting average, the club lost ten more than it won in the first half. Both Carpenter and Daubert moved up to Pittsburgh later in the summer. As losses piled up, fans stayed away. On July 8, 1916, the Senators decided to return the franchise to the league and disband the team. Barrett cited "poor business" as the reason. Powell blamed the poor attendance on the streetcar company for charging ten-cent fares from downtown, double the previous year's charge to the old park.[32]

By the time Charleston disbanded Huntington was also in trouble. Indeed, the club was unable to pay players' salaries. At that point, two Huntington residents, J. W. Pool and Phil C. Jacks, attempted to purchase the strong Lexington, Kentucky, club with the intention of moving its players to Huntington. League President Joe Carr stepped in to void the purchase. Knowing Huntington was ready to fold, Carr prepared to shut down the league, which he officially did on July 18. Without sadness, *The Huntington Advertiser* wrote, "Baseball, as far as the Ohio State League is concerned, is dead in Huntington."[33] In fact, professional baseball would be dead in Huntington and Charleston for the next fifteen years.

After professional baseball wound down in central West Virginia in mid-summer 1916, only the Panhandles continued to have pro teams. Martinsburg in the Eastern Panhandle had a team in the Blue Ridge League beginning in 1915. The team continued playing into 1918 when the effect of World War I caused a disruption in league play. It would, however, begin again after the war and continue until the Great Depression.

Up the Ohio River from Huntington in the Northern Panhandle where Wheeling had lost its team, local interests managed to regain a professional team in 1915 after being without a team in 1914. When Wheeling was without, Harry "Pop" Shriver worked tirelessly to bring a professional team back to town. During the winter of 1914–15 Dick Padden, a nine-year major league veteran who operated a bowling alley in Martin's Ferry, joined Shriver's efforts. The two attended the Central League winter meeting in January 1915 in hopes of getting Wheeling back in the league. Louis Heilbroner, president of the league, was interested in expanding from six to eight teams. Shriver and Padden reported back to Wheeling mayor H. L. Kirk that a place in the league was available. Kirk called a meeting for February 22, 1915, where ten men reorganized the Wheeling Athletic Association that they incorporated with capital stock of $10,000. A week later the membership elected H. C. Whittaker president, Padden secretary, and Shriver business and field manager.[34]

As was so often the case in Wheeling, the first problem after getting a Central League franchise was finding a place to play. Floods had destroyed the previous grounds, the park on Wheeling Island. To make matters more difficult, the team needed a place to play Sunday games outside the Wheeling city limits. Padden convinced the others in the corporation to buy Breitstein Field across the Ohio River in Martin's Ferry. An enclosed park with grandstand seating for 2,500 fans was readied for Opening Day. Despite the fact that the new home of the Wheeling Stogies was actually in Martin's Ferry, Ohio, Mayor Kirk led a parade of 120 automobiles from City Hall to the park. In a concession to its location, both Kirk and Martin's Ferry mayor Newton Wyckoff threw out first balls.[35]

The new Stogies of 1915 disappointed their organizers. Manager Pop Shriver expected former major league star John "Goat" Anderson to power the club. He also had high hopes for recent West Virginia collegians Greasy Neale of West Virginia Wesleyan College and Arch Reilly fresh from Marshall College's 1915 state champions. Both would make the majors, although Reilly failed to stick. Shriver batted an anemic .121, while Anderson and Reilly had mediocre years. By July, with the team near the bottom of the standings, Shriver handed the reins to young Reilly. The change made little difference.

The only Wheeling standout was Neale. The former college football and baseball great already had three years of professional experience. He had played two years with London, Ontario, while still in college, returning there in 1914 to bat .320. Neale had started the 1915 season with Saginaw, Michigan, until that team collapsed. At Wheeling in 1915 he batted .351. That would have led the Central League, but he lacked the required number of at-bats to qualify. Wheeling sold him to the Cincinnati Reds following the season.

Shriver and Whittaker continued to run the Stogies in 1916. Shriver brought in a new manager, Harry Smith, and a whole new cast of players. The team continued playing at its Martin's Ferry site, now called League Park. In mid-season John Anderson took over as manager and the club showed improvement, settling for a fourth place finish in the eight-team league.

Once the United States entered the Great War in February 1917, it became difficult for professional baseball to justify its existence or to continue holding the attention of fans. In Wheeling, Shriver, Padden, and Whittaker—the driving forces behind professional baseball since 1914—needed little excuse to drop out. Unlike Perkins before them, the trio was unwilling to continue losing money. Even though the other Central League cities tried to continue in 1917, Wheeling was not willing.

Baseball, of course, was not dead in 1917, just the professional variety. After the early collapse of the Ohio State League, semi-pro teams continued in Huntington and Charleston. W. W. Turner organized a Huntington team called the Independents. It found games against clubs from Ashland, Kentucky, Ironton, Ohio, and Charleston. In the state capital, former Senators manager Biddy Beers ran a semi-pro team until Powell took it over. In 1917 they played teams from former Ohio State League cities, but by 1918 teams in both Charleston and Huntington were reduced to playing other local clubs. Both Charleston and Huntington had City Leagues made up of teams representing men's civic organizations, company teams, neighborhood teams, and the YMCA.[36]

In Wheeling amateur ball also continued. An Inter-City League included teams from Follansbee, St. Martins and Moundsville, West Virginia, and Steubenville, Ohio, among its members. Teams representing industries in the Wheeling and surrounding towns continued to play as well. Stroehman Bakery, managed by Frank Bero, was the best of the lot.[37] Each year, however, there were fewer teams, and after World War I, grassroots baseball would operate with a much reduced participation level.

6

"The City Is Baseball Crazy"
The Martinsburg Dynasty, 1914–1934

Martinsburg created a baseball dynasty unmatched by any professional team in West Virginia history. No team duplicated Martinsburg's three-peat as Blue Ridge League champions between 1922 and 1924. The Blue Sox captured another title in 1929. Before and after their league years, 1915–1929, the city enjoyed outstanding semi-pro teams. Along the way, Baseball Hall of Fame greats Lefty Grove and Hack Wilson started their professional careers in Martinsburg.

After twenty barren years, baseball returned to the Eastern Panhandle in the 1890s as town teams began to appear in the region. Martinsburg came to dominate the region's baseball, as it did the economy and culture. From the time the Baltimore and Ohio Railroad pushed through the region in 1842 Martinsburg was a railroad hub. The Civil War had played havoc with the city as Union and Confederate armies vied for control of the important railroad. In the 1870s and 1880s bitter labor conflict wrenched the town to its core. By the 1890s the appearance of a thriving textile industry and the growth of commercial apple farming and processing in the upper Shenandoah Valley reduced the importance of the railroad to the city's economy. As Martinsburg's population increased to 7,500 in 1900 and to over 10,000 by 1910, and as its industrial economy grew, a new generation began to turn to baseball.[1]

Baseball had briefly excited Martinsburg's youth in the mid–1890s. Local product Jack Boyd pitched for Washington for three years. Martinsburg's first league team came with the formation in 1895 of the Cumberland Valley League. Martinsburg joined teams from Carlisle and Chambersburg,

Pennsylvania, and Hagerstown, Maryland, in a short-lived league. The league managed to survive its modest thirty-six game schedule in July and August, but did not regroup the following summer.[2]

Another opportunity for Martinsburg to join a league did not appear until two decades later. In the spring of 1914 the Maryland cities of Hagerstown and Frederick proposed a new semi-pro league and invited Martinsburg to join. Max von Schlegel, dynamic thirty-year-old owner of the *Martinsburg Journal*, took the lead in creating a Martinsburg Baseball Association. He became president, with John L. Bateman as secretary. They had little trouble in getting stock subscriptions. By the end of May construction started on a wooden grandstand, bleachers, and a fenced field on John Street at Illinois Avenue, a block off King Street, on property donated to the city by Walter Lambert. The park in the Rosemont section of the city was variously called Lambert Field and Rosemont Park. The team adopted the name "Black Sox." The name was intended as descriptive only; the appellation lacked the evil connotation it would get five years later when Chicago's White Sox threw the World Series.[3]

As manager of Martinsburg's Tri-City League team, the club brought in William "Country" Morris, just graduated from the Maryland Agricultural College (University of Maryland). First baseman Morris brought two college teammates with him, third baseman Burt Shipley and second baseman Kenneth "Mike" Knode. Shipley soon ended up in a Martinsburg hospital with appendicitis. Knode began a pro career that would lead to the majors. With the college lads leading the way, Martinsburg handily won the only Tri-City League championship. Following the season, Martinsburg won four straight games from Cumberland, Maryland, champions of the George's Creek League.

The arrival of a team with uniforms, out of town players, and a park with stands charging admission looked big-time to Martinsburg. Suddenly, "the city is baseball crazy," *The Martinsburg World* put it. Soon an eight-team city league appeared. It included teams sponsored by the Moose Club and the YMCA as well as work based teams and neighborhood clubs. Town teams reappeared in neighboring Shepherdstown and Charles Town. An African-American team, the Wonders, claimed to be the "colored champions of West Virginia."[4]

After the success of 1914, the leaders of the Tri-City League teams decided to expand their circuit into a professional league. Charles H. Boyer of Hagerstown provided the leadership in the effort to line up three other cities. Boyer had previous experience in Organized Baseball, having served as president of both the South Atlantic League and the Virginia League. Max von Schlegel of Martinsburg and Frank K. Schmidt of Frederick willingly joined Boyer. They agreed that Chambersburg should be the fourth team. Gettysburg became the fifth city, even though the team lacked an enclosed park. Nixon Field at Gettysburg College had no fence either in the outfield or around the park. Not until March 1915 could a sixth city be found. Hanover, Pennsylvania, east of Gettysburg would continue in the league until its demise, despite limited success on the field.[5]

The newly created Blue Ridge League quickly gained admission into Organized Baseball as a Class D league. After electing Boyer president, the organizers set an 80 game schedule. In order to keep expenses close to the bone, they established a roster size of thirteen, including the manager. This meant that all managers would be playing-managers. They also created an $800 a month salary cap for each team. Since managers commanded a higher salary than most of their players, typically $75 to $125 per month, money left for other players averaged $40–$60 per month.

The Martinsburg club of 1915 adopted the nickname "Champions," based on their 1914 Tri-City League pennant. The team continued at Rosemont Park, one of only two league fields with an outfield fence, Frederick's Fairgrounds being the other. Like most parks of the era, Martinsburg's field had a wooden grandstand with roof behind home plate and bleachers down

Boys once played baseball from sun-up to sundown and all year long. The winter's frigid temperatures did not deter this group of boys in 1915. The group standing is the first nine; the "muffins" are on the front row (Unknown).

the baselines and, like most minor league parks of its day, it had a skinned infield, barren of grass. On Opening Day, an automobile parade, with the City Band playing, led 1,500 fans to the park.

William G. "Country" Morris remained in Martinsburg to guide the club in its first few seasons in Organized Baseball. His 1915 club put on a stretch run but finished second to Frederick. Burt Shipley played a steady shortstop, Morris batted clean-up, and future major leaguer Alan "Lefty" Clarke pitched effectively.

The star of the 1915 team was a rail-thin, twenty-five year old outfielder from Washington, D.C., named George Reggis Rawlings. "Reg" or "Reggie" quickly became Martinsburg's favorite son. Six feet tall but weighing only 165 pounds, the outfielder could run, field, hit for average, and hit for power. In his first Martinsburg season he led the club with a .325 batting average. Moreover, the bachelor came with a steady, sober and polite demeanor, which contrasted with the popular image of ballplayers of the deadball era. He would remain Martinsburg's favorite player for the next two decades, and a resident of the city until his death in 1954.[6]

No longer champions, Martinsburg changed its nickname to Mountaineers for the next few seasons. At the beginning of the 1916 season, Boyer resigned as league president to devote full time to his Hagerstown team and to avoid conflict of interest charges. Max von Schlegel supported Hagerstown businessman James Vincent Jamison, Jr., to succeed Boyer as league president. Jamison had been treasurer of the Tri-City League in 1914. Blue Ridge expanded its schedule to 100 games and raised the salary limit to $1,100. After some discussion, the league continued its policy of not playing Sunday games.

The Mountaineers came within a hair of the championship in 1916. By August the rivalry between Martinsburg and Chambersburg heated up to the point that Chambersburg tried to avoid going to Martinsburg by claiming it feared injury from rabid Martinsburg fans. No injuries occurred, and Chambersburg swept a double-header on Labor Day to capture the pennant. Country Morris' club won 56 games, three more than Chambersburg, but the Pennsylvania team played seven fewer games, losing four fewer than Martinsburg. That gave Chambersburg a .569 winning percentage and a one-half game edge over Martinsburg, which finished with a .560 percentage.[7]

The 1916 Mountaineers possessed outstanding pitching. Marvin Goodwin led the Blue Ridge with 19 wins. Goodwin also led with 165 strikeouts. At one point in the season he pitched thirty-five consecutive scoreless innings. He became the first Martinsburg player to make the Big Leagues. Goodwin pitched three games for Washington in September following the

Mountaineers' season and stayed in the majors for seven seasons. Frank Colley won 17 games and Alan "Lefty" Clarke notched 14 victories. All three pitched over 200 innings.

The club possessed solid fielding to support the pitching, but lack of hitting hurt the team. Rawlings had, for him, a down year at the bat, hitting only .279, but he led the league outfielders in fielding average. Rookie first baseman Luzern "Lu" Blue from Washington, D.C., also displayed smoothness in the field, but he hit a meager .216. At the conclusion of the season, Goodwin, Rawlings, outfielder Lee Percy and third-baseman Henry "Shorty" Long made the league all-star team. Following the season, Morris went south to coach basketball and baseball at Clemson College for the 1916-17 season.[8]

When the United States declared war on Germany in 1917, von Schlegal stepped down as club president. He turned his energies to organizing the home guard in Martinsburg. Lewis H. Thompson, a clothier with a business on Queen Street, succeeded von Schlegal as president of the club. The newspaperman did agree to serve as the Blue Ridge League secretary, and he remained the power behind Martinsburg baseball until 1923 when he sold the *Martinsburg Journal* and moved to Baltimore.

The 1917 Mountaineers, who finished second for the third consecutive year, believed they were robbed of the league title. Martinsburg held a 3½ game lead on August 13, before going into free fall. By the last day of the season, Martinsburg still had a chance to capture the league title if they could sweep the Labor Day double-header from Hagerstown. In fact both games went to Hagerstown. The frustration of three second place finishes came out when Martinsburg protested that Hagerstown had used an ineligible player. The player in question, Hanson Horsey, wrote Morris that he had not signed a contract. The Hagerstown club contended that Horsey had signed, but the "contract was mislaid." President Jamison, however, ruled against Martinsburg.

Hitting carried Morris' 1917 team. The duo of Clarke and Colley pitched well, winning 17 and 16 games. Clarke even pitched a no-hitter for nine innings on June 15; unfortunately the innings were the tenth through the eighteenth. The effectiveness of the mound staff dropped off sharply after Clarke and Colley. Shortstop Johnny Bates set a new league home run record with 15 round-trippers. Outfielder Les Perey topped the league with 84 runs scored. Rawlings' batting average again topped .300. Lu Blue matured into an outstanding minor league player and major league prospect. He banged out 35 doubles and eight home runs. Playing with the assumed name of Kenny Thompson, their second baseman was really Kenneth "Mike" Knode. He had played on the 1914 Martinsburg team, and in

1916 was at the University of Michigan, where he captained the football team as well as playing baseball. Baseball proved to be his best sport and he climbed to the majors in 1920.[9]

Hall of Fame umpire Bill McGowan later told the apparently apocryphal tale of Blue hitting two grand-slam home runs in the same game, one batting left-handed and the other from the right side. Recently, extensive research has failed to unearth such a game. Blue did attract the interest of major league scouts, and, at the end of the season Martinsburg sold Blue's contract to Detroit. He played twelve seasons as a regular in the majors, mostly with the Tigers.[10]

The Blue Ridge League experienced troubles but managed to finish the 1917 season. In mid-season the league moved the Chambersburg franchise to Cumberland, Maryland. Gettysburg limped to the end before dropping out. Every team in the league suffered financial losses. This was true across baseball. As the United States entering the Great War fans turned their attention to other matters. In fact, only one other league at the Class C or Class D level finished the season.

With the country at war, it may have been folly to try to play in 1918. League President Jamison was determined to continue. In Martinsburg, Max von Schlegel and his *Journal* urged the league to keep playing, while the rival *Martinsburg World* favored abandoning baseball during the war. Gettysburg and Hanover chose not to play. The league decided to go with just four teams, and reduced the monthly salary cap to $900 and roster size to twelve. Then, just a week before the season was to open, Frederick threw in the towel, claiming the rail trips to Cumberland would be too costly.[11]

To make the fourth team for 1918, the league turned to Piedmont, West Virginia. The tiny home of West Virginia Company's pulp and paper mill had so little flat land that the town ball field was across the Potomac River on the floodplain in Maryland. Piedmont, however, had a baseball tradition. Mill workers there had fielded teams for over two decades. A professional team played there briefly in 1906, 1907 and 1916. Long-time resident Bill "Baldy" Louden had gone to the majors from the 1906 team. Piedmont wanted Louden as its manager, but Minneapolis owned his contract. So the new club settled on Arthur "Shorty" Smith as manager. Traditionally, Piedmont teams had used the nickname "Drybugs" after an insect that populated the area; the Blue Ridge League team maintained the tradition.[12]

The 1918 season proved to be short-lived, lasting only until June 15. Smith managed to field a team in Piedmont in two weeks, aided by the league delaying its opening until May 28. With Rawlings in the armed forces, Country Morris' other players struggled and Martinsburg's attendance suffered. Changing starting time to twilight did not help. After three weeks, the Mountaineers had won only six of their sixteen games. Von Schlegel convinced Hagerstown to vote with him to suspend operation. Cumberland and Piedmont, the league leaders, wished to continue. League president Jamison cast the deciding vote to suspend operation. Although Cumberland finished one-half game ahead of Piedmont, the Drybugs could claim the league's top pitcher in Ben Schaufele, who finished with a 5–0 record and a 2.88 ERA. Piedmont and Cumberland attempted to form a semi-pro league with Fairmont and Clarksburg but wartime reality quickly ended the effort.

Not surprisingly, neither Jamison nor any of the teams attempted to reorganize the league in 1919. Although the war ended in November 1918, the post-war treaty, its failed ratification, the Red Scare, recession, the influenza epidemic, strikes and labor violence, and the Women Voting Rights and Prohibition amendments combined to make 1919 the most traumatic non-war year since 1860.

By 1920 the country longed for a return to what President Warren G. Harding called "normalcy." The country's sense of normal very much included baseball. Jamison announced the Blue Ridge League was ready to operate again. Five of the original members answered his call to a meeting in February 1920. Martinsburg, Hagerstown, Frederick, Chambersburg, and Hanover sent representatives, as did Waynesboro, Pennsylvania. The only change they made to the league format was to raise the roster size to fourteen.

Changes had taken place in Martinsburg since the abortive 1918 season. Lewis H. Thompson, by then president of the Shenandoah Valley Bank, regained the club presidency. Rosemont Park had fallen into a state of disrepair after two years of neglect. The outfield fence had lost boards and sagged badly, and the whole place needed paint. Country Morris, who had managed the club since 1914, guiding it to 165 wins plus the 1914 Tri-City League championship, moved up the road to Waynesboro. Piedmont resident Bill Louden replaced Morris at the helm. Loudon brought six years of major league experience to the job, but this was his first managerial experience. Louden did not experience the managerial success of Morris. His team won one more game than they lost, but that placed them in the second division for the first time in a full season schedule.

The best thing Louden did as manager was to sign a left-handed first baseman-pitcher named Robert Moses Groves. When he reached the majors, "Lefty" dropped the "s" on his name. The son of a coal miner, Groves hailed from Lonaconing, Maryland, across the Potomac River and up the mountain from Piedmont. He dropped out of school after the eighth grade and started playing baseball in 1917. By 1919 Groves had developed a local reputation for his fastball and hard hitting. When Louden went looking for Groves the new manager found him working as a mechanic in the Baltimore and Ohio Railroad yards in Cumberland. Groves managed to get a thirty-day leave from his job to try his hand at pro ball.[13]

Groves' stay in Martinsburg was too short to help the club much on the field. After a few games at first base, Louden gave Groves his first start in pro ball on May 21, 1920. The six-foot, three-inch Groves stared down hitters with an expression that intimidated them. Although he lost 4–1 he struck out ten batters, and word of his blazing fastball soon spread around the league and beyond. In Baltimore, Jack Dunn, who owned and managed the most successful minor league team of its day, heard of Groves. Dunn sent a scout, Harry Frank, to look over Groves and another young left-hander named Cecil "Cy" Slaughter. Frank brought back such glowing reports on Groves that Dunn sent his son, Jack, Jr., to Martinsburg. On June 25 with his thirty-day furlough now up, Groves threw a two hit shutout against Hagerstown. Dunn immediately made Martinsburg an offer they could not refuse. In exchange for Groves, the Orioles gave Martinsburg $3,000, enough to make the needed repairs on the park, especially a new outfield fence.[14]

Jack Dunn got more than his money's worth in the deal. Grove pitched five years for the Orioles before Dunn sold him to the Philadelphia Athletics for a record price of $100,600. The big fireballer won 109 games for Baltimore, pacing the team to pennants each year. Once he reached the majors he became the best left-handed pitcher of all time. He won 300 games, led the American League in strikeouts seven times, and in earned run average nine times. Not a bad trade for an outfield fence.

Manager Louden also signed a promising rookie first baseman from Baltimore named Johnny Neun. The slick-fielding switch hitter went on to play seven major league seasons where he batted a solid .289. With Martinsburg, he batted .271 behind Reg Rawlings' .311, Louden's .308, and third baseman Joe Brophy's .303. The pitcher Baltimore passed on, Cecil Slaughter, led the Blue Ridge League with 16 wins. Teammate Ross Roberts matched Slaughter in victories.

Martinsburg fans became even more excited by the 1921 team. New manager Joe Ward quickly had a falling out with the team president Lewis H. Thompson and got his walking papers two weeks into the season. Fans applauded the appointment of Reg Rawlings to replace Ward as manager. Rawlings had become the most popular player in town as well as the team's most reliable. The quiet, unassuming Rawlings may not have been cut out for managerial chores.

Despite some talent, the team slipped under Rawlings' reign. Reggie had his best season to date, batting .355 and hitting a team record 17 home runs. Neun came into his own, batting .342. Following the season, Martinsburg sold Neun to Birmingham and he made it to the Big Time in 1925. Infielders Dave Black and Joe Brophy kept the fans abuzz with their hustle and spirited play. The pitching staff, however, could not boast of even one hurler with a winning record.

Most of the 1921 opening day lineup consisted of holdovers. The one promising newcomer, a catcher named Lew Wilson, managed to break his leg in the first game. Lewis Caldwell Wilson, who answered to the nickname "Stouts," came to Martinsburg from Chester, Pennsylvania, for a tryout along with an infielder William Maitland. Their manager in the Delaware County League, former major league player Bris Lord, recommended the two to Martinsburg president Lewis H. Thompson. Wilson gladly signed for $175 a month. After sitting out most of the summer with his broken leg, Wilson returned for the final thirty games, but his leg did not allow him to catch; he would be an outfielder for the remainder of his career. During Wilson's brief return, he slugged five homers and batted .356.[15]

Stouts Wilson found a home in Martinsburg. Wilson came from the hardscrabble side of the tracks. Born out of wedlock to a sixteen-year-old mother who died when he was seven, he lived with an alcoholic father who saw no need for Lewis to attend school. Short but strong, Lewis worked as a laborer when not playing ball. Little wonder he had no desire to return to the tough streets of Chester. The nickname "Stouts" reflected his build. At five feet, six inches tall, he carried 190 pounds on size six feet. Later he acquired the nickname "Hack" because of his resemblance to wrestler George Hackenschmidt. Locals remembered him as friendly, "open and easy to talk to." In his first off-season in Martinsburg, Wilson worked in a sock factory and courted Virginia "Jen" Riddleburger, a divorcee ten years his elder.[16]

The Martinsburg Blue Sox, as the team was called in the twenties, reigned in the Blue Ridge from 1922 to 1929. They ran off three straight titles in 1922, 1923, and 1924. They shared a title in 1927 and won again in 1929. No other professional team from West Virginia has enjoyed such success in an eight-year stretch. Martinsburg had become a dynasty.

Rawlings gladly turned over the managerial reigns for 1922 to H. Burton "Burt" Shipley. The new manager had played for Martinsburg in 1914, 1915 and 1918. During the winters he had coached at the Perkiomen School in Pennsylvania and Marshall College before moving on to coach baseball and basketball at the University of Delaware. Shipley could not join the Blue

Sox until after the season started. Second baseman Dave Black ran the club until Shipley's arrival. The thirty-year-old manager possessed the right balance of toughness and fun, organization and flexibility. Players liked him and responded to his style. The following year, Shipley returned to his alma mater, the University of Maryland, where he coached basketball from 1923 to 1948 and baseball from 1924 until 1960.

The lively ball came to the Blue Sox in 1922. That season Lew Wilson smashed the league home run record by slugging 30 round-trippers. That represented nearly a fifty percent increase over the previous record. Rawlings also broke the record hitting 26 dingers. Dave Black, who held the previous record, finished third in the league with 19 homers. The team smacked 123 home runs in 99 games. As a point of comparison, Babe Ruth's New York Yankees led the majors that year with 105 home runs in 154 games. Wilson himself hit more than the entire Hanover team. The tandem of Wilson and Rawlings had more homers than all teams except Hagerstown. In a single game against Frederick the Blue Sox hit seven home runs.

Rawlings was the league's Most Valuable Player. The dynamic duo of Wilson and Rawlings accounted for most of the batting titles. Rawlings had the highest batting average, with a .371 mark. He led the league in at-bats, hits, and runs, and, of course, finished second behind Wilson in home runs. Although runs batted in were not counted at the time, league historian Mark C. Zeigler credits Rawlings with a record 108 RBIs and Wilson with 94. Wilson set a league record with a .717 slugging average.

The 1922 Blue Sox were more than just the Rawlings-Wilson show. Third baseman Dave Black batted .308. Shortstop Joe Brehaney led the league with 34 stolen bases. James Hensel "Hank" Hulvey won 13 games pitching and batted .321 as the regular right fielder. Pitcher Ross Roberts led the league with 15 wins, and Frank Colley notched 12 victories. Walter Seaman posted a 9–3 record, and belted three homers in a game against Frederick. All in all, it was a wonderful season.

Following the regular season, the *Baltimore Sun* sponsored a "Five State Series" pitting the Blue Ridge champions against the winner of the Eastern Shore League. In the series the Blue Sox swept Parksley, Virginia, in four straight. The Blue Sox smashed four home runs in winning the first game 8–3. In game two, shortstop Jim Brehaney homered and Walter Seaman threw a shutout in a 3–0 win. The third game went 11 innings before Brehaney's suicide squeeze scored the winning run. Returning to the friendly confines of Rosemont Park, the Blue Sox wrapped up the series aided by a triple play in the third inning.[17]

After his great 1922 season, it was obvious Wilson had a bright future in baseball. The Blue Sox sold Wilson to Portsmouth of the Class B Virginia

League for $500. That, added to the $3,000 the team got for Groves, meant the Martinsburg club received $3,500 for two future Hall of Fame players, hardly an example of great business sense. Wilson married Jen Riddleburger toward the end of the 1923 season. They bought a comfortable house on John Street in Martinsburg. Wilson enjoyed socializing around town and hanging out at the Elks Club. His income and status took a leap when the New York Giants purchased him from Portsmouth for $11,000.[18]

Rawlings, however, remained the favorite of Martinsburg fans despite Wilson's power display. Years later, Wilson's biographer allowed, "West Virginia old-timers consider ... Rawlings to be a better player than Wilson."[19] After the 1922 season, Rawlings married a Martinsburg girl. The next spring, the lure of higher salary and the challenge of faster play led him to Portland, Oregon, of the Pacific Coast League. Homesick for his bride and familiar surroundings, he quickly managed to convince Portland to ship him back east. Portland sent him to Waynesboro, where his old manager, Country Morris, did Rawlings the favor of trading him back home to Martinsburg for a marginal player.

Even without Stouts Wilson, Martinsburg repeated as Blue Ridge League champions in 1923. Lewis Thompson developed a relationship with the Philadelphia Athletics that would last through 1929. It began with Earle Mack, son of Philadelphia Athletics owner and manager Connie Mack, taking over as the Blue Sox manager. As a youngster, Earle had played in five games for his father between 1910 and 1914. By the time he arrived in Martinsburg, Mack had thirteen years in the minor leagues. He had demonstrated managerial skills at Moline, Illinois, in the 1920–22 seasons. Philadelphia newspapers speculated that he would succeed his father as manager of the Athletics.

Mack guided the 1923 Blue Sox to a 68–29 record. That record represented a .701 winning percentage. No team would have a better single season record in Blue Ridge League history. The Blue Sox cruised to a seventeen game lead over their nearest challenger. Martinsburg led the Blue Ridge in batting average and home runs, and outscored other teams by over 100 runs.

Rawlings enjoyed an even more spectacular season than he had the year before. No player ever dominated the Blue Ridge League as Rawlings did in 1923. He won his second straight batting championship with a .376 batting average. He also led the Blue Ridge in at-bats (386), hits (145), doubles (28), home runs (25), total bases (260), and runs (104). He became the first and only player to score 100 runs in a season.

Unlike 1922, the 1923 Blue Sox had pitching and fielding as well as hitting. Playing first base, Earle Mack contributed a .321 batting average.

6. "The City Is Baseball Crazy" 101

Dwight Hulvey, George Quellich, Ed Sherling, Red Farrell, and Fred Lucas also batted over .300, although Sherling and Lucas played only a portion of the season. Quellich, Sherling and Lucas would go on to the majors.

The Blue Sox possessed the league's outstanding pitcher in Horace "Doc" Ozmer. Earle Mack was so impressed with Ozmer that he sent the pitcher to his father early in the season. Connie let Ozmer pitch two innings on May 22 before returning him to Martinsburg. After his return, Ozmer dominated the Blue Ridge League. He became Martinsburg's only pitcher ever to win 20 games in a season. His 25–5 record was the most wins and best winning percentage in the league. He also led the league with 142 strikeouts. Early the following season, the Blue Sox sold Ozmer to Shreveport of the Texas League, but he never again reached the majors. Hensel Hulvey, brother of Dwight, recorded a 13–7 record and finished third in the league in strikeouts. At the conclusion of the Blue Sox season, Earle took Hulvey to Philadelphia, where he pitched one game for the Athletics.

Charles "Lefty" Willis was no Lefty Grove, but in 1923 Martinsburg fans drew flattering comparisons. The Blue Sox signed Willis, a seventeen year old from nearby Leetown, West Virginia, off the campus of Shepherd College. The well-proportioned youngster (6'1" and 175 pounds) showed

Manager Earle Mack's 1923 club coasted to a Blue Ridge League pennant with a .701 winning percentage, the highest ever posted by a West Virginia team (Mark Ziegler).

great promise in his first professional season posting a nifty record of nine wins against three losses.

Despite the Blue Sox's regular season success in 1923, they lost the Five State Series to Dover, Delaware. Before the series began, Manager Mack allowed, "overconfidence may prove our downfall."[20] He was right. After winning the first two games in Martinsburg, the Blue Sox lost three straight in Dover. Rawlings, as usual, was not to blame for the downfall; he batted .443 for the series and hit four home runs. Quellich also batted .400.

The Blue Sox captured their third straight title in 1924. The team accomplished the feat of winning three in a row with a different manager each season. For the 1924 season, Connie Mack kept Earle in Philadelphia on the Philadelphia Athletics bench. Mr. Mack, however, watched out for Martinsburg; he recommended Pete Curtis for the managerial job, and the Blue Sox hired him. Curtis' previous managerial experience had been with the Strawbridge and Clothier Department Store team in the Philadelphia city league.

The 1924 team captured the pennant by the narrowest of margins. The winner was not decided until the last day of the season. The Blue Sox needed to win both ends of a morning-afternoon Labor Day double header from Hagerstown in order to beat out the Hubs for the league title. Ed Andrews pitched a two hit shutout to win the first game for Martinsburg. A crowd of 5,129, the largest in Blue Ridge history, turned out for the morning game. With the pennant on the line, the Blue Sox captured the second game 5–3 behind Ed Sherling's three home runs. With the two wins, the Blue Sox nosed out Hagerstown by the slimmest of margins; the Martinsburg team finished with a .608 winning percentage while Hagerstown had a .606 record. It could not have been closer.

Rawlings again led the Blue Sox to their 1924 Blue Ridge title. He captured his third consecutive batting crown with a personal high .379 batting average. For the second time he led the league in home runs with 21 round-trippers. His league-leading 31 doubles were a career best for him, as were his seventeen stolen bases. Rawlings also led the Blue Ridge League in hits (151) for the third time.

Others contributed to the Blue Sox attack. Second baseman Dave Black and outfielders Dennis "Denny" Sothern and Ed "Shine" Sherling always seemed to be on base when Rawlings came to the plate. Black led the league in bases on balls. Sothern batted .321 and Sherling chipped in with a .313 average. Both Sothern and Sherling reached the majors; indeed, Sherling went to Mack's Athletics before the season ended. Rawlings had reason to wonder about baseball's reward system. In the three championship years, Rawlings out-hit Wilson, Quellich, Sothern, Lucas, and Sherling. These five outfielders made the majors, but Rawlings remained in Martinsburg.

Lefty Willis matured into the mainstay of the staff in 1924. The local favorite had a fine 14–9 record and was second in the league in strikeouts. The following season Willis made the grade with the Philadelphia Athletics. There he greeted Lefty Grove when Baltimore sold its Lefty to Connie Mack in 1926. The two former Martinsburg pitchers had quite different major league careers. Willis lasted but three years in the Big Show. Grove played in the majors until 1941, and, of course, won 300 games.

After the 1924 Blue Ridge League season ended, Martinsburg closely followed the 1924 World Series to see how favorite son Hack Wilson performed on the biggest stage in baseball. The Giants regular center fielder, he had batted a solid .295 in the regular season. The Giants' roster included, as well, pitcher Wayland Dean, a twenty-one year old from the coalfield town of Richmond, West Virginia. Both had a disappointing series. Dean pitched just two innings. Wilson hit a weak .233 as the Washington Senators won the only World Series championship in the team's history.

Martinsburg's reign as the dominant team in the Blue Ridge League came to an end in 1925. Hagerstown won two straight titles in 1925 and 1926. The Blue Sox fell to third place both seasons. Rawlings' production fell off a notch and the supporting cast was not able to pick up the slack. Reg still led the league in home runs in 1926 with 19 and batted .335 and .320. Dave Black, Dennis Sothern, Earl Stanwood and Frank Burke hit over .300 in 1925. Black won the team Most Valuable Player award as he batted .319 and led the league in stolen bases. The 1926 club had five regulars who hit over .300.

First baseman Mickey Keliher led Martinsburg's potent attack in 1926. A veteran minor league slugger in his mid-thirties, he had played briefly for Pittsburgh in 1911 and 1912, but he had knocked around the minor league for the next fourteen years. After his league-leading .370 average in the 1926 season, he turned to managing, winning the 1927 Blue Ridge title for Chambersburg. He died young in 1930.

Pitching let the team down in 1925 and 1926. Harry Fishbaugh did win seventeen games in 1925, but the pitching staff had little behind him. The 1926 club with five .300 hitters had no pitcher who won even ten games; Bob McIntire's eight wins topped the staff. The weaker teams hurt attendance. At the close of the 1926 season, the club faced a $2,000 debt.

Martinsburg faced a crisis before the 1927 season. A conflict arose over the title to the land on which the ballpark was located. In the end, the team was forced to find a new home. The club managed to rent land adjoining Rosemont Amusement Park (later War Memorial Park) six blocks north of the old park. The new Rosemont Park, just outside city limits, was bounded by Park Avenue, Louisiana Avenue, Race Street, and Delaware Avenue.

James G. Maples, who had recently assumed the club presidency, and C. P. Howell, the treasurer, launched a drive to raise $12,000 in stock sale. They did not make their goal, but they got enough to build a new park before the season. The new Rosemont Park included a covered grandstand seating 1,000, right field bleachers, and a "colored grandstand." Because the club started $2,370 in debt, the *Martinsburg Journal* lamented, "gone is the high salaried player."[21]

The 1927 Blue Sox fared better than expected. The team started slowly, but fortunately the Blue Ridge League had introduced a split season format in 1926 in the hope of sustaining fan interest among also-rans late in the year. The Blue Sox started slowly, but got hot in the second half and torrid in the stretch run, winning their final eleven games to edge Chambersburg for the second half title. Rawlings raised his batting average to .351, his best since 1924. Bob McIntire, the main reason for the team's turnaround, won 13 games and led the league in strikeouts. Playing the outfield when not on the mound, he complemented Rawlings with a .316 batting average. The *Martinsburg Journal,* however, awarded a gold watch, emblematic of the team's Most Valuable Player, to Frank Burke. He not only managed the team, but he hit .290 as the regular first baseman, and, as a pitcher, he compiled an 11–2 record.

After the successful second half surge, the Sox entered the playoffs against first half winner Chambersburg with unbounded optimism. Earle Mack and Lefty Grove came down from Philadelphia to watch the playoffs. The Blue Sox, however, disappointed their fans, dropping the post-season playoffs to Chambersburg.

Following their second-half success in 1927, Martinsburg crashed in 1928. The team started well, finishing second in the first half of the season. Then nothing went right. A last place finish in the second half assured the Blue Sox their worst finish since 1920. Rawlings was the main reason for the collapse. His .258 batting average was the lowest by far in his twelve-year career, and his measly six home runs the lowest since 1915. Rookie outfielder Ed Millek took up some of the slack, hitting .320 and leading the league in hits, but that output did not compensate for Rawlings' dismal showing. Bob McIntire was a workhorse on the mound, pitching a league-leading 228 innings, but could only win eight games against ten losses.

After Rawlings' disappointing 1928 season, Martinsburg let the fan favorite go to Hagerstown. In over 1,000 games for Martinsburg, he had compiled a .331 batting average. In his twelve years as a Martinsburg pro he hit 172 home runs. He had three Blue Ridge League batting crowns to his credit, as well as having led the league three times in hits and home runs. Blue Sox fans were happy for him when he rebounded in 1929 to hit .321

with Hagerstown. No one doubted he was the Blue Ridge League's all-time outstanding player.

Given the club's lingering debt, Maples, Thompson and other investors were delighted when the Philadelphia Athletics assumed operation of the club in 1929. Newspapers dubbed the club the "Macklets." Fortunately for Martinsburg, Roger "Doc" Cramer was part of the contingent of players the A's sent to Martinsburg. Philadelphia had signed Cramer, a big, six feet, two inch, 185 pound brash kid from New Jersey, as a pitcher. He got the assignment to pitch Opening Day, but it quickly became apparent that his future was not as a pitcher; that season he walked 28 batters in 44 innings. Most of the season he played third base, although he logged in a few games in the outfield, the position he played for the next twenty years in the major leagues. Cramer batted a franchise high .404! Even Rawlings never reached the magical .400 level. Cramer banged out 31 doubles to tie Rawlings for the club record, thirteen triples, and five home runs for a league leading 217 total bases. Years later he remembered, "I liked Martinsburg. But you know, if you're having a good year, it doesn't much matter where you're playing." When the Blue Sox season ended, he headed directly to Philadelphia.[22]

With Cramer leading the way, the Blue Sox captured their fourth regular season title of the decade. Cramer had support from second baseman Joe Luciano (.333) and Art Wooding, the Blue Sox catcher since 1924, who enjoyed his best season, hitting .315. Pitcher Harry Griffith, although wild, won 18 games, as did George Malichy. Al Jones chipped in with 14 wins. Cramer, by the way, finished 2–2 as a pitcher.

Earle Mack compared the 1929 club favorably with his 1923 team. The '23 had better hitting he thought, but he allowed as how the 1929 team may have had stronger pitching. That was before the pitching let the Blue Sox down in the playoffs against Hagerstown. Of course, Mack had not been around to see the 1922 team of Hack Wilson and Reg Rawlings. That crew must be ranked the best Martinsburg team.

Following the Blue Ridge season, Martinsburg's attention turned to the World Series, where Hack Wilson was on baseball's biggest stage against the Blue Sox parent club, the Philadelphia Athletics. Having been traded from the Giants to the Chicago Cubs in 1926, Wilson went on a five-year rampage that earned him a spot in the Baseball Hall of Fame. He led the National League in home runs in 1926, 1927 and 1928. In 1929 he drove in over 100 runs for the fourth consecutive year, leading the league with 159 RBIs. The Cubs roared to the National League pennant. John "Sheriff" Blake of Ansted, West Virginia, helped the Cubs by winning 14 games that year.

Unfortunately, Wilson and Blake wore goat horns after the Series. After

Philadelphia won game one, Wilson went three for three in game two, but the Athletics won again when Lefty Grove, pitching in relief, shut the door on the Cubs. Chicago then captured the third game as Wilson collected two hits. In game four the Cubs appeared to be on their way to tying the Series when they took an 8–0 lead into the seventh inning. After the A's made the score 8–4, Wilson to his lasting dismay lost an easy fly ball in the sun, allowing three runs to score. Sheriff Blake then entered the game to put out the fire. He could not get anyone out and became the game's losing pitcher. Although Wilson had the highest batting average in the series, a resounding .471, it would be his muff that people remembered.

The Great Depression, which followed fast on the heels of the World Series, hit Martinsburg quickly. Despite the team's successful 1929 season, the parent Philadelphia Athletics reported a loss of $11,000 to $13,000 on the Martinsburg operation. The A's were World Champions but Connie Mack disliked losing money more than losing games. The growing financial crisis frightened him. Early in 1930 the Athletics decided to pull out of Martinsburg. Lewis Thompson, who again assumed the leadership of Martinsburg baseball, was "dumfounded" and "highly discouraged." His hope of convincing Mack to change his mind was dashed when Earle Mack came to town and confirmed his father's intention to pull out. Thompson then tried to find other major league backers, but to no avail. Local businessmen failed to step up to invest in baseball. Briefly, Thompson and league president Jamison hoped Winchester, Virginia, would join with Martinsburg in a shared franchise. In April, Thompson thought he had an out of town buyer, but that too fell through.[23]

Martinsburg could not answer the bell for the 1930 season. The Blue Ridge League limped through the 1930 season with four teams, and then it too collapsed. Martinsburg fans did not know it at the time, but Organized Baseball was over in the Eastern Panhandle.

Martinsburg's fans did enjoy the exploits of Hack Wilson in 1930. That year he captured the National League's Most Valuable Player award. No wonder. That season he drove in the all-time major league high of 191 runs. He also led the league in home runs with a career high 56, just four fewer than Babe Ruth had hit in 1927. It was Wilson's fourth home run title. Pitchers tried not to give him good pitches, resulting in his leading the league in base on balls. He would never have a season like that again, but no one has had a more productive one.

Rawlings and the other Blue Sox who stayed in Martinsburg continued playing semi-pro ball. They wore their old Blue Sox uniforms and played weekends at Rosemont Park. A semi-pro Blue Ridge League reappeared in 1934. Wilson joined the team as player-manager in 1935. They played teams from the Washington, Baltimore, Winchester, and the old Blue Ridge towns, occasionally traveling to the Norfolk area. When they could not schedule better teams, they played clubs from the Bi-County Industrial League. It was easy for Wilson to get away from his pool hall and sporting goods store, but the enterprise did suffer from Hack's lackadaisical attitude. The pair of Rawlings and Wilson had terrorized the Blue Ridge League in 1922, but by 1935 Rawlings was 45 years old and Wilson a 35 year old alcoholic. Still, local opponents preferred to walk Wilson than to pitch to him.[24]

The fun proved short-lived. Wilson's life became tragic after 1935. He was descending into the bottle, divorce, unemployment and perhaps venereal disease. Rawlings' age was finally catching up to him. By the time Wilson left Martinsburg in 1939, the city's baseball days were over. Wilson moved a lot after leaving town — western Pennsylvania, Chicago, back to Martinsburg, and finally to Baltimore where he died in 1948. The Martinsburg Elks paid for his burial at Rosedale Cemetery and for an impressive tombstone with crossed bats. Rawlings stood quietly at the unveiling of the marker. He had to know an era had ended.[25]

7

"Baseball Was the Miners' Sport"
Coalfield Baseball, 1920–1941

Southern West Virginia has always been the heart of Appalachia. There the mountains rub shoulders and the valleys tighten. Flatland virtually disappears. The region consisting of Mercer, Raleigh, Fayette, Wyoming, McDowell, Logan and Mingo counties has remained physically, economically, and culturally isolated since the days when Daniel Boone tromped these hills. The English and Scots-Irish who settled the area continued to be clannish and suspicious of strangers until recent times. Beginning in the nineteenth century, outlanders described these folk as a backward, hard drinking, poor, feuding, brawling people left over from another time. The image of the archetypal hillbilly came from these mountains.[1]

This pre-industrial world of the mountains began to change in the 1880s when the Norfolk and Western Railroad pushed tracks through the region to remove its natural resources. By the beginning of the twentieth century, "King Coal" came to dominate the economy of the southern counties. Hundreds of investors, mostly from out of state, leased land from the railroad in search of the wealth that came from black diamonds. While other industries went through massive consolidation in the first decade of the century, coal remained characterized by destructive cutthroat competition. Nowhere was this truer than in Southern West Virginia.

Following World War I, the miners' efforts to organize a union and the operators' determination to destroy the hated union led to bitter industrial warfare. Coal operators had their private armies, the local law enforcement, state troopers, and the National Guard on their side. They evicted miners from their homes. When miners erected tent colonies, the operators burned them and drove out the miners and their families. Operators and their agents brought in strikebreakers, gassed, shot, even bombed their fellow West Virginians. The operators had the power and wielded it fiercely. By 1922 the coal operators had won a complete victory over the United Mine Workers Union and its organizers and supporters. The coal wars left miners discouraged and economically depressed. According to historian David Corbin, miners increasingly relied on alcohol to wash away their cares, and fatalism to carry them back into the mines.[2]

Following the wars of 1919–1922, coal operators began slowly to introduce practices that came to be called "welfare capitalism." This constituted a subtler defense against unionization than violent forms of intimidation. In the mid-twenties, especially after 1924, profits soared in the southern West Virginia coalfield and coal operators could afford to invest some of their gain on means to keep their workers peaceful and wages low. The fundamental ideal of welfare capitalism, according to coal historian John Hennen, was to create a "satisfied, stable, and productive work force."[3]

A primary object of welfare capitalism was "to bind workers to employer." What better way to do that than to give the coal camp a baseball team? Rooting for a team bearing the company name reinforced the sense of the individual identification with the company. Colleges had long understood the value of students rooting for the school's sports teams. Two coal companies established the earliest models for welfare capitalism. The Raleigh Coal and Coke Company, just south of Beckley in southern West Virginia, and the Consolidation Coal Company, headquartered in Fairmont, saw advantages for the company in providing recreation programs for their employees. The Raleigh company formed the Raleigh Mining Institute to orchestrate its recreation program. Consolidation established an Employment Relations Department in 1917. Each moved quickly to sponsor a baseball team. At Raleigh, the company-owned Raleigh Mining Institute's park, known as RMI Park, became the center of baseball in the Beckley area throughout the 1920s and 1930s. Raleigh teams, both white and black, played there, as did Beckley's professional and semi-professional teams.[4]

Coal operators in southern West Virginia did not immediately jump on the baseball bandwagon. Bluefield, however, the unofficial capital of the southern coalfields, demonstrated the popularity of baseball to the rest of the southern West Virginia coal towns. Bluefield had a tradition of baseball dating back to 1904. Local businessman W. L. Otley sponsored a town team there in 1906, and a strong semi-pro team had played there in 1912. After World War I, the boys of Bluefield played lads from just across the state line in Graham, Virginia, in a much-ballyhooed July 4, 1920, game at the fairgrounds on the border between the two states. Fans filled the grandstand and automobiles lined the outfield, attesting to the potential of the sport as a spectator event. The following summer teams from Bluefield, Poca-Bramwell, Princeton and McComas began playing each other on Sunday afternoons.[5]

In isolated Logan County, site of the four-day Battle of Rich Mountain in 1920, baseball began to come alive in 1922, seemingly as a way for miners, townspeople and operators to forget the recent struggles. A Logan town team soon found competition from the surrounding coal towns of Omar, Holden, Man and Monitor. At the model town of Holden, the Island Creek Coal Company constructed a fine wooden ballpark. Monitor, a coal patch town outside Logan, combined with even smaller Gay to form the strongest team in the area in both 1923 and 1924.[6]

The first real baseball boom in the coalfields occurred in 1924. Bluefield, as was usual in the region, led the way in establishing the new cultural pattern. Local businessmen Fred Fox and Fred Hawley formed a new team with the intention of bringing professional baseball to the city. In doing so they undertook the most ambitious baseball operation yet seen in Southern West Virginia. The fairgrounds offered a place to play that allowed them to charge admission. Hugh "Ike" Shott, owner of the influential *Bluefield Daily Telegram*, declared the team a good idea and threw the weight of his paper behind the proposal. Dick Neberger took over as manager and recruited players, mostly from the region, and in May the team began play as Bluefield-Graham. When the adjoining Virginia city of Graham changed its name to Bluefield, the team adopted the nickname of Blue-Grays.[7]

The Blue-Grays looked east and south for competition and obtained a spot in the newly created semi-professional Blue Ridge League, not to be confused with the Class D league with the same name. Bluefield was the only West Virginia entry in the league that included teams from Virginia and North Carolina. The team played on Wednesdays and Saturdays, alternating home and away games, and then played at home on Sundays. Neberger's team of town boys had trouble competing, and by late July the initial enthusiasm wore thin. The team, tired of losing games and money, withdrew from the league.

The excitement the Blue-Grays had generated in May and June spawned numerous other teams in the city and surrounding region. Less talented than the Blue-Grays, the amateur teams brought the enthusiasm of the newly converted to the sport. Boys and young men organized church teams. Neighborhoods sprouted clubs, although these teams seem to have been of the sandlot variety, composed of teenage boys. Whenever they had enough players, they arranged a game; usually they just played pick-up games among themselves. Businesses, including the *Daily Telegram* and Dupont, sponsored teams. Indeed, there were several teams from the Norfolk and Western railroad yard. Uniforms represented a kind of dividing line between recreational and more serious teams. Uniforms, of course, required money and money typically came either from charging for admission to the team's games or from a sponsor.

In the coal towns of the Pocahontas coalfield to the west of Bluefield, the example of the Blue-Grays created a virtual explosion of teams each wishing to trump their neighbors. Coal operators in this relatively prosperous region took the lead in establishing teams to carry their towns' names. Bramwell to the west of Bluefield was one of the first to field a team. Bramwell had become a town of company offices and mansions for coal operators. The wealthy residents happily donated land for a diamond and money for uniforms. Lawrence Tierney, the coal camp operator at Powhatan, population under 500, wanted to prove his equal to the big mules in Bramwell. Across the county line in McDowell County on the recently paved State Route 8 (later W.Va. Route 52) teams formed at Maybeury and Elkhorn-Northfork. In the county seat of Welch, wealthy young John Blakely organized a town team. South of Welch, in the U.S. Steel Company–owned town of Gary, Mine Superintendent Colonel Edward O'Toole wanted a winning team and was willing to pay. He expanded Gary's roofed park into a horseshoe stretching from first to third base. It was the finest ballpark in the coalfields. By August 1924 strong teams also emerged in the McDowell County company towns of Coalwood and Berwind.[8]

Almost as soon as these teams were formed, the organizers began recruiting players from outside town. The competitive juices of the coal operators drove the initial process of bringing in outside players to augment local talent. Not content with pride in their teams' successes, they began betting their counterparts large sums of money on the outcome of games. With money as well as bragging rights at stake, quality players quickly became in great demand.

When mines recruited baseball players, the recruits seldom actually went into the mines. Sebert Toney, Jr., of Berwind remembered "they were given a real cushy job ... topside." Clerking in the company store, doing office work if they possessed basic literacy, doing repairs on company houses, and stringing utility lines were favorite jobs for players. They had time off to practice or play. By August 1924 these teams played almost daily.[9]

Coalfield historian Stuart McGehee put his finger on the importance that baseball came to have for coal operators. As he pointed out, because flat land was scarce, it was precious. Miners' homes and those of the bosses more often than not clung to hillsides, but the companies willingly committed large chunks of flat land to the baseball field. None of the fields resembled the manicured parks of today. All had dirt or skinned infields. A smooth dirt surface could play fast and true, very much like Astroturf fields fifty years later, but very few reached that level of quality. As an old coalfield veteran recalled, bad bounces were common, and "if the ball took a bad hop and hit you in the face, well, that was too bad."[10] Most fields had wooden stands, open wooden bleachers actually, perhaps four to seven rows deep. At Gary and a few of the better fields, grandstands had a wooden roof. At all, home plate was located dangerously close to the backstop and stands, where a chicken wire screen offered spectators some protection from foul balls. Dugouts were uncommon; players sat on benches. Since few fields were enclosed, most were without outfield fences. Home runs, generally, came from long hits between outfielders and speed on the base paths, not from hitting the ball out of the park.

Bluefield's Blue-Grays appeared to have the advantage over the coal camp teams. After withdrawing from the Blue Ridge League in July, the Blue-Grays played whatever teams it could line up. They managed to log in at least fifty-three games by mid–September. The city's population and the team's admission revenue seemed to favor the Blue-Grays. The club brought in two outstanding pitchers to strengthen the team. Vic Sorrell came to Bluefield from North Carolina and never left, making his home there even while playing in the majors. He used the Blue-Grays as a springboard to Detroit, where he played from 1928 until 1937. John "Chick" Smith, a Kentucky native, was already over thirty and on the way down after reaching the majors in the teens, but he could still retire semi-pro batters.

Despite their pitching, the Blue-Grays could not dominate the competition. The mine teams countered by bringing in top-flight players of their own. The Elkhorn-Northfork All-Staters found Clarence "Lefty" Thomas, a promising young Virginian who was good enough to pitch for the American League champion Washington Senators the next year. Future major league pitchers Harry "Hoge" Workman, John Woods and Guy Morrison dotted the rosters, as did outfielder Herman Layne. Gary brought in a University of Cincinnati student named Ethan Allen. Playing the outfield and batting cleanup, Allen quickly established himself as one of the two best hitters in the coalfields. He went on to play thirteen years in the major leagues, 1926–1938, compiling a career batting average of .300. After his playing days, Allen coached baseball at Yale University from 1946 to 1968. Poca-Bramwell's first baseman Charlie McMillan, whose fame never reached beyond the coalfields, was the other top hitter.[11]

7. "Baseball Was the Miners' Sport"

Interest in baseball increased even more in October 1924 when the Cincinnati Reds barnstormed through southern West Virginia. Their games at Huntington, Williamson, Gary, Welch, and Bluefield brought out huge crowds. The host cities put together an "all-star" team from the local area to play the professionals. Although the "all-stars" fared poorly on the field, fans flocked to see major league players.[12]

In 1925, Frank M. Archer, who had assumed the operation of the Blue-Grays, took the lead in forming the first league in southern West Virginia. The Coalfield League of 1925 had only four teams: the Bluefield Blue-Grays, Pocahontas-Bramwell Indians from Mercer County, Colonel Edward O'Toole's Gary Coal Diggers, and the Coalwood Robins from McDowell County. The league opened on Memorial Day and continued until mid–September. Bluefield, under manager Ray Price, started fast, but faded when Sorrell left to pursue a professional career. Sorrell returned in time for the Blue-Grays to square off against Gary in a five game series for the league title. Bluefield's pitching stopped Allen and his fellow Gary hitters.

Coalwood got the attention of the entire league in 1925 when Shufflin' Phil Douglas came to town. Already thirty-five and with a serious drinking problem, he had spent nine seasons in the majors winning 93 games plus two in the 1921 World Series. In his last season with the New York Giants, he won 11, lost only 4, and posted the best ERA in the National League. Before the 1922 season ended, Douglas self-destructed. After being forced by the Giants to enter a detox center, forced to pay for his own treatment, and being fined by manager John McGraw, Douglas committed the unforgivable. He wrote to a friend on the St. Louis Cardinals offering "to [go] to a fishing camp and stay there" if he received "some inducement" from the Cardinals. McGraw labeled Douglas "the dirtiest ball player I have ever seen," and Commissioner Kenesaw Landis suspended him for life. *The Sporting News* blamed his indiscretion on his reduced mental capacity. It described Douglas' mental processes as "those of a child" and concluded he was "sub-normal at his best."[13] A native of the East Tennessee mountains, Douglas had little or no education and few skills. All he knew was how to pitch. If he could not pitch in New York, he would pitch in Coalwood, West Virginia. It must have seemed like home; he would have no problem finding alcohol in the coal town.

The league failed to reorganize for 1926, but teams operated in hundreds of coal patches, camps and towns throughout the hills of Southern West Virginia. Welch, Berwind, Gary, Coalfield, Bishop, War, Kimball, Iaeger, Powhatan, Keystone, and North Fork operated teams in McDowell County. Phil Douglas left Coalwood, but teenage hotshot Paul Derringer replaced him. Derringer would pitch in four World Series and log 223 wins in 15 big-league seasons between 1931 and 1945. In Wyoming County, Mullens, Pineville, Glen Rogers, Glen Morrison and Oceana fielded teams. Logan County teams included Holden, Monitor, Omar, and Peach Creek as well as the town of Logan. Fewer teams operated farther west in Mingo County: Red Jacket, Matewan, Kermit and Williamson were the contenders.[14]

The major explosion of teams occurred in Raleigh County, which rapidly became the heart of coalfield baseball. In his town, "Major" Walter P. Tams, paternalistic owner of mine and town, prided himself on having the best recreation facilities in the county. His team, the Tams Majors, like his town, carried his name. In Glen White, population 700, miners in 1919–20 had trashed the mine and burned the coal tipple of the Koppers Coal Company. Five years later the miners took pride in their baseball team, the Glen White Koppers. Other teams included Stonecoal and Hot Coal, Cranberry and Crab Orchard, Loup Creek and Winding Gulf, Raleigh, Lester and Stotesbury, Amigo, Beaver, Cirtsville, Fireco, Mabscott, McAlpin, Stansfield, Sprague, Sullivan, Price Hill, Skelton, Lillybrook, Mead, Helen, Fayette, and Pax.[15]

After the fast times of 1924–25, most teams settled into playing only on Sundays. Even without imported players, games remained highly competitive, hard-fought affairs, often in the stands as well as on the field. Former Gary manager A. N. Harris recalled: "The enthusiasm for a particular team often caused fights, individual and mob." There is no evidence of players or umpires being killed, but Harris and Bob Bowman, who went to the majors from the coalfields, remembered guns being fired at games.[16]

Despite the competition, games took on greater importance as social events. In the mid-twenties, visiting teams typically arrived by train. The N&W ran special trains for games between teams from the larger towns, Welch, Gary, Bramwell and Bluefield. Later, automobiles, with as many as possible piled into Model T Fords, brought spectators to away games. Men, women and children, virtually the entire town, turned out for games. It was not uncommon to have as many women spectators as men. Fans overflowed the small stands, lined the foul lines and even stood in the deep outfield, or they sat on hillsides outside the park.

If flat land was precious in the hills, leisure time in coal country in the twenties was "precious time," to use a term Robert and Helen Lynd coined in their study titled *Middletown*. In the non-union mines of Southern West Virginia, miners still worked six days a week, leaving only Sundays for relaxation. A. N. Harris remembered: "All week long the citizens of McDowell County looked forward to the baseball game to be played on Sunday afternoons." A native of Berwind, a coal camp in McDowell County, recalled: "Sunday in Berwind was Baseball." Another reflected: "Berwind and Baseball were synonymous." The same could be said for most coal towns. After the games, a more festive atmosphere usually replaced the enthusiasm of the competition. Women broke out baskets of food, often for the visiting players as well as for the home team. Men broke out a bottle; miners always seemed to know where they could obtain a bottle of homebrew.[17]

Ballplayers, local or outsiders, had a special status in the coal camps. As one old-time player remembered, "Your wife would wash your uniform and hang it out on the line. You could see that uniform while walking back home from the mines and you'd feel that pride all over again." Historian Crandall Shifflett's understated summary rings true: "Baseball was the miners' sport."[18]

Strong African-American teams began to appear in the mid-twenties. Southern West Virginia had a sizable black population, most of whom originally came to the area from the South as strikebreakers. In McDowell County over one-third of miners were black. In neighboring Logan County, African-Americans constituted twenty percent of the population in 1931. While work in the mines may have been integrated, the topside world remained strictly segregated. Players on the early mine teams were as white as their home uniforms, but by the mid-twenties coal operators began to rethink the exclusion of black miners from the ball field. For the same reasons companies sponsored white teams—to create loyalty to the company, as a barrier against unions, and as a means of social control—they saw fit to form teams of African-American employees. Teams like the Bishop Miners, Raleigh Clippers, Holden Bear Cats, Tams Black Sox, East Gulf-Stonecoal Giants, Slabrock Indians, Gary Grays, Coalwood Monarchs, and New River Giants played home games on the same fields as the white locals. The black and white teams from the same town, however, almost never played each other.

Segregation had some advantages for African-American teams. Because there were fewer black teams in the coalfields, they traveled farther to find games than their white counterparts. Black squads also welcomed opponents from greater distances. Teams from Virginia, Ohio, and Pennsylvania commonly played African-American nines, whereas white coalfield teams seldom had an opportunity to test their skills with distant opponents. Beginning in the twenties, the famous Homestead Grays barnstormed through the region, playing at enclosed parks. Other Negro League teams soon followed.[19]

The center of coalfield baseball moved into Raleigh County in the late twenties. As it did, the seriousness of the game took a quantum leap. In

1927 a Beckley newspaper, the *Raleigh Register,* formed the Raleigh County League for coal mine teams. So many teams wanted to join that to make as many happy as possible the organizers formed two divisions, an "A League" and a "B League." The "leagues" were really divisions of the same league. Each league initially had eight teams, all from coal towns, with one exception, that being a team representing Beckley Baking. The A loop consisted of Eccles, Beaver, Glen White, Cirtsville, Fireco, Mabscott, Glen Morgan and Beckley Baking. The B grouping included teams from Stansford, Sprague, Raleigh, Sullivan, Cranberry, Price Hill, Lester, and Shelton. Teams played against others in their division on Sundays and holidays. The two league winners met at the conclusion of the scheduled season for the county championship. Eccles, managed by former West Virginia Wesleyan captain Doctor Doff D. Daniels, beat Lillybrook for the first league title.[20]

At the same time, a twilight league came together in Beckley. Unlike the mine league, it provided an opportunity for "mediocre players" and youngsters. The newly formed American Legion team played in the league, as did teams from service clubs, the Kiwanis and Lions, and teams composed of employees of town businesses. High school teams also made their first appearance in 1927 in Beckley, Lester, and Oak Hill.

Before the summer of 1927 ended, another league called the Coalfield Association appeared in McDowell County. Welch, Coalwood, Gary, and Bramwell entered teams. Coalwood, featuring the pitching of young, strong future Cincinnati Reds all-star Paul Derringer, fielded the strongest team. The Welch Senators boasted about brand new Blakely Field with a covered grandstand seating 500 fans. Built by former player John Blakely, who was rapidly amassing a fortune in insurance and movie theaters, it rivaled Gary as the best in the county.

The organization of coalfield baseball took a further leap in 1929 with the creation of the semi-pro Tri-State League. This organization, modeled on Organized Baseball leagues, consisted of teams from three of the state's largest cities—Huntington, Charleston and Parkersburg—plus Beckley, Williamson, and a team from Ashland, Kentucky. Lou H. Barringer of Charleston, who had experience as president of the short-lived professional Mountain States League, served as the league's executive. He drafted a 20 game schedule with matches on Saturdays and Sundays. All the teams played at enclosed parks where they charged twenty-five cent admission.

Several experienced baseball men, in addition to Barringer, played leadership roles in the league. Johnny "Stud" Stuart, the boss at Huntington, had four years of major league experience with the St. Louis Cardinals, 1922–25. He also coached Marshall College's baseball team. Watt Powell, who had played on and managed the Charleston team in the Ohio

State League before World War I, ran the Charleston club. At Beckley, Roy Elkins, a "gas and baseball man," started the team, but Eccles' Doc Daniels soon took charge.

As mine teams had done in 1924, Tri-State League owners loaded up with talent. Stuart signed former New York Giants pitcher Wayland Dean for Huntington. The Beckley Black Diamonds brought in Duke University shortstop Bill Werber, who was good enough to play for the New York Yankees the next year. Kelsey Jennings quit organized ball to play for Beckley because he made more money than he would playing for Wilkes-Barre of the Eastern League. He became the loop's leading hitter in 1927. Powell's Charleston Statesmen captured the first half of the split season. Dean, however, led Huntington to the second-half flag and then to a playoff victory over Charleston.

Once the fast semi-pro league started, the Raleigh County League fell by the wayside, at least for the duration of the Tri-State loop. Logan, left out of the Tri-State League, developed a strong league system. A Twilight League provided playing opportunities for the newly created American Legion team for youngsters and for men of the city service clubs. The next year the league changed its name to the Logan Service League to better reflects its purpose. A Logan County Industrial League provided a setting for mine teams from Omar, Holden, Lorado, Monaville, Henlawson, Merrill and Dehue.[21]

Logan replaced Parkersburg in the Tri-State League of 1930. Known as the Indians, the Logan team reached into the Deep South for a veteran minor league star from Alabama named Holt "Cat" Milner. For Logan, Milner batted a resounding .493, leading the Indians to the first half championship. Beckley, with Kelsey Jennings, the leagues' top pitcher as well as one of the best hitters, captured the second half. In a five game playoff, Beckley prevailed over Logan three games to two. Jennings won the deciding game at Logan before a crowd reported at 3,000. The fans overflowed the 500 seat grandstand, filled the bleachers, and stretched down the foul lines and around the outfield fence.[22]

Even though the country suffered through the worst depression in its history and the coal industry teetered on the brink of collapse, the Tri-State League cities showed a profit in 1930. The experience so buoyed the teams' operators that they jumped at the opportunity to enter Organized Baseball with full-blown professional teams in 1931. When the Class C Middle Atlantic League decided to expand to twelve teams for the 1931 season, Doc Daniels in Beckley, John Stuart in Huntington and Watt Powell in Charleston wasted little time in joining the expanding league.

In the wake left by the shift of the largest Tri-State cities to the professional ranks, Beverly Maynard of Williamson took the lead in forming a successor league. His 1931 semi-pro Ohio Valley League included Logan, where T. M. Higley and Dr. L. E. Farnsworth ran the team; Huntington, owned by Hol Slutz; tiny Kenova, where Sheral Edler put together a team; and Maynard's Williamson Colts. The loop only lasted through the 1931 season. Huntington's club could not compete against the professional team in town, and Kenova proved too small to support a team. A new Tri-State League reappeared in more modest form. Composed of smaller towns like Kenova, Cedroe and Barboursville, it lasted for several more years.[23]

Bluefield, left out of the league building, attempted to find a niche in the hierarchy of baseball. Businessman Emmett A. Cain operated a team that had played on his East End field since 1924. In 1933 he found a spot for it in yet another Virginia based semi-pro Blue Ridge League. Cain constructed a park, bearing his name, which opened in June 1933. He then turned the team over to a group headed by Charles Nordscik and Frank M. Archer. On the field, this edition of the Blue-Grays, led by pitcher Bob Bowman and catcher Dan Rainey, beat out Mount Airy, North Carolina, for the league title.[24]

In the thirties, coalfield ball reverted to county-based organizations. Logan, McDowell, Mercer and Raleigh counties had their own leagues. Toward the end of the decade the Logan, McDowell, and Mercer circuits merged into a Tri-County League that lasted until World War II. In McDowell, Amonte won in 1933. Bishop captured the flag in 1934 thanks to the late-season addition of Henry "Nick" Cullop, who had a five-year major league career, and who would hit over 400 minor league home runs. Then the Iaeger Red Birds, representing the Red Bird Mining Company, won in 1935.[25]

In Mercer County, the Elkhorn team, with Bob Bowman pitching, dominated until he left to play professionally in 1937. Bowman, who became a 29-year-old major league rookie in 1939, had entered the mines at age 16. Baseball got him topside. After he turned professional, sportswriters asked Bowman to comment on the grind of playing every day. He responded: "Pitchin' every day beats workin' in the mines." With Elkhorn he felt greater pressure to win because "the boys ... were betting their shirts.... I had to win or else."[26]

Raleigh County remained the most rabid baseball area throughout the 1930s. Indeed, much that has been written about baseball in the coalfields, its mythology and legends, is really about Raleigh County in the Great Depression decade. In the early 1930s, the growing economic depression had an effect on the mine teams. As "the bituminous industry was sliding toward bankruptcy" the coal companies, of necessity, cut their expenses.

Many no longer felt they could afford the luxury of a baseball team. By 1932, the Raleigh League was reduced to half the teams it had before the Wall Street crash, despite the efforts of *Raleigh Register* sports editor Needy McQuade, who served as league president.[27]

Even with fewer teams, the Raleigh County League remained the strongest league in the coalfields. The mining camp of Glen White established the first mini-dynasty in coalfield ball. They won the Raleigh League in 1932, 1933, and 1934 before losing in a playoff to Scarbro in 1935. Glen White, a town of 700, was five miles southwest and off any main roads from Beckley. Back in 1919, miners there had trashed the mines and burned the tipple, but by 1932 miners flocked to the Koppers Coal Company baseball field for home games.

The arrival of pitcher John "Sheriff" Blake in Glen White in 1932 turned the Glen White Koppers into the best mine team in the state. Blake became as much of a legend in the mine camps as John Henry. The native of Ansted, West Virginia, had gained a reputation as the star pitcher for West Virginia Wesleyan College before World War I. He had been a major league pitcher since 1920; he posted double-digit wins for six years with the Chicago Cubs, including a 17–11 record with an eye-popping 2.47 earned run average in 1928. Wildness kept him from being a truly outstanding major league pitcher. When the Philadelphia Phillies released him, Blake returned to West Virginia rather than go to the minor leagues of professional ball. Once he got to Glen White he stayed put, pitching for the mine team as long as it lasted. The wildness served him well in the coalfields, where batters feared for their lives when facing Blake. He might put the ball in their ear, on purpose or not. In addition to Blake, longtime coalfield star Charley McMillan provided power in the lineup. Blake found a job in Glen White for Earl Webb, a buddy from their Chicago Cubs days, and he provided additional clout for Glen White.[28]

The unionization of the southern West Virginia mines in 1933 presented more problems for coalfield baseball. Coal companies, whose goal in sponsoring baseball teams had been to keep workers happy and the union out, now had less reason to put resources into baseball. Even so, somehow the teams survived. The United Mine Workers picked up some of the slack by sponsoring teams when the company dropped baseball. The UMW even created its own league beginning in 1933 and continuing through the decade. Another technique for supporting teams was in the unofficial check-off on payday. After the union and operators signed a collective bargaining agreement, miners had their union dues deducted from their paycheck. The mine team stood next in line, asking miners for a fifty-cent donation each payday to support the team. Miners seldom refused.[29]

By the mid-thirties the leagues had reestablished a rhythm that carried them until World War II. The Raleigh County A and B leagues operated with eighteen teams and the UMW league had eight more. Scarbro replaced Glen White atop the league in 1935. Because steady jobs were hard to come by in the Great Depression, even for a former major league ball player, several were glad to take work and play ball at the mines. In addition to Webb, other former big-leaguers included Henry "Pete" Rice, a ten-year veteran with the St. Louis Browns, who roamed the outfield for the Amigo Red Birds, and pitcher Jim Brillheart, cut loose by the Red Sox in 1931 but who still had a little left in his arm.

There were also local products on the way up to the majors. Tom Cafego, a Coalwood boy who played the outfield for Scarbro, emerged as the league's top hitter in the mid-thirties. No one from the coalfield was surprised when he made the major leagues in 1937. After being cut from the majors, he returned to Scarbro. Pitchers John Gorsica, Max Butcher, and Arnold "Lefty" Carter used the mine teams as a springboard to the majors.

African-American teams also flourished in the thirties. Although less numerous than white teams, black clubs were not in short supply in Southern West Virginia. Among the better teams were the Raleigh Clippers, Holden Bear Cats, Slab Fork Indians, New River Giants of Sprague, Tams Black Sox, Keystone Giants, Kyle Cardinals, Glen Rogers Red Sox, Gary Grays, Berwind Cubs, and the East Gulf–Stonecoal Giants. Other African-American teams came from Amigo, Winding Gulf, Price Hill, Scarbro, Eccles, Mullens, Bishop, and Hemphill. At White Sulphur Springs, waiters and porters at the Greenbrier resort organized a team. Bluefield had two teams of Norfolk and Western railroad workers. The independent Huntington Quicksteps joined the field in the late thirties.[30]

The best of the black teams were the Holden Bearcats in Logan County, the Raleigh Clippers from the mining camp of that name outside Beckley, and the Kyle Cardinals in McDowell County. The Clippers' Grover Lewis was to black fans what Sheriff Blake was to whites. He had played for the Homestead Grays in the twenties, 1925–1929, before returning to Raleigh County. He managed the Clippers from 1931 into the 1950s. Lewis was the Clippers' power hitter in the thirties. He was the best but not the only outstanding player. Second baseman Tommy "Toots" Sampson, a magician in the field, left to play for the Chicago American Giants, Birmingham Black Barons, and New York Cubans between 1938 and 1949. Nathaniel Smith held down the shortstop position from 1931 until World War II. Outfielder S. G. "Garson" Totten went on to play for the New York Cubans in the 1940s.

The Clippers had their way with local African-American teams, except in 1935 when Summerlee laid claim to the county title and 1940 when the Slab Fork Indians bested the Raleigh team. Not content with beating local teams, the Clippers scheduled African-American teams from Roanoke and Richmond, Virginia, Charlotte and Wilmington, North Carolina, and various Ohio towns. Their biggest games were against barnstorming Negro League teams. The Birmingham Black Barons and Memphis Red Sox made occasional visits, but the Pittsburgh teams, the Homestead Grays and Pittsburgh Crawfords, were annual attractions. These games were played at the Beckley professional team's RMI Park. While the Clippers regularly attracted crowds of 500 for their games against local teams, they could draw 3,000 white as well as black fans against the Grays and Crawfords. Local fans took a special liking to the Crawfords' Oscar Charleston.

On occasion, African-American teams played white clubs, but not often. In 1940 the black Slab Fork Indians, winner of the newly formed Tri-County Negro League, took on Raleigh League winner Stotesbury. In that game the white club prevailed 19–9. The same year, black and white all-star teams from Raleigh County faced off in a three game series. The teams were evenly matched. The white club won two games, each by just one run. Earl "Red" Martin, just three years from being the top hitter in all the minor leagues, was the batting standout for the white stars. Ex-major league pitchers Sheriff Blake and John Gorsica started each game for the white club. Grover Lewis' "colored all-stars" picked up a 6–3 victory in the series. Angus Evans, former Clipper outfielder, remembered "no racial tensions on the diamond. We played ball."[31]

The town of Holden in Logan County had the reputation of being a model town. It and Tams prided themselves on having the best recreation facilities. Holden had a nice little enclosed ballpark with grandstand where white and black teams played. Like the Clippers, Holden played the Homestead Grays and Pittsburgh Crawfords to packed houses. Holden was the strongest black team in Logan County throughout the decade beginning in 1930, when the Bearcats beat a county all-star team. In 1937 they beat a strong Clipper team to stake a claim to being the best in the state. Holden amassed a thirty game winning streak in 1938, but lost a five game series billed as the West Virginia championship to Kyle of McDowell County.[32]

The formation of the Mountain State League as a Class D league under the umbrella of Organized Baseball in 1937 reduced the appeal of the coalfield teams everywhere, but less in Raleigh County than elsewhere. In fact, the Beckley Bengals of the Mountain State League lasted only two seasons before going under for lack of attendance, but the mine teams in the Raleigh County League continued to operate and draw big crowds until World War II.

The quality of play may have dropped a notch in the late thirties. Blake's Glen White team no longer dominated the league after the mid-thirties. The Lillybrook Coal Company's town was home to only 550 people, but it grew fine ballplayers for the town's Reds. The infield of local favorites Virgil "Snooks" Keaton and the McGraw brothers, John, Willard, and Gene, was unmatched for over a decade. "Lefty" Tudor, the best coalfield pitcher in the late thirties, pitched for the Reds. They led the Reds to B-League titles in 1936, 1937, and 1939. The Reds finally took the county championship in 1939, beating the Eccles Admirals. Tudor was the winning pitcher of the title game, backed by Willard McGraw's two homers. When Tudor shifted to Stotesbury in 1940, his new club nipped Scarbro for the A League title, and then beat Pete Rice's Amigo Red Birds for the county championship. Amigo came back to win in 1941 when John Kerzit struck out sixteen Mullens batters in the championship game.[33]

In Mercer, McDowell and Logan a Tri-County League continued until the end of the decade, and a small Tri-State League operated in the southwest corner of West Virginia. The Tri-County League limped along as a six-team league. Princeton, Pocahontas, Bramwell, and Macoma always had teams, but otherwise membership resembled a swinging door. The town team from Princeton, the seat of Mercer County, was the most consistent member. Only Barboursville gave continuity to the Tri-State circuit.[34]

Leagues catering to the less skilled players, variously called twilight, church or service leagues, largely went by the wayside in the 1930s. Softball offered a recreational brand of ball that was less dangerous and more accessible to inter-generational players. The large ball sport grew by leaps and bounds in the larger cities of Huntington and Bluefield during the early years of the Depression decade. As World War II approached, the popularity of softball spread to smaller coalfield cities and towns. Urban businesses, retail stores and manufacturing firms began sponsoring softball teams. A few businesses even provided teams for women employees. Softball would continue to grow during World War II.

As war approached, the culture of the mine communities and the communities themselves began to change. New Deal highway dollars had paved roads and union wages allowed more miners to own their own automobiles. As miners acquired cars, some began to live away from their place of work. The Works Projects Administration and Civilian Conservation Corps funded the development of parks and recreation facilities. As automobiles and paved roads made miners more mobile, families found other recreation for a Sunday afternoon. Other cracks began to appear in the tight coal patch communities. The companies began to sell off their houses to miners. With prohibition a thing of the past, beer joints cropped up to provide a place to drink away from the ball field and often away from family. As defense industries began to create a demand for labor in the industrial cities of Ohio, Southern Appalachian Mountain families began leaving the dangerous struggle to mine coal for safer manufacturing jobs.

Baseball had brought people together in the twenties and thirties. Historian David Corbin describes miners of the 1920s as alcoholic and fatalistic, and that image no doubt describes many residents of the coal towns. Baseball pulled miners, their families and their communities in a different direction. The game connected towns in a shared experience and raised the spirit of the entire community. At baseball games, residents bonded into a community. Baseball obliterated distinctions. Miners and mine owners were on the same side, as were Catholics and Protestants, Hungarians and Scots-Irish. Of course, there had always been limits to baseball's ability to create community; blacks and whites remained largely separate on the playing field, as they did in other areas of their lives. By 1940, however, as war clouds gathered, baseball had little chance of holding the communities together in the face of massive social and demographic changes. The days of the coals camps and coalfield baseball were not yet over. The coal towns would have a boomlet after the war, but the heyday of coal and coalfield baseball had passed.

8

"Hit the Ball and Run Like Hell"
The Middle Atlantic League, 1925–1942

From its formation in 1925 until World War II, the Middle Atlantic League (MAL) stood head and shoulders above all other lower classification leagues in Organized Baseball. Baseball men thought it the toughest and fastest league of its class. Players who made it in the MAL would surely get a shot at the big show. Indeed, over 400 players used the league as a springboard to the majors. Historian Robert Obojski called it "the toughest Class C circuit in the history of organized baseball."[1]

The league originated in the efforts of Dick Guy, former sports editor of the *Pittsburgh Leader,* to make a job for himself when the paper folded. An old baseball man, he had been president of the Pennsylvania-Ohio-Maryland League before World War I and later operated the semi-pro Pittsburgh Collegiates. In January 1925, representatives from the mid-size cities of Wheeling, Fairmont, and Clarksburg, West Virginia, Cumberland, Maryland, and Johnstown and Erie, Pennsylvania, met with Guy in Pittsburgh to launch the Middle Atlantic League. The league entered organized baseball as a Class C circuit. Before the season started, Scottdale, Pennsylvania, replaced Erie, thereby reducing travel distances.

Leadership of the league quickly changed hands. After the founders elected Guy president, he arranged to swap positions with Pittsburgh oilman Ray Archibold, who originally held the Wheeling franchise. When Archibold tired of the job's details, as he soon did, Guy backed Elmer Daily for the presidency. Daily would hold the post for twenty-six years. In addition, he would serve as president of the Pennsylvania State League from 1934 through 1942.

Baseball men in the Mountain State knew Daily well. He had attended Bethany College, played baseball there and coached the 1911 team. After stints pitching for Pennsylvania teams in Shamokin, Williamsport, Altoona, and Washington, Daily returned to West Virginia in 1912 to finish his playing career in organized baseball with Fairmont. Following a brief stint as baseball coach at Fairmont Normal College, Daily moved on to coach at West Virginia Wesleyan College, where he won a state championship in 1914. From Wesleyan he returned to Bethany College as athletic director and baseball coach. A short, dapper, cigar smoking man, Daily possessed enormous energy, a salesman's gift of gab, and a quick mind as well as knowledge of the sport.[2]

In North Central West Virginia, Clarksburg and Fairmont welcomed the return of professional baseball after nearly a decade. During the absence of pro ball, Clarksburg had surpassed Fairmont as the region's dominant city. The decline of the northern coalfield after World War I cut into Fairmont's economy. Meanwhile Clarksburg's glass, chemical and gas industries had boomed. By the mid-twenties, Clarksburg's population exceeded that of Fairmont.

Clarksburg's power elite backed the new MAL team. This contrasted sharply with the pre-war period when civic leaders showed little interest in baseball. In 1925 the Clarksburg Chamber of Commerce pushed for a team. So did Virgil Highland, president of the largest bank and owner of the city newspapers. Highland lined up supporters. The list of team officers read like a who's who of the city: D.E. "Dan" McNichol of McNichol Pottery, president; Prosecuting Attorney William E. Stathers, vice-president; and William O. Merrills, a printing and engraving man, secretary-treasurer. The remaining members of the board of directors were Rolland Glass head Eugene Rolland; T. B. Cain, president of West Virginia Business College; Washington I. Booth, president of Clarksburg Trust Company; and George W. Stoner, vice-president of Parson-Souders Department Store. Theater owner Jack Marks headed the booster club. The team, called the "Ghosts" for unspecified reasons, played at the fairgrounds at Norwood Park in suburban Nutter Fort, easily accessible by trolley or automobile. The park did have some downsides. The skinned infield was some distance from the grandstand, creating poor sight-lines. A greater financial problem existed in the commitment of Nutter Fort Town Marshall D. J. Reed to enforce a ban on Sunday games. Before the season started, however, the powers that be persuaded Reed to moderate his attitude and the new team played on Sundays.[3]

Fairmont's bragging point remained its South Side Park. No longer the only steel and concrete park in the minors, it was still a classic little park. Fred L. "Joe" Doringer headed the Marion County Baseball Association, a stock company that owned the club. Doringer would later spend ten years in the West Virginia House of Delegates. Informal support came from Brooks Fleming and James E. Watson, two of the city's wealthiest citizens. The initial subscription allowed the team to purchase its own bus at a time when other teams rented buses or crammed into automobiles for travel to away games. Fairmont drew nearly 5,000 to their opening game.[4]

Wheeling's growth was slowing, but it remained the largest city in West Virginia with a 1920 population of over 56,000. It was still famous for its line of tobacco products; Marsh and Sons' stogies and Block Brothers' Mail Pouch chewing tobacco gave Wheeling national recognition. Steel, iron and tin plate, however, had supplanted tobacco in importance. The mills north and south of downtown along the Ohio River churned out smoke at a prodigious rate. Workers and their families living on the hillsides behind the mills could not escape the soot and odors. The middle class was rapidly moving to suburbs away from the river out along Wheeling Creek and the National Road, around the mountain from the factories and downtown. Wheeling Island, site of the fairgrounds and the ballpark, was rapidly filling up with housing.[5]

With the economy humming in 1925, the league enjoyed a hugely successful inaugural season. In the profit-loss ledger all teams finished in the black. On the field, the Johnstown club, featuring future Hall of Fame member Joe Cronin, easily captured the pennant. Clarksburg was the only West Virginia team to finish with a winning record, but like Fairmont and Wheeling, it finished well down in the standings. Still, fans in all three cities had reason to be pleased with the new circuit.[6]

Although Richard Guy's Wheeling Stogies finished fifth, their fans enjoyed two of the most popular and best-remembered players in the city's history. Two Irish brothers named Rooney captivated Wheeling. Art, an outfielder, led the league in base hits and in stolen bases. Dan, a catcher, batted .359 and led the MAL in doubles. Neither would make the majors in baseball, but both had long careers in sports. Dan entered the priesthood and went on to become athletic director at St. Bonaventure College. Art, a good natured and loquacious Irish lad, seemed to end up running things. Before the season ended he took over the reins of the Stogies. He had a penchant for horses and racetracks. Legend has it he used his track winnings to purchase a National Football League franchise for Pittsburgh in 1933. The longtime owner of the Steelers won the hearts of Pittsburgh fans even though his team seldom had winning seasons.

In the MAL's second season, Fairmont and Clarksburg settled on new and more appropriate nicknames for their teams. In the initial season, when Cy Ferry managed Fairmont, the club had accepted the label "Fairies." In 1926 a new manager, Joe "Hooker" Phillips, demanded a different nickname. "Black Diamonds" was the logical choice for a city whose economy revolved around coal. Clarksburg jettisoned the "Ghosts" in favor of "Generals," referencing the city's pride in being the birthplace of Confederate General Stonewall Jackson. Changes took place in Wheeling also, but the club retained the Stogies moniker. Guy sold the franchise, at a tidy profit, to a group of Wheeling businessmen who put together a stock company to purchase the team. Gibson Bradford became president of the new group.

Old-time Fairmont fans remembered the new manager, Joe "Hooker" Phillips, from the pre-war Pennsylvania–West Virginia league where he starred for Uniontown. He drove the Black Diamonds to a first place finish in the second half of the 1926 split season. Pitcher Art Cousins led the late season charge, as he became the MAL's first twenty game winner with a 21–7 record. Despite having the league's best overall record, Phillips' club lost the playoffs to Johnstown.

The three West Virginia teams finished with winning records in 1927. Wheeling had the top hitter in Karl "Doc" Weber, who led the Middle Atlantic League with a .340 batting average. Stogies pitcher Claude Gillenwater posted a MAL best 1.66 earned run average to go with his 13–3 won-loss record. Fairmont's William "Chick" Helmick topped the league pitchers with 18 wins. Clarksburg player-manager Earle "Greasy" Neale had the league's best hitting team, helped by his .321 average. However, the Generals also had the worst fielding club.

In the 1928 season, two West Virginia teams squared off in the postseason playoff series. Wheeling won the first half of the split season. Fairmont needed a sweep of a double-header on the last day of the season to nose out Cumberland for the second half title. The Stogies playing-manager Bill Prysock was in his twentieth year of minor league ball, having started with Grafton in 1909. Prysock's lineup featured batting champ Bill Prichard. On the mound the Stogies relied on Billy Thomas (15–9), Bill Gwathmey (12–6), and George Dresher, who had pitched a no-hitter late in the season. Fairmont countered with outfielders Howard Holland, who topped the loop in home runs (20) and RBIs (96), and young stud Julius "Moose" Solters, on his way to a nine-year major league career. The Black Diamonds had even better pitchers in Howard "Ace" Roberts and Art Cousins. Roberts led the MAL with 213 strikeouts, and was the league's hardest pitcher to hit; opposing batters averaged a mere .213 average against him. Ace boasted of a no-hitter among his 14 wins. Cousins posted an 18–12 record.

Fairmont's Black Diamonds romped their way to the 1928 Middle Atlantic League championship. Wheeling won the first game of the best of seven game series, thanks to five RBIs from Bill Prichard. Fairmont won the next two, both in ten innings, before big crowds in Wheeling. The series then shifted to Fairmont. Wheeling evened the series when Thomas won his second series game. The Black Diamonds broke the series open as William "Chick" Helmick (12–6 in the regular season) and Roberts shut down the Stogies in games five and six.

After taking care of MAL business, Fairmont took on Hanover, Pennsylvania, pennant winners of the Blue Ridge League, in a series sponsored by the *Baltimore Sun*. Behind the outstanding pitching of Cousins and Roberts, the Black Diamonds disposed of Hanover three games to one in a best of five series. The downside of this series was that only 500 attended the final game in Fairmont.

Despite their on-field success, the Black Diamonds were experiencing serious financial problems. The 1928 strike of coal miners cut deeply into the club's attendance. Only 800 showed up for the first game, the lowest ever to attend an Opening Day at South Side Park. By mid-season the club fell $4,500 into debt. Fortunately, a $5,000 one-shot investment from an anonymous donor, possibly Brooks Fleming, paid off the debt. A local newspaper lamented that "a black cat must have crossed their pathway ... there has been nothing but grief for the club owners all season." Travel costs to and from Hanover combined with disappointing attendance left the team with no profit to show from the post-season games. The sale of Roberts to the New York Yankees (he failed to stick) and Holland to Baltimore netted $2,500, but the team looked to an austere budget in 1929.[7]

In Clarksburg, the Generals fared poorly on the field in 1928 because of dreadful pitching, but their fans enjoyed an exciting offense. Third baseman Bill Prichard led the MAL in batting with a .370 average, but Clarksburg sent him to Wheeling near the end of the season. "Jo-Jo" Morrisey, a product of Holy Cross College, hit .319. He would become the only General to advance to the majors. Outfielder Dewey Stover hit .348 and led the 1928 circuit in stolen bases.

Wheeling continued to play well in 1929, again winning the second half and finishing in a first place tie with Charleroi in the overall standings. The Stogies lineup included six .300 hitters led by Gerald "Gee" Walker's .373 average. In addition, hustling outfielder Frank "Dollie" Doljack batted a respectable .270; he would be in Detroit's lineup the following season. Gwathmey won 19 games and future Yankee Tommy Bridges won ten. For the second straight year, the Stogies lost the playoffs, managing only one win while losing four to Charleroi.

8. "Hit the Ball and Run Like Hell"

The stock market crash that followed on the heels of the 1929 season had an impact on baseball for the next decade. As unemployment rose and investment dollars disappeared, teams and leagues across the country began to fall like dominoes. Forty-three fewer cities fielded teams in 1931 than in 1929, and the downward spiral continued until 1934.

Despite the crash, Clarksburg overflowed with optimism in 1930 when Earle "Greasy" Neale returned as player-manager of the Generals. Neale was West Virginia's most famous sports figure. Before World War I he had led West Virginia Wesleyan College to its greatest football and baseball seasons. After graduation, he played professional baseball in summers and coached college football in the fall. In 1919 Neale reached the pinnacle of the baseball world when he played centerfield for the World Champion Cincinnati Reds. Indeed, Neale had been the Reds' leading hitter in the World Series. While playing baseball, the two-sport star also coached football. At tiny Washington and Jefferson College he led his team to the 1921 Rose Bowl. Later, during the twenties, he became head football coach at the University of Virginia and then in the early thirties he took on the head football job at the University of West Virginia. Perhaps his greatest coaching success came in the late 1940s when his Philadelphia Eagles captured back-to-back National Football League titles.[8]

Clarksburg, Fairmont and Wheeling staged a tight race to the wire in the second half of the 1930 season. Wheeling faded first despite the hitting of future big leaguers George McQuinn, Ervin "Pete" Fox, and Frank Doljack. Wheeling did generate the most memorable moment of the 1930 MAL season. On July 13 Stogies owner Charles Holloway turned on the lights for the first night game in Wheeling and the MAL.

The final day of the season, September 1, 1930, dawned with the Generals clinging to a one-half game lead over Fairmont thanks to a 6–5 win over the Black Diamonds the day before. The two then played three games on one day, a single game in the morning to make up a rainout, and a double-header in the afternoon. Fairmont won the morning game 4–1 behind the pitching of ten year minor league veteran Cecil Slaughter, a 16 game winner who posted a league leading 3.23 ERA. The win gave Fairmont the league lead. Before a record crowd of over 5,000 fans, Clarksburg swept the afternoon doubleheader 4–1 and 4–2 to take the title. Veteran pitcher Dick "Red" Proctor pitched both ends of the twin-bill, winning the first game 4–1 and holding the Black Diamonds to five hits to gain the victory in the final game.[9]

The 1930 Clarksburg Generals were a team of veteran players. Neale led the Generals on the field as well as on the bench. He batted .332 and stole 21 bases. "Red" Proctor, like Earle Neale a former major leaguer, won a

Middle Atlantic League record 24 games. After their exciting second half finish, the Generals blew a three game to one lead in the playoffs against Johnstown. Proctor suffered a season ending injury when hit by a line drive in game six. The Johnnies came from behind to win after Proctor's forced departure. Without Proctor, Clarksburg also lost game seven and the series. Nevertheless, the 1930 Generals would be remembered in Clarksburg as the city's finest team.

Following the first Depression season, Middle Atlantic League President Elmer Daily realized minor league baseball faced dark days ahead. Daily began searching for a plan to insulate his league from the growing crisis. After Jeannette bailed out for 1931, Joe Cambria, owner of the Hagerstown team in the defunct Blue Ridge League, approached Daily about a franchise in the MAL. Then Doff D. "Doc" Daniels, owner of a semi-pro team in Beckley, contacted Daily. At that point Daily made the daring decision to expand rather than contract. No twelve-team league existed in organized baseball, but Daily opted for such an experiment. Watt Powell jumped at the opportunity to get a franchise for Charleston. Daniels and Powell had little trouble in convincing Johnny Stuart of Huntington to follow suit.[10] The twelve-team MAL of 1931 began with six West Virginia cities (Beckley, Charleston, Clarksburg, Huntington, and Wheeling).

The ownership of the new West Virginia teams came straight out of the semi-pro Tri-State League where Daniels, Powell, and Stuart had operated teams in 1929 and 1930. All three operators brought extensive baseball experience to the MAL. Stuart had pitched four years for the St. Louis Cardinals. Daniels played on West Virginia Wesleyan's championship team of 1914 and captained the 1916 team. He had operated teams in Eccles and Beckley since 1927. Powell had been operating professional and semi-pro clubs in Charleston since 1916. Each team had established parks and an existing fan base, plus Charleston and Huntington had previously fielded teams in organized baseball, albeit before the First World War. So Daily correctly expected them to make a successful transition to the MAL.

Before July of 1931, Daily's dream began to turn into a nightmare. First, Hagerstown threatened to go belly-up. Joe Cambria met the crisis by transferring his franchise to Parkersburg, West Virginia. He made this move on June 23, although the "Hubs" did not play their first game in Parkersburg until June 28. The Ohio River city had never been a strong baseball town and the city did not offer Cambria's team a warm reception. The team tried to promote catcher Gordon "Babe" Phelps, the league's best player who hit .408 for the season. Parkersburg, however, did not buy. With an absentee landlord and no pre-season buildup, neither the city nor its newspaper took to the newcomers. When fewer than 200 showed up for the first double-header, Cambria realized his mistake. After only a week as the Parkersburg Hubs, the team moved to Altoona, Pennsylvania.[11]

Next, trouble erupted in Fairmont. The team had spent money in the off-season to install lights at South Side Park. The Depression hit Fairmont hard, and the Black Diamonds soon found they had lost their fan base. Then in late July, manager Jim Walsh and six players went on strike for back pay. Team president Joe Doringer signed replacement players from the semi-pro Marion County League, but they were overmatched. Although Doringer managed to raise enough money to pay back salaries and to see the team through the 1931 season, there would be no long-term investment. Unlike the 1928 crisis, there were no playoff games to generate additional income to pay the bills.[12]

During the 1931 season, Daily worked without pay, and according to one supporter, "without sleep." Only Charleston made money, although Beckley broke even. Somehow, to Daily's credit, the league limped to the end of the season with its full complement of twelve teams. His twelve team experiment, however, was viewed as a prescription for disaster; it would not be tried again for be a long time.[13]

Of the new teams, Charleston was the best organized. The capital city had enjoyed prosperity in the twenties and witnessed a building boom. The twenty story Kanawha Valley Bank, the stately Boone Hotel, and a new state capitol nearing completion anchored the new downtown. Watt Powell gave the franchise strong leadership. He raised $11,000 in stock funds, enough to install lights at Kanawha Park. Former major league first baseman Dick Hoblitzel, who had played for Clarksburg and Wheeling on his way up, came in as manager and provided instant credibility. Without stars, Charleston completed the first half of the 1931 split-season one game behind Cumberland. The Senators then went on a roll and took the second-half flag. Their regular season record was the league best. In the first home playoff game between first and second half winners, the Senators drew a then–MAL record 5,500 fans. The series, however, went to Cumberland.[14]

Beckley finished a strong third. Their thirty-two year old player-manager Frank Welch looked back on a nine-year major league career. The solid, 5'9", 175 pound veteran slammed 38 home runs. His homer total not only led the MAL, but also led all minor leagues in 1930, and set the all-time MAL record. He also drove in a league high 122 runs. Beckley managed to do well at the box office thanks in part to an established tradition of supplementing their income by playing exhibition games against barnstorming teams. The House of David and Homestead Grays were staples in Beckley, as the Pittsburgh Crawfords would be later in the decade.

In the off-season of 1931–32, Daily faced difficult choices. The northern

West Virginia cities lobbied for a six-team West Virginia league but they were in no position to dictate policy. Others called for a reduction in the $3,000 monthly salary limit. The small Pennsylvania cities of Charleroi, Jeannette, Altoona and Scottdale quickly bailed out. Fairmont and Wheeling soon followed the Pennsylvania towns, returning their franchises to the league.

Fairmont's economy had never recovered from the mine strike of 1928 and the subsequent decline in the region's coal production. The onset of the Great Depression only worsened the already depressed coal economy. A contributing factor to the team's demise may have been team president Joe Doringer's decision in 1929 to become program director of Fairmont's first radio station. The demands of the radio job detracted from his ability to help the team. Finally, when local sporting goods dealer Frank Ice obtained a court writ to attach the team uniforms for payment of debt the club gave up all hope of continuing in organized baseball.

In Wheeling, owner Charles Holloway had spent heavily to upgrade his park, including lights for night ball. His investment did not pay dividends. Night games were not the panacea for Wheeling's attendance problems. Tom Hopkins, sports editor of the *Daily Intelligencer*, lamented, "For the last two years [Holloway] took it on the chin financially." In one last effort to save the franchise Holloway and Daily campaigned for a working agreement with a major league team. The New York Giants expressed interest, and Holloway offered a sweetheart deal on the park rental, but the Giants backed away. In April 1932 an opportunity to keep baseball in Wheeling appeared in the person of Joe Cambria. After moving his 1931 franchise from Hagerstown to Parkersburg to Youngstown, he offered to take over the Wheeling operation. Holloway, however, wanted nothing to do with Cambria, who had shown no loyalty to any city. Holloway chose to let the Stogies die rather than sell to Cambria. The loss of a team in Wheeling took the MAL down to six cities.[15]

In the six-team MAL of 1932, Charleston and Beckley produced the second all–West Virginia playoff. Beckley raced out to win the first half, but Charleston came on strong to capture the second half. A rookie and a veteran arrived from Alabama to power the Beckley offense. Rookie Fred Sington, who had been an All-American football player at the University of Alabama, dominated the league as no one had before. He became the first and only Triple Crown winner, leading the MAL in batting with a .368 average, in home runs with 29, and RBIs with 110. He also topped the league in runs with 110. Thirty-two year old "Cat" Milner had led the Tri-State League in 1930 with a resounding .493 batting average for Logan. The Riverview, Alabama native, whose given name was Bloomer Holt Milner, had ten years of professional experience when he arrived in West Virginia. He would continue playing until 1942 and then manage until 1954. He offered simple advice to young players like Sington: "Just hit the ball and run like hell."[16] With Beckley in 1932 Milner batted .336 and drove in 84 runs. One player Milner advised was third baseman Lou Chiozza, whose 187 hits constituted a MAL record and who had a 34 game consecutive hitting streak during the season.

Charleston's Watt Powell also hired one of the all-time great minor league players in Danny Boone. Powell handed the reins of the club to Boone, who already had five years of managerial experience. Like Milner, Boone hailed from Alabama and had begun playing professionally in 1919. Unlike Milner, Boone had experienced life in the majors, albeit as a pitcher and early in his career. More recently, in the previous six years he had played and managed at High Point, North Carolina, where he rewrote the Piedmont League record books, winning four batting titles. When he retired as a player after the 1933 season, he had 214 homers and a lifetime .356 average. With the 1932 Senators he hit .349, slammed 17 homers and drove in 92 runs.[17]

In the Beckley-Charleston playoff series, Boone and pitching ace Wayne LaMaster took control. LaMaster pitched a four hitter in the opener while Boone slammed three homers. After Charleston won game two, the series switched to Beckley, where the Black Knights tied the series thanks to Milner's hitting and Kelsey Jennings' pitching. After LaMaster won game five, Boone's bat carried Charleston to the championship in game six. For the series, Boone batted .350 with four homers and ten RBIs.[18]

After the 1932 season Clarksburg lacked funds to make the final payroll. Jack Marks' Booster Club took over the team and paid off its bills. By that time, though, the city elite had little time for baseball. Banks, manufacturing and retail businesses faced perilous times in the trough of the Depression. Initial organizers of the team had earlier passed control of the team to upstart banker Harley Clark, who now just wanted to cut his losses. After a valiant effort to sell stock, Marks' group failed to raise the necessary money to keep the team alive. Virgil Highland's newspaper blamed Franklin D. Roosevelt's bank holiday for the failure.[19] In reality, Clarksburg baseball lacked both leadership and money.

The failure of baseball in Clarksburg pointed to a cultural paradigm shift that altered forever baseball's relationship to its community. At the very time Jack Marks and his group of baseball boosters were trying to mobilize capital to keep the Generals solvent, all eyes of Clarksburg sports fans and the local newspapers were focused on Victory High School's successful run for the state basketball championship. Both Victory and Washington

Irving High School drew more fans for basketball games than attended the Generals games in the summer. Unlike professional baseball, high school basketball required little capital mobilization. Fans could identify with the high school kids; they were, after all, from the community, not outside mercenaries brought in for the summer. Exactly when high school basketball supplanted baseball as West Virginia's favorite spectator sport is hard to pinpoint, but the shift had taken place in parts of the Mountain State during the Depression years. Robert and Helen Lynd had observed this phenomenon in their classic study *Middletown*, admittedly in Indiana, noting: "more civic loyalty centers around basket-ball than any other one thing."[20]

A perceptive observer of West Virginia mores, Jennings Randolph, while a resident of Clarksburg had foreseen a cultural shift that endangered the centrality of baseball. After graduating from nearby Salem College, Randolph became sports editor of the *Clarksburg Telegram*. From that vantage point he noticed that the Roaring Twenties were creating many alternative entertainments to baseball, especially radio and motion pictures. Just as dangerous for the sport were the infatuation with the automobile, dances, tennis and golf. Teenagers were not flocking to the sandlots to play baseball to the same extent as had the previous generation. That did not bode well for the future of the game. By 1932, Randolph himself had found his own alternative to covering sports, the intoxicating world of New Deal politics.[21]

Unlike Clarksburg, Wheeling had reason to feel upbeat in 1933. After a year out of the league, Daily arranged for the New York Yankees to pump new life into the Stogies. New Yankee farm director George Weiss leased Stogie Park, put together a local group to run the club, and promised to stock the team with Yankee farmhands. Weiss was as good as his word. He sent Earl Mann, a creative and ambitious thirty-year-old, to Wheeling as general manager. Mann soon moved on to become the long-time owner of the Atlanta Crackers of the Southern Association. Jack Sheehan came with Mann as field manager. Weiss even decked the Stogies out in Yankee pinstripes, absent only the New York logo.[22]

No less than six future major leaguers came to Wheeling. They led the Stogies to the league title. Two new college graduates, first baseman John Aloysius "Buddy" Hassett right out of Manhattan College and shortstop Jimmy Hitchcock from Alabama Polytechnic Institute (Auburn), were the mainstays. They each batted .332 for Wheeling. Hitchcock, Auburn's first football All-American, had only a brief stay in the majors, but Hassett played seven years, batting .292.[23] Catcher George "Skeets" Dickey could not compare with his older brother, the Yankee great Bill Dickey, but he would play in the Big Leagues. Three Stogie pitchers bound for the Big Time gave

Wheeling the best pitching in the Middle Atlantic League. Lefthander Kemp Wicker posted the best earned run average in all of the minor leagues (2.00) and won 14 games. Joe Vitelli topped the staff with 16 wins against nine losses while Jim Tobin had a 13–7 record. With that lineup the Stogies nipped Zanesville by three games in the final overall standings.

Wheeling's success proved short-lived. The Yankee connection, which benefited the Stogies in 1933, failed them in 1934. Weiss restocked the Stogies with first year pros, except for pitcher Atley Donald and catcher Warren "Buddy" Rosar. The youngsters were not ready for MAL pitching. Indeed, the 1934 Stogies were dreadful. Wheeling finished dead last, 33½ games behind the league leader. Wheeling fans felt victimized by New York ownership and dropped away as fast as the Stogies' pennant chances. Weiss obviously gave up on Wheeling and Wheeling on him. After the season, Weiss strung Wheeling along, not announcing his intention for 1935. When Weiss finally announced the transfer of the franchise to Akron, Ohio, Wheeling greeted the news without a whimper.[24] The city's experience with the Yankees had demonstrated the pros and cons of major league ownership.

Wheeling, the birthplace of baseball in West Virginia, the home of the state's first professional team over half a century before, the city with the most years in organized baseball, was without a team. For a brief moment it appeared that baseball might not die in northern West Virginia. Dick Guy, who had started the MAL, reappeared with a proposal for a new West Virginia–Pennsylvania league. He proposed a Class D league that would include Wheeling, Fairmont, and Clarksburg with three Pennsylvania cities. Wheeling backers actually organized a team and brought in sixty players for try-outs before the proposed league collapsed in mid–April 1935.[25]

Charleston struggled in 1934, but Huntington and Beckley contended for the pennant before coming up short. Wayne LaMaster's pitching was about all Charleston fans had to cheer. In his third year with the Senators, he led the MSL in wins with seventeen and in strikeouts with 168. He would move on to the majors. Huntington manager Eddie Dyer would also make the majors as pilot of the St. Louis Cardinals. He managed to coax Huntington to a third place finish without benefit of stars or prospects. Beckley, on the other hand, was loaded with prospects. First baseman Frank McCormick's only minor league stop came that year in Beckley. The Cincinnati Reds paid for him to travel by bus from New York City to Beckley for a tryout. Signed for $100 a month, he remembered the good and the bad of the year. While he "enjoyed it," he also remembered "you had to eat hot dogs by the roadside and [sleep] all night on the bus, and the times when the bus broke down and you had to get out in the middle of the night and push the darn thing along a country road until you found a garage ... [and] the clubhouses that didn't have showers."[26] No less than seven teammates also moved up to the majors, outfielders Jimmy Outlaw and Gus Brittain, infielder Jose Gomez, and pitchers Lee Grissom, Whitey Moore, Earl Cook, and Russell "Red" Evans.

Despite a winning team and exciting players, attendance at Beckley's games declined drastically in 1934. By the end of the summer, the club faced a bleak financial ledger. The Black Knights could not obtain a formal working agreement with a major league team as Wheeling had with the Yankees, Charleston with Detroit, and Huntington with the St. Louis Cardinals. The Cincinnati Reds did send a few players, as did the Memphis Chicks of the Southern Association, but Beckley got no financial help. By the end of the 1934 season the club faced a deficit even after selling eight players. *The Raleigh Register* cited lack of a working agreement, poor attendance and mounting transportation costs as the source of the problem. As Daily's league moved westward the distance between Beckley and the other cities increased, pushing up transportation costs; Beckley to Dayton was 300 miles on narrow two-lane roads. The loss of paying fans remains more difficult to explain. Despite the Depression, the city's economic outlook remained brighter than that of the industrial cities in northern West Virginia. Semi-pro coalfield teams continued to draw well in Raleigh County. Local theater man C. D. Crawford, who had taken over as business manager, blamed lack of parking at RMI Park and insufficient bus service for the problem.[27]

In February 1935 a new ownership group emerged to save the team, at least for a year. J. Lewis Bumgardner, wealthy corporate lawyer, had just stepped down as the first president of Beckley College. He agreed to head the Smokeless Coal Athletic Association, which took over the club from Doff D. "Doc" Daniels. The new head made it clear his group would not long support a team that bled dollars.[28]

Unlike Beckley, baseball in Huntington gained new life when the team became a farm club of the St. Louis Cardinals. Now called the Red Birds, Huntington enjoyed its finest MAL season in 1935. Huntington won the first half of the split season but slipped in the second half. Playing-manager Benny Borgman provided glue to the team as an all-star shortstop. Pitching, however, gave the Boosters the edge over the rest of the league. Mike Martynick won 21 games and led all minor leagues with 299 strikeouts. Despite the affiliation with St. Louis, Borgman had few prospects. None made it to the Cardinals, although catcher Hugh Polland did play in the majors during the war years. Borgman's boys, nevertheless, won the playoffs, besting Dayton four games to two.

Each year in the thirties the MAL seemed to lose another West Virginia city. After the 1931 season Fairmont folded. A year later Clarksburg dropped out and Wheeling left for a year. Wheeling departed for good following the 1934 season. Then Beckley returned its franchise to the league in fall of 1935. The new management in Beckley had changed the team name from Black Knights to Miners, but failed to nail down a working agreement with a major league team. Their 1935 roster consisted of players whose talent lay in the future and could be signed on the cheap. Not surprisingly this policy led to a cellar finish and depressing attendance. Daily, who was tilting the MAL westward, replaced Beckley with Canton, Ohio.[29] Beckley had proven a good breeding ground for players. In the city's mere five years in the MAL twenty-two future major leaguers wore Beckley uniforms; only Charleston would produce more.

Fans in both Charleston and Huntington enjoyed watching some outstanding performances in 1936. Charleston became a Cleveland farm team and compiled the second best record in the league. Senators' outfielder Barney McCosky led the MAL in batting with an even .400 average. He would go on to hit .312 over eleven years in the Big Leagues. Fellow outfielder Ralph Hodgin hit .337; he would play six years in the majors. Pitcher Cletus "Boots" Poffenberger went from Charleston to Detroit, where he won ten games in 1937. Huntington first baseman Walter Alston never became a big league star, in fact he batted only once in the majors. That at-bat came for the St. Louis Cardinals at the end of 1936, after he had slugged an MAL high 35 home runs for the Red Birds. He would, however, return to the majors as manager of the Dodgers from 1954 to 1976, and be installed in the Hall of Fame in 1983. Huntington's skinny (6'2", 160 pound) shortstop Marty Marion batted only .268, but seemed magical in the field, leading the league in putouts and assists. A decade later he would earn the National League Most Valuable Player trophy. Huntington also featured pitcher Mike Martynik, who again led the league with 226 strikeouts.

Before the start of the 1937 season, dual disasters struck in Huntington. The city's experience as a St. Louis Cardinals farm team had brought a championship in 1935, but after experiencing a bad team in 1936, Cardinals General Manager Branch Rickey pulled the plug on Huntington and moved his farm club to Portsmouth, Ohio. Major stockholder John Stuart, team president Harry Hutton, and league president Daily expressed optimism about getting another agreement. Before that could happen the Ohio River went on a rampage. In January 1937, the Ohio River pounded Huntington with the worst flood in recorded history. League Park, right on the riverbank in downtown, took the brunt of the waters. It seemed obvious to observers that the park could not be usable by May. League President

Daily moved quickly, replacing Huntington with Springfield, Ohio.[30] With the departure of Huntington, the state of West Virginia, which had once had six teams in the MAL, was down to one, Charleston.

The capital city continued to grow in the Depression years. Its mayor, Daniel Boone Dawson, although a Republican, proved to be aggressive in getting federal funds and projects from the Democratic administration in Washington. He found money for new bridges, a municipal auditorium, new schools, streets, and public housing projects. In addition, the expansion of the state government brought jobs and people to the city. By 1937 it had passed Wheeling in population. Baseball was part and parcel of the city dynamism.[31]

Watt Powell's Senators experienced mediocre second division seasons in 1937 and 1938, but Charleston fans continued to support the team. Night games at Kanawha Park were part of the reason. Exciting players also helped. Nineteen-year-old Danny Litwhiler, who played on the 1937 team, was on his way to an eleven-year major league career. The 1937 Senators also included outfielder Hugh Holliday (12-87-.342) and catcher Jack Tighe (6-59-.302) who enjoyed all-star years. Neither reached the majors as players, but ten years later Tighe became manager of Detroit. The 1938 team won only 59 games; Jim Morris won 20 of them and posted the best earned run average in the MAL, yielding just 2.75 runs per game.

Things began to look up for Charleston when Ed Hall took over as manager. He led the Senators to second place finishes in 1939 and 1940 before the team slipped to the second division in 1941. Hall helped his own cause by leading the club in RBIs his three years at the helm. Pitchers George Diehl, who went 12–5, and Willard "Bill" Donovan, who had a 2.41 ERA, and MAL All-Star catcher Sig Broskie of the 1939 team would go up to the Boston Braves. The 1940 team enjoyed outstanding pitching despite dreadful support in the field. Steve Mlinsarik won seventeen games, and Bob Haas led the league with a 2.25 ERA. Future big leaguers Bryan Stephens and Ed Klieman came on fast to win nine games. Klieman became Cleveland's ace reliever in 1947 and 1948. George Binks and Hank Edwards provided what little pop the team could muster. In 1941 Klieman became the ace of the staff, winning sixteen games with a 2.22 ERA. Erv Palica, who would spend nine years in the big leagues, won twelve. Youngsters John Blatnick and Gene Woodling showed promise but struggled more with MAL pitching than they would against major league hurlers.

Despite Pearl Harbor and America's entry into World War II, baseball continued in the summer of '42, but all was not the same. Players were going into the service. Travel was restricted and gas rationing was on the horizon. Even though American troops had not yet seen significant combat, people were being reminded, "There's a war going on." Civilians followed the government's urging to collect scrap metal and newspapers. Baseball seemed less important. The signs pointed to 1942 being the last season for the MAL, at least for the duration of the war.

The Charleston Senators went out in style. They finished the 1942 season with 75 wins, the most in their MAL history, to garner their first pennant in a decade. They led the league in team batting with an unimpressive .258, but 1942 was the lightest hitting season the MAL experienced. As a team the Senators totaled only ten home runs. Manager Jack Knight's team started fast and stayed in first place the entire season except for five days. They had four .300 hitters. Shortstop Frank Yankovich, who failed to make the majors, led with a .319 average, followed by three who did make the big show, outfielder-catcher Joe Tipton, outfielder Johnny Blatnick, and catcher Ralph Weigel. Their pitching carried the Senators. Lefty Bob Kuzava led the league with twenty-one victories against six losses. After the war he spent ten seasons in the majors. Don Bayliss won seventeen and led the league with a 1.52 ERA. Chuck Byers also notched seventeen wins.

By the beginning of 1943, most minor leagues had disbanded for the duration of the war. The Middle Atlantic League was no different. The league formally closed up shop at its winter meeting on February 21, 1943. In announcing the unanimous decision to cease operations, Daily stated the obvious: "Suspension ... is the only course open to us" for the duration of the war.[32]

As Watt Powell packed away the team's equipment and locked up Kanawha Park for the last time, he had no way of knowing that he would be dead before the next game would be played in Charleston or that the game would be played in a park named in his honor. He could, however, look back with satisfaction on twelve years in the Middle Atlantic League. He had seen professional baseball fail in Wheeling, Clarksburg, Fairmont, Parkersburg, Beckley and Huntington. His Senators had captured two outright league titles and sent twenty-three players to the majors. In the process Charleston had become the strongest professional baseball city in West Virginia.

9

"Dark and Dusty"
The Mountain State League, 1937–1942

The Southern West Virginia coalfields experienced the Great Depression differently than most of America. Happier days came to the coalfields after the election of 1932. Franklin D. Roosevelt's New Deal provided an opportunity for John L. Lewis's United Mine Workers to organize the coalfields. Proclaiming "the President wants you to join the union," Lewis's union quickly organized West Virginia miners in 1933. The National Recovery Administration, with its codes of fair competition, and later Guffey Acts, gave coal operators a level playing field. Going into the mines continued to be fraught with danger, but jobs existed. By 1939 there were 17,000 more men employed in coal mining in West Virginia than in 1932. With the union behind them, and operators no longer competing with each other by cutting miners' pay, mine wages began to inch higher.[1]

Like coal, minor league baseball managed to survive the Depression years, and after the arrival of the New Deal, bush league baseball began to improve. The number of minor leagues grew from fourteen when FDR took office to forty-four in 1940. Part of the explanation for this phenomenon was the introduction of night baseball in 1930. With the advent of night games, baseball, like the movies, became the favored and affordable entertainment outlet in hard times. Unlike motion pictures, which were an individual or, at most, a family outing, baseball served as a focus for the community.

The reelection of President Roosevelt in 1936 generated a renewed optimism in the country. A new sense of the possible touched a former player, manager, and would be magnate named Ray Ryan. Without a job in baseball after over thirty years in the sport as player and manager, he decided to create his own league. The native of Piketon, Ohio, looked the part of a former catcher — short, stocky, gray-haired and talkative. He had played and managed in a dozen cities beginning in Lancaster, Ohio, in 1906. His stops included Roanoke, Virginia, where he caught every game in 1909. The Chicago White Sox drafted him off the Roanoke roster, but he failed to stick in the Big Leagues. Back in the minors his stops included Wheeling, where he managed the Stogies in 1913, Meridian, Mississippi, Cedar Rapids, Iowa, and Allentown, Pennsylvania, where he managed in 1935. In the 1920s, he had played coalfield ball in Gary and Welch. He had relatives in Bluefield. So he knew the southern Appalachians and he sensed that the relatively peaceful times offered an opportunity to bring professional baseball to the region.[2]

Joe F. Carr, promotional director of the National Association of Baseball Leagues, urged Ryan to reconstitute the Appalachian League. Carr, who doubled as president of the National Football League, had known Ryan for over twenty years. An Appalachian League had existed in the early twenties in East Tennessee and Southwest Virginia. Carr gave Ryan letters of introduction. With Carr's letter in hand Ryan began a canvass of prospective towns in the winter of 1936–37. His initial effort to center a league in the triple cities of Bristol, Johnson City, and Kingsport, with other towns along U.S. route 11 from Wytheville, Virginia, to Morrisville, Tennessee, fell flat. Only Johnson City and the hamlets of Elizabethton and Newport, Tennessee, and Pennington Gap, Virginia, showed real interest. In the end he laid claim to the Appalachian League designation and started the 1937 season with only four clubs.[3]

By February 1937, Ryan had developed bolder plans. He believed Roanoke and Bluefield would create a solid core for a new league. When his Roanoke contacts let him down he looked west from Bluefield with a vision of a West Virginia league. In the cities with experience in fast semi-pro leagues — Bluefield, Welch, Logan, and Williamson — Ryan found baseball men who wasted little time in expressing interest. Ryan also received queries from Oak Hill, Fayetteville, Mt. Hope and Mullens, but he judged them too small. Promoters in Ashland, Kentucky, pressured Ryan for admission, but by that time he was committed to an all West Virginia circuit.[4]

Bluefield possessed a larger middle class than other cities dependent on the coal economy. On the eastern edge of the rich Pocahontas coalfield, Bluefield became the unofficial capital of the southern coalfield when the Norfolk and Western Railroad made the town its headquarters. Bluefield dominated a vast coal hinterland not only because it was the railroad hub, but also because it provided the insurance, legal, banking, financial, and wholesale supply needs for the area. The prosperous white-collar residents had been excited about the future of the city since before World War I. Exuding civic pride, Bluefielders boasted they lived in an "Air Conditioned City" where the high temperature in July and August averaged 80–81 degrees. Its population dwarfed that of other cities in the coalfields with a 1930 count of 19,339, plus another 4,000 in neighboring Bluefield, Virginia, and it continued to grow through the thirties. The Depression had given Bluefield's power structure pause, but as New Deal dollars for highway and bridge construction improved the city's infrastructure and rapidly linked Bluefield with the major coal towns and county seats of the southern coalfield, optimism returned. The idea of a professional baseball team appealed to the city's self-image.[5]

Thomas C. Scott, who owned a semi-pro team, the Bluefield Blue-Grays, quickly jumped on Ryan's bandwagon. Scott wasted little time. In March 1937 he managed to raise $5,000 in stock sales and confidently aimed for a $10,000 capitalization. Scott had a lease on Cain Field, a less than state-of-the-art park in the East End of Bluefield. An enclosed park with small wooden grandstand, Cain Field could seat 1,500 by the addition of bleachers, including one for "colored fans," down the baselines. So Scott was ready to start building a team.[6]

Newly paved roads also gave miners from hundreds of coal camps access to the larger towns in the southern West Virginia coalfields. West from Bluefield, Welch, the seat of McDowell County, was only thirty-five miles away on newly paved W.Va. Route 52. Its population of 5,376 may have been less than Ryan hoped for, but he knew the town, having played there for the semi-pro Welch Senators in the 1920s. That team's owner, John W. Blakely, was the city's wealthiest businessman, owner of the largest insurance company in West Virginia, and the city's mayor. The idea of a professional team appealed to Blakely's civic pride. A decade earlier he had dedicated Blakely Field for his coalfield team. Its grandstand only sat 500 fans, it lacked dressing rooms, and was showing wear and tear. Blakely, however, knew his way around politics. He wasted no time in arranging for the Works Projects Administration to refurbish his park, raising its seating to 1,500, constructing a clubhouse and surrounding it all with a massive stone wall. An arched doorway and huge green doors cut into the stone wall gave the place the look of a medieval fortress. The left-field wall tucked into the mountain behind it, but right field required a prodigious poke to clear the wall. The stones in the wall made for some crazy bounces, not to mention a danger to outfielders. At Ray Ryan's suggestion, Blakely formed a stock company, the McDowell Athletic Club, capitalized at $10,000, to operate the team.[7]

9. "Dark and Dusty"   143

Williamson, seventy-seven miles west of Welch along a narrow, winding, dangerous mountainous road, is the seat of "Bloody Mingo" County. Its population of 9,410 stretched out on a large floodplain across the Tug River from Kentucky. The Norfolk and Western Railroad owned a wooden, enclosed park across the river in West Williamson, Kentucky, that had been home to numerous town teams. E. S. "Lefty" Hamilton and William S. "Gus" Lindberg, himself a former coalfield player for Bramwell and Williamson, heeded Ryan's call and moved to organize a municipally owned team.[8]

Logan, with 4,396 residents, had an even smaller population and was more isolated than Welch or Williamson. Ryan, however, needed towns. Located in a narrow valley bounded by the Guyandot River on one side and the railroad and mountain on the other, Logan had no place in town to play. Town teams played in Whitman, a village some three miles out of Logan where the local coal company had an enclosed park. Even without its own park in town, Logan prided itself on its strong semi-pro team of the early thirties and an active industrial league. Harry S. Gay, Jr., operator of the Gay Coal Company, who had been an early and staunch supporter of coalfield baseball, headed the organizing effort in Logan, and served as the first president of the Logan Athletic Corporation.[9]

West Virginia's largest city fell into Ryan's lap when Huntington lost its franchise in the Middle Atlantic League. When the Ohio River overflowed its banks and flooded League Park in January 1937, the MAL quickly transferred the franchise, believing it impossible to play in Huntington in the 1937 season. Johnny "Stud" Stuart, former major league pitcher and Huntington's best known baseball man, thought otherwise. By mid–February he was ready with the $900 forfeit fee needed to lock up a spot in the league. Huntington had negatives for Ryan. It extended the travel for league cities; eighty-four miles on only partly paved roads from Williamson, Huntington stood a hard day's drive from Bluefield. On the other hand, Huntington's population of 75,000 was more than enough to support a Class D league team. The city had a tradition of professional baseball; teams operated there from 1910 to World War I and from 1931 through 1936. Its League Park, on the banks of the Ohio River at Ohio Avenue and 8th Street West, boasted lights for night ball and the largest seating capacity in the proposed league.[10]

The Mountain State League (MSL) formally came into existence at a March 27, 1937, meeting in Welch. Five teams made up the circuit: the Bluefield Blue-Grays, Logan Indians, Welch Miners, Williamson Colts, and Huntington Boosters. Only Huntington had a park with lights, but the others promised to install them as soon as possible. The teams elected Ryan as president with a salary of $1,200. The new president announced he would set up the league office in Bluefield. They agreed to a 14 man roster and a $1,000 per month salary limit, and affirmed a 110 game schedule beginning May 12. It would operate as a Class D league.[11]

Ryan still needed a sixth city. He tried to talk up the virtues of Oak Hill, but everyone understood that Beckley, with a population of nearly 10,000 and site of a Middle Atlantic League team, was the logical sixth. The city had a pro team in the Class C Middle Atlantic League from 1931 through 1935. J. Lewis Bumgardner had been the last president of the MAL team. When Ryan went to Beckley, Chamber of Commerce secretary W. A. James made it clear Bumgardner would be the decision maker. A wealthy and widely respected lawyer and civic booster, he had recently stepped down as the first president of Beckley (Junior) College after its accreditation. He had folded Beckley's MAL franchise following the 1935 season because of declining attendance, mounting red ink, and a poor team built on the cheap. Bumgardner refused to be rushed by Ryan, other league cities, or public opinion. His asking price for joining the league was a working agreement with a major league team that included players and $1,500 toward start-up costs. By mid-April he still refused to budge. Other team presidents correctly saw Bumgardner's demands as blackmail, but with less than a month before the season's start, time was running out. Ryan, Carr and Watt Powell, owner of Charleston's Middle Atlantic League team and a farm club of Detroit, put pressure on the Tigers to accept Bumgardner's terms. When they did, the new league was ready to begin operations.[12]

The first worry of minor leagues had always been survival. In the inaugural season of the Mountain State League, Huntington threatened to cripple the league. The cost of readying the park after the January flood left little money for players' salaries. Huntington management, mainly manager John Watson, underestimated the quality of play in the new league. Watson on Stuart's advice drew heavily from local talent. Eight members of the starting lineup came either from the Huntington area or from Marshall College. The local lads proved no match for the rest of the league. As losses piled up, fans stayed away. The team turned the franchise back to the league on July 23. Ryan put the Boosters on the road while he tried to find new backers. Finally, on August 1, 1937, he gave up and collapsed the franchise. Ryan quickly reorganized the schedule, creating an unbalanced split season.[13]

The Beckley Bengals benefited from Bumgardner's insistence on having a working agreement with a major league team. The Detroit Tigers sent ten farm hands to Beckley, including the league's best pitchers. The Bengals ran away with the inaugural Mountain State League title, posting a record of 65 wins against 35 losses. Teenage pitcher Charles "Major" Bowles collected sixteen victories, the most of any Mountain State League pitcher. The tall right-hander would pitch for Connie Mack's Philadelphia Athletics in two wartime seasons. Lefty Ed Schumacher posted a nifty 2.70 earned run average, the MSL's best, to go with his 13–5 record. Joe "Chip" Kenis finished with the same record as Schumacher and allowed only 3.06 earned runs per game. Another Detroit farmhand, catcher Lawrence "Tuck" Steinbeck, led the league with 20 home runs.

Beckley's brightest star, however, was not a Detroit farmhand but a city resident and veteran minor leaguer named Earl "Red" Martin. A Mississippi native, Martin had made his home in Beckley since playing for the Black Knights of the Middle Atlantic League in 1933 and 1934. He started the 1937 season with Scranton of the New York–Pennsylvania League but was released after batting only .244 eleven games into the season. He returned home where he signed with the Bengals. Martin quickly became the league's outstanding player. He dominated the league statistics in runs-batted-in, doubles, triples, and total bases. His .406 batting average not only was the highest in the MSL, it was tops for all minor league players.[14]

Following the inaugural season, Ryan orchestrated a playoff series between his two leagues. Beckley proved too good to even make the series close. Manager Eli Harris' Bengals swept Appalachian League champion Pennington Gap Bears in four games. Beckley then beat the Class C Charleston club of the Middle Atlantic League two straight games to cap a brilliant season. No one doubted Beckley had the best team in the state.

The league's top prospects, in addition to Beckley's outstanding pitchers, were Logan's seventeen-year-old pitcher Millard Howell and Bluefield's pitching sensation Marvin Garner. Howell's teammates gave the Kentuckian the nickname "Dixie," and it followed him to the major leagues, where he labored for six seasons. With Logan he established himself as a workhorse, leading the league in 1937 with 233 innings pitched and in strikeouts with 153. Garner joined Bluefield after his classes ended at Kent State University and posted a 10–2 record. Sports writers recognized him as the best lefty in the league. Following the season, Beaumont of the Texas League purchased him for $1,000, but, unlike Howell, he could not build his MSL start into a major league career.

Every team could point to prospects who would make it from the Mountain State League to the Big Leagues. Beckley's Murray Franklin would not blossom until the following year. Bluefield's Bob Bowman pitched only briefly for his hometown team before joining faster company. Catcher Sig Broskie of Welch, first baseman Al Gardella, who started the season at Huntington and finished at Beckley, and outfielder Walt Sessi of Williamson went on to have a the proverbial cup of coffee in the majors.

Ryan could take pride in the MSL's inaugural season. After he found a new group to operate the Huntington franchise, all six clubs returned for 1938. In addition, Ashland, Kentucky, continued to campaign for a franchise, but Ryan resisted an odd number of teams. By the end of the 1937 season, all the parks except Bluefield and Logan had lights for night ball. In Logan, Troy Walker, who had taken control of the team in mid-season, used the off-season to build a new park. Monitor Park, two miles outside town, had wooden covered grandstands and top grade lights. Also before the 1938 season, Williamson became the second league club with a major league affiliation when it signed a working agreement with the St. Louis Cardinals.[15]

In 1938 Beckley again boasted the best hitter in the minor leagues. Shortstop Murray "Moe" Franklin enjoyed a monster season. He had won the shortstop job mid-way through the 1937 season, but gave fans little reason for believing he would destroy MSL pitching the way he did in 1938. He batted .429 to win the silver bat presented by Louisville Slugger to the top hitter in the minors. His batting average was the highest ever achieved by a professional player for a West Virginia team. No player has topped that average in the years since. The 24-year-old Chicago native also led the league with 26 home runs, 13 triples, and 304 total bases. Franklin made the majors, working his way up to Detroit in 1941 and 1942, but he never had a year approaching 1938.

Red Martin slipped just a notch in 1938. He batted a resounding .392, second to Franklin. He also hit 14 homers with 94 RBIs. No one in the league would match Martin's back-to-back seasons and no pair of teammates would hit the number of homers, RBIs, and total bases that Franklin and Martin did in 1938. Unlike Franklin, however, Martin, having found a home in Beckley, had little desire to venture far from home to further his career.

Despite the hitting of Franklin and Martin, Beckley lost the 1938 regular season pennant to Logan. The Logan Indians' new playing manager, Eddie Hock, a 39-year-old minor league veteran, anchored a slick fielding and hustling team. Hock was a hard-nosed, hustling player whose uniform always seemed dirty and rumpled. His pro career began in 1920 at the top when he played one game with the St. Louis Cardinals. He tasted major league life again briefly in 1923 and 1924, but the last eighteen years of his career were spent in the low minors. By the time he finally took off his uniform for good in 1942, Hock had collected 3475 base hits. All but one of his hits came in the minor leagues. His 2944 singles still stand as a minor league record. Hock would remain in the MSL until its demise. His 656 base hits stand as the all-time league record, as do the 571 games he played.

Hock's 1938 Logan team won with a balance of fielding, pitching, hitting, and hustle. The Indians' top pitcher, rookie Vernon Kohler, recorded a 15–3 record to go with his league leading 216 strikeouts. He posted a fine 2.24 earned run average. Sherley Slone won 14 games. Thanks to Hock's work in the middle infield, the Indians led the league in fielding average. Their all-star first baseman, Robert "Buck" Hershey, led the club with a .343 batting average and with 108 runs-batted-in.

Despite its regular season success, Logan lost the post-season playoffs, introduced for the first time in 1938, to Beckley. In addition to Franklin and Martin, the Bengals lineup included future major league brothers Al and Danny Gardella, and Raleigh Singleton, who led the league with 42 stolen bases. In the playoffs, it was pitcher John Gorczyca who shut down the Indians, giving the league pennant to Beckley.

The league experienced some outstanding pitching in addition to Logan's Kohler. Earl Brinegar of Williamson posted an 18–2 record. His winning percentage of .900 would never be bested. Vic Sorrell, a ten-year veteran with Detroit, where he won 92 games, joined hometown Bluefield during the season and posted a league leading 1.37 earned run average. John Gorczyca of Beckley had 18 victories against seven losses. He simplified the spelling of his name to Gorsica before he made the Detroit Tigers roster in 1940.

Few fans noticed a rookie pitcher for Williamson named Stanley Musial. He would, of course, become the only Mountain State League player to be inducted into the Baseball Hall of Fame. In 1938, in his first year of professional baseball Musial was far from being "Stan the Man," the most feared hitter in the National League for over a decade. Local sportswriter Jim Van Sant labeled the Donora, Pennsylvania, native the "Keystone Kid." A seventeen year old left handed pitcher playing ball between his junior and senior years in high school, he gave Mountain State fans little reason to take note of him. Pitcher Musial compiled a modest 6–6 record with a 4.66 ERA. The 80 walks he gave up against only 66 strikeouts in 110 innings documented a serious wild streak. At bat he could muster only a .258 batting average, hardly an auspicious beginning in professional ball. In Williamson his $65 a month salary allowed him to room at the Mountaineer Hotel and to idle his days away playing pool. Despite Musial's limited success, manager Nat Hickey took a liking to the youngster and encouraged him to return in 1939.[16]

Logan rose to the top of the MSL at the box office in 1938 as well as on the field. Troy Walker's investment in his new park paid instant success. Back in 1919–1920, some 5,000 miners had attempted to march on Logan before being stopped by state police, private mine guards, the National

Before Stan Musial became known as "Stan the Man," he was a seventeen-year-old pitcher for Williamson of the Mountain State League. Locals dubbed him "The Keystone Kid," but his manager thought the young pitcher too wild to be a prospect. But could he hit! (National Baseball Hall of Fame Library, Cooperstown, N.Y.)

Guard, and the U.S. army. In the summer of 1938, miners poured into Logan from the surrounding coal camps for a very different reason, to root for the Indians. Capacity crowds of 3,000 filled the park for an exhibition against the barnstorming House of David team, the first night game and the final playoff game against Beckley. Despite having the smallest population in the league, Logan attracted 50,000 spectators, the most of any league city in 1938.

League President Ryan faced a potential crisis when charges were leveled against Welch manager Ed Krajnik and General Manager Pat Flanagan for betting on games. Since the Black Sox scandal of 1919, betting on games had been a cardinal sin in organized baseball. Krajnik was a fiery little manager who was "continually stirring things up." That made him enormously popular in Welch and the manager that fans in other cities loved to boo. Supporters of the two pointed out that they bet on the Miners to win. To Ryan, it mattered little who they bet to win. Ryan acted quickly, suspending the pair for sixty days. The team released the duo, but many ardent fans in Welch never forgave Ryan.[17]

After the success of the 1938 season, Ryan, ever the baseball entrepreneur, hoped to enlarge the MSL from six to eight franchises. An Ashland group headed by local lawyer Robert T. Caldwell actively sought a franchise. Ryan again courted his contacts in Roanoke, where interest in pro ball had resurfaced. Both cities possessed larger populations than any MSL franchise except Huntington.

Before Ryan could execute his expansion plan, trouble appeared on a number of fronts. In January 1939, Huntington owners William M. Martin, Bert Wilson, and Ezra Midkoff sold the franchise to a Florida man, Harry M. Hatcher. The new owner was not new to baseball, also owning the team in Montgomery, Alabama. Still, the sale troubled Ryan because absentee landlords lacked local roots or long-term commitment to the city.[18]

Further bad news came from Williamson, where the Norfolk and Western Railroad sold the South Williamson ballpark to real estate developers. General Manager E.S. "Lefty" Hamilton was pushing the city of Williamson to fund a new park but the success of his efforts remained uncertain until March 1939. Finally, it appeared Williamson would get a new park in time for the start of the season.[19]

The league's greatest crisis occurred when Beckley President Lewis Bumgardner and General Manager Roy Elkins announced Beckley's withdrawal from the league. The Bengals had been the most successful team on the field in the first two years, winning one regular season title and two playoffs. Bumgardner had been determined to run the league's classiest operation, and to do so he operated with the highest budget. Attendance, unfortunately, failed to support Bumgardner's budget. Also, Bumgardner's health was failing and he wished to retreat from public life. Manager Eli Harris tried to put a new ownership group together but he failed to get the necessary financial backing from the community, despite Beckley's seeming financial health. Harris then announced his plans to retire from baseball and to open a bowling alley in Beckley.[20]

Without Beckley, Ryan needed Ashland just to bring the Mountain State back to a six-team league. Thus, the Kentucky city became the first and only non–West Virginia team in the league. Their presence necessitated changing the league name from Mountain State to Mountain States League in 1939.

With the MSL back to six teams again, Ryan used Roanoke as the keystone for a revised Virginia League. For 1939 Ryan cobbled together a circuit consisting of Roanoke/Salem, Harrisonburg, Lynchburg, and Staunton. So when Watt Powell, owner of the Charleston Senators, proposed to take over the Beckley franchise, Ryan rebuffed him in order to avoid an uneven number of teams. Meanwhile Ryan expanded his Appalachian League to include Kingsport and Greenville, Tennessee. Ryan at that point became president of all three leagues.[21]

The best off-season news came from Bluefield, where new team leadership of F. M. Archer, president, and Wayne Austin, business manager, finally convinced the city to build a new stadium at the old agricultural fairgrounds on the border between West Virginia and Virginia. In the twenties the area had been converted to a recreation park, baseball field and airfield. It possessed trolley service from downtown plus plenty of parking for the increasing number of fans who came to games by automobile. Tree covered hills beyond the outfield fences provided a setting as picturesque as any park in the country. Named for Harry Bowen, a Bramwell coal operator, the park opened on May 14, 1939, even before the field had any grass. At a time when most minor league parks and all Mountain State League parks were wood construction, the steel and concrete grandstand made the park a state of the art facility. Its roofed main grandstand sat 2,500. An additional 1,000 could be accommodated in bleacher seats. Admission to the grandstand cost 40 cents and bleacher seats could be had for 25 cents. Lights for night games made it the finest park in the MSL. Little wonder Bluefield led the league in attendance in 1939.[22]

The Williamson Red Birds also played in a new park. Montezuma Park in West Williamson, just off the N&W main line and hard by a railroad tunnel, had a low grandstand of wooden seats but with a metal roof. Williamson's new park attracted the largest opening day crowd of 1939. Bluefield's new park could not compete because it was not ready for the season opener. Montezuma Park, with less seating capacity than Bluefield's Bowen Field, would not maintain its attendance lead.

In their new park, the Red Birds set a fast pace and coasted to the regular season pennant in 1939. In one stretch they won twenty of twenty-two games. Soft spoken, twenty-six year old Harrison Wickel managed the team and led it at the plate. "Wick" drove in a league leading 142 runs. He would collect more RBIs than anyone in MSL history. He also batted .368 with 23 homers. Alabama born first baseman John Streza, also an all-star, led the league with 185 hits and 294 total bases. Outfielder Bill Shewey led in batting (.376) and stolen bases (48). All-Star outfielder Walt Sessi, who would play briefly in the majors for the St. Louis Cardinals, also had a banner year. His .372 batting average and 125 RBIs were second in the league, and his

21 homers ranked third. Pitcher Howard Smith won 19 games and lefty hurler Tony Kvadis notched 17 wins.

Stan Musial won nine games against only two losses for Williamson. His was the best winning percentage in the league, but his record was misleading. Wildness caused manager Wickel to lose confidence in the young left-hander. Wickel wrote the parent Cardinals describing Musial as "the wildest pitcher I have ever seen."[23] On the other hand, Musial's .352 batting average suggested future greatness as a batter.

Huntington, after two basement finishes, made a surprisingly strong run to finish third behind Williamson and Welch. Twenty-year-old left-handed pitcher Russ Meers set the all-time league record by striking out 297 batters. Meers pitched briefly in the majors both before and after World War II. Teammate John Patterson, who notched 18 wins, was rated the MSL's best right-handed pitcher. Sportswriters selected Mike Powell as the manager of the year.

Bluefield's new park proved even more popular than Williamson's Montezuma Field. Spurred on by large crowds of boisterous fans, Bluefield finished strong. Player-manager Vic Sorrell saved his pitching arm for the late season push and the playoffs. Despite their fourth place regular season finish, Bluefield came alive in the four-team playoffs. They beat Welch two games to none. In the final game, former major league pitchers, now player-managers, Vic Sorrell and Sam Gray locked up in a pitching duel. Gray's 3.04 ERA was the league best, but Sorrell ranked a close second. With the series on the line, Sorrell proved the better pitcher. The Blue-Grays then upset Williamson three games to one to gain the playoff championship. Williamson's lone victory came in game two when Musial collected five hits, including a home run. Following the MSL playoffs, Bluefield took on Virginia League champion Harrisonburg. After losing the first two games in Harrisonburg, the Blue-Grays ran off three straight victories at home to take the series three games to two. Jack Talbott pitched a neat four-hitter to win the deciding game before an overflow crowd at Bowen Field.[24]

Williamson repeated as regular season champions in 1940, becoming the MSL's only back-to-back champs. This time they won the playoffs as well. The Red Birds just nosed out Logan with 76 wins to Logan's 75. Wickel again led the way for Williamson, batting .319 and driving in 129 runs. Bill Shewey repeated as stolen base leader with 59 steals, and also topped the circuit with 134 runs and 21 triples. Second baseman Pat Capri had an all-star year batting .317 with 105 runs batted in. He would play briefly for the Boston Braves during the war years. Pitcher Harold Sharp won a league high 18 games and mound mate Ernest Peters posted the best winning percentage with a record of 17–5. In the post-season playoffs, Williamson knocked out Bluefield and then beat Logan three games to one.

Despite the success of Williamson's pitching duo of Sharp and Peters, other outstanding pitchers dotted MSL rosters. Logan's top pitchers took a back seat to none. Joe Pennington matched Sharp with 18 wins while Harry Potts posted a 16–9 record and led in complete games. Bluefield player-manager Vic Sorrell continued his mound dominance with a 1.98 earned run average.

Welch's young right-hander, Vern Bickford, led the league in strikeouts and posted a 15–11 won-loss record with a 3.50 earned run average. Sportswriters identified him as the MSL's top prospect. Before moving up to the major leagues, Bickford won more games (49), struck out more (520), and pitched more innings (690) than any pitcher in the history of the Mountain State League. After World War II, he joined Warren Spahn and Johnny Sain in the Boston Braves pitching rotation, where in 1948 he helped that team to its only National League pennant.

Sportswriters around the league selected Welch's Clarence "Buck" Etchison as the circuit's outstanding player for 1940. The big first-baseman just missed winning the Triple Crown. He finished in a tie with Ashland's Worthington Day for the highest batting average, both with a .363 average. Etchison also led the league with 132 runs-batted-in, and his 24 homers were just two behind Logan's Stan Wentzel. Feared by league pitchers, he also led in walks with 95. Etchison and Wentzel both went on to play for the Boston Braves during World War II. Wentzel, who played eighteen years in the minors, had only the proverbial cup of coffee with Boston. Etchison became a regular before entering military service.

Huntington, now called the Aces, finished last as usual in 1940. The team's pathetic 33–87 record was the worst showing in MSL history. Before the season, the club lost its park. League Park, hard by the Ohio River, fell to the wrecking ball to make way for a much-needed floodwall. Long Civic Park on upper Fifth Avenue was readied for opening day, except for lights, which were not installed until a month into the season. The team's fourth consecutive losing season contributed to Huntington fans losing interest. By mid-season, absentee owner Harry Hatcher was desperate to unload the team. In July he blackmailed Huntington by threatening to sell the team to Beckley interests. To make his point he came north to meet with Roy Elkins and Beckley Chamber of Commerce leaders. In response, a Huntington group headed by Walter Arnold purchased the team from the Florida owner.[25] Rebuilding the team would not happen overnight, but local ownership seemed a promising beginning.

In 1941 Logan nosed out Williamson, reversing their 1940 finish.

Williamson possessed the best hitting team. The Red Birds recorded the highest team batting average of .290. Williamson's player-manager Harrison Wickel was the league's outstanding player. His 147 RBIs and 53 doubles would stand up as the highest single season marks in league history. He also batted .356, with 20 homers, and a league leading 303 total bases. The Red Birds also featured outfielder Hal Rice of Morganette, West Virginia, and catcher Del Rice, no relation to Hal. Both would have productive careers with the St. Louis Cardinals after World War II.

All Logan's player-manager Ed Hock did was win. He had help from teammates. Logan hitters were no slouches, topping the league in home runs. Terrance "Tennis" Mounts led the MSL with 24 home runs and finished second to Wickel in RBIs with 129 and total bases with 295. Stan Wentzel finished second in homers, one behind Mounts. Both Mounts (.333) and Wentzel (.311) batted over .300. Logan's pitching was unmatched. Joe Pennington became the league's first and only twenty game winner, notching 21 wins against 6 losses. He also led in strikeouts with 229. Teammate Harry Potts recorded a 17–8 mark and finished second in the league in strikeouts. Pitcher Arnold Carter won only 11 games but would make the majors even if his more productive teammates did not.

Huntington finished last again, but their fans enjoyed watching Don Smith, the league's top hitter. Smith was the MSL's third .400 hitter in its first five years, batting a lofty .404. A speedy contact hitter, Smith set a league record with 191 base hits. He also stole 61 bases, second all time in the MSL. Smith possessed little power, however, and never advanced to the majors.

Edison "Eddie" Guinter, the only player to participate in all six seasons of the MSL's existence, had his best season in 1941. Guinter's three seasons with Logan included their 1938 championship season. In 1939 he set a league record with 113 bases on balls. He split the 1940 season between Huntington and Welch. After being sold to Ashland in 1941, he stole a league record 85 bases. He also hit a career high .349. Guinter holds more MSL career records than anyone, including Wickel and Hock. He scored the most runs, hit the most doubles, triples, and home runs, stole the most bases, collected the most bases on balls and hit for the most total bases. He ended up second to Hock in games, at-bats, and hits, and followed close behind Wickel in RBIs.

The summer of 1941 would, of course, be the last good baseball season for some years. After the Japanese attack on Pearl Harbor took the United States into World War II, all organized baseball, the majors and the minor leagues, questioned whether there would be professional baseball during the war. However, the Mountain States League nearly came apart for reasons unrelated to the war. Ashland team president Randall Stevens and lawyer Robert T. Caldwell led a fight to oust Ryan as president. Ashland and Huntington, the westernmost cities, felt Ryan spent too much time with his other baseball interests, which took him east away from the league. The Ashland group gained greater leverage when Ashland advertising executive E. Clark Bobbett purchased the Williamson franchise. Bobbett and Huntington owner Walter Arnold joined the campaign against Ryan. In Welch, Blakely, an ally of Ryan from the beginning of the Mountain States League, gave up control of the club. New business manager L. E. Harville blamed Ryan for what he perceived to be high league operating costs. With his support there were enough votes to oust the league founder. At the league meeting in early February 1942, Caldwell had the votes to be elected president. Wells Gaynor, Huntington sports writer, and Roy Elkins, former general manager of Beckley, were elected co–vice presidents. Caldwell was also elected secretary-treasurer. Bluefield sports writer Stubby Currence termed the vote "one of the dirtiest deals of its kind that I have known." Despite his conviction that "Ryan did a Herculean job," control of the MSL had passed to new hands.[26]

Caldwell took an aggressive approach to league affairs. He wanted to continue operation despite the war, and quickly got all the clubs to agree to field teams in 1942. He then managed to get the National Association of Baseball Leagues to upgrade the MSL's classification from Class D to Class C, even though its cities had a combined population lower than any other Class C league. The salary cap for each team increased from $1,200 to $1,500 per month. When he made up the 130 game 1942 schedule, for the first time all games, except Sunday's, would be played at night.[27]

In a maneuver that added to the conspiratorial view of Ryan's ouster, Caldwell orchestrated a shift in ownership whereby Bobbett gained control of the Huntington franchise. Shortly after the league's winter meeting, Bobbett obtained the lease on Long Park in Huntington. Then, after the Huntington franchise was returned to the league, Caldwell passed it on to Bobbett. Then, in mid–March 1942, William "Gus" Lindberg took over the Williamson franchise. Lindberg, along with Lefty Hamilton, had run the baseball operation in Williamson from the inception of the MSL.[28]

The league seemed topsy-turvy in 1942. Perennial tail-ender Huntington finished on top. A working agreement with the St. Louis Browns provided a major boost for Huntington. Logan, the 1941 champions with 80 wins, plunged to the bottom of the league standings with just half as many wins as in the previous year. With World War II underway and mines working three shifts, attendance dropped all across the league.

Huntington, now called the Jewels, won a league record 82 games in

1942 and posted the highest team batting average in league history with a .297 mark. The Jewels' .661 winning percentage was also the highest in the league's existence. Future major league outfielder Ken Wood hit .318 with 25 homers and a league leading 126 RBIs. Slick fielding second baseman Ed Bachman led the Jewels team with a .331 batting average and in the field turned the most double plays. In addition, manager Art Scarein had the league's finest pitching staff. Bob Peterson and Bob "Ribs" Raney won 17 games; Bob "Whitey" Hartman and Cliff Fannin won twelve games. Raney, born Frank Robert Donald Raniszewski, and Fannin were eighteen-year-old kids in 1941. Both would appear briefly in the majors after World War II.

Welch finished second behind Huntington. A working arrangement with the Boston Braves brought the Miners player-manager Don Manno. The minor league veteran quickly established himself as the league's outstanding player of 1942. Manno led not only the MSL, but also all minor leagues with 34 home runs and 136 runs scored. In addition, he topped the league in batting (.381), hits (174), triples (14), and total bases (346). His 34 home runs set the Mountain States League record. It was the only time a league batter clubbed over 30 homers. Manno's total bases mark of 346 was also the highest recorded during the MSL's existence.

As great a year as Manno had, he was not all Welch had in 1942. The working agreement with the Braves also brought Welch young catcher Bob Brandy, an MSL all-star in 1942 who made it to the Braves in 1946 and 1947. Seventeen-year-old Tim Triner pitched 24 complete games and won 17, but he only made it to AAA on the organized baseball ladder. It also led pitcher Vern Bickford to the Braves, but not before he won more games than any other pitcher in Mountain State League history.

World War II sounded the death knell for the MSL, as it did for most of minor league baseball. Forty-one leagues opened in 1941, but only 26 completed the 1942 season, and just ten opened in 1943. The MSL was one of the casualties of war. By mid-season all six teams were operating in the red. With the economy booming, the mines worked three shifts and there was plenty of overtime. Workers had less time for baseball. With higher salaries and lower attendance all six teams reported losses by mid-season. Players were going into military service. Gasoline rationing made it virtually impossible for leagues like the MSL to operate. Besides, ironically, continuing to play "the National Game" seemed somehow unpatriotic with a war going on.

10

"Ain't Nobody Got Time for Nothing No More"

The Post-War Years, 1945–1955

When World War II ended in 1945, boys put away their model airplanes—the P-51 Mustangs, the twin fuselage P-38s, the Navy Hellcats, and B-24, B-25, and B-17 bombers. Out came new baseball bats, balls and gloves. Leather had been needed for the war effort, so balls and gloves had been hard to come by. Now, not only were gloves available, there were wonderful new models, larger with more padding and deep pockets. How could a kid miss a ground ball with these trappers?

Like the economy, baseball boomed after the war. Professional teams were fewer than before the war, but the ones remaining set attendance marks not dreamed of before the war and not matched in the half-century afterward. During the Depression years or even in the Jazz Age, baseball operators could not dream of attracting over 100,000 fans for a season; 50,000 had been big news in the pre-war years. From 1947 to 1952 Charleston, Bluefield and Welch drew record crowds. Below the professional level, baseball became organized and bureaucratized. At the collegiate level, the West Virginia Intercollegiate Athletic Conference (WVIAC) began to crown a champion. Morris-Harvey College dominated the league with four consecutive championships. West Virginia University's team emerged from twenty years of doldrums to become the power of the Southern Conference. At the high school level, the West Virginia Secondary School Activities Commission (WVSSAC) began a state high school tournament that has continued annually to the present. Over fifty American Legions offered opportunities for teenage boys, and Little League baseball gave pre-teen lads experiences unimaginable when the local sandlot had been the only ballfield for kids. The Wheeling Legion nine and a Fairmont Little League club made their respective World Series. The post-war period produced some of the best West Virginia natives ever to pull on a major league uniform, and produced the first African-American player to make the Big Time.

The American economy shifted into overdrive in the fifties, but baseball, especially minor league baseball, suffered a crash from which it has never fully recovered, despite the revival associated with the movie *Bull Durham*. The high water mark of minor league baseball came in 1949 when 448 teams attracted 39,670,065 customers. After a slight dip in 1950, the downward spiral became dizzying in 1951. Five years later attendance and the number of teams had dropped by fifty percent. Only Charleston was left with a team in 1956, the low water mark for professional baseball in the Mountain State.

At the end of World War II in August 1945, Ray Ryan moved to put his Mountain States League back together. When the league dissolved after the 1942 season, its members included Bluefield, Welch, Williamson, Logan

Integration came in the 1950s. Henry Louis Gates, later professor of theology at Harvard University and currently chairman of Afro-American Studies at Harvard, standing at left, was scorekeeper for the 1962 Piedmont Little League team shown here (West Virginia Archives and History Library, Charleston, W.Va.).

and Huntington in West Virginia, and Ashland, Kentucky. In 1942, Ashland people had orchestrated Ryan's ouster from the league he had founded. Understandably, he wished to replace Ashland, and he had Narrows, Virginia, in mind. He quickly found support in Welch, Williamson, Logan, and Narrows. To his surprise, Bluefield put up a roadblock.[1]

Charles Elliott, who had ascended to the Bluefield club presidency in 1942, had a vision different from that of Ryan. Rather than looking west along the Norfolk and Western Railroad line, he looked south to the Appalachian League. That venerable circuit, which ironically Ryan had launched in 1937, had somehow managed to survive throughout World War II. It was the only Class D league to play each year. Because of its tenacity, the Appy had become a favorite of National Association President Judge William G. Bramham.

The Appalachian League needed to expand from its core cities in East Tennessee. Bluefield was attractive to league president Carl A. Jones for several reasons. Its population exceeded that of other possible cities. It had drawn well before the war, and its park was nicer than any in the league. Bramham quickly got behind Jones' plan.

Jones and Bramham arranged for Ed Smith, an Army captain awaiting discharge, to join with Elliott in running the Bluefield franchise. Smith had operated the Bristol team in the Appy in 1941 before going into service. Before that he had worked in the front offices in both Cincinnati and Brooklyn. Jones quickly arranged for the Appy to admit Bluefield and Pulaski, Virginia, at a hastily called December meeting.

The move blindsided Ryan. He quickly lined up his son Joe and Judge Thomas H. Scott to head a Bluefield franchise in his Mountain State League. Ryan maintained that the Bluefield territory belonged to the Mountain State League, and asked Bramham to nullify the Appy's move. Back in 1937 when Ryan formed the Appy and the Mountain State leagues, he had strong backing in the national office from Joe Carr, director of promotions for the minors. Carr, however, had died in 1939. Bramham ruled that the Mountain State League had failed in 1942 to file papers to have the league put on the suspended list. In other words, the MSL ceased to exist in 1942, so the Appy was free to move into the Bluefield territory. Ryan asked for a meeting with Bramham to "sort out the Bluefield mess," but Bramham would not reverse his ruling.

Ryan still believed he could plant a league, but his efforts failed to bear fruit. Not content with taking Bluefield, the Appy next stole Welch and New River (Narrows) from Ryan. In December 1945, both agreed to join with Ryan, but when he failed to solidify his league by February 1946, they jumped to the Appy. Ryan then called an organizing meeting in Huntington in hopes of forming a more expansive league from Huntington, Williamson, Logan, Beckley, Charleston, Clarksburg, Fairmont, and Parkersburg, with Wheeling, Ashland and Portsmouth, Ohio, as backups. Putting together a league of six teams from this grouping of cities proved to be a chore. In the end it did not matter. Bramham brought down the hammer on Ryan's efforts. No new league, he ruled, would be approved after March 1, 1946. Ryan was checkmated.[2]

With Ryan out of the way, and Bluefield and Welch firmly in the Appalachian, the league moved to finalize details for the 1946 season. The league would play a 120 game schedule. Each team would be allowed a roster of fifteen, plus three war veterans, with the salary cap set at $1,800 per month. In Bluefield, Smith arranged a working agreement with the Boston Braves, but the team kept the traditional nickname of Blue-Grays. Welch had even less time to prepare than did Bluefield. Mayor L. E. Rodgers successfully pushed the city to appropriate money to renovate Blakely Field. Team president Quinto Bary convinced civic clubs to purchase season tickets. For the first time local radio carried the Welch Miners' games. Still, fewer than 1,500 turned out for Welch's first Appy League game, 1,000 less than in Bluefield.[3]

On the field, Bluefield and Welch never moved far from the bottom of the standings in 1946, but Bluefield jumped to second place in 1947. Smith departed Bluefield after one season, allowing Elliott to take over as president and Jim Morse as business manager. The Braves sent George Lacy to manage the club, and stocked the Blue-Grays with talented players. First baseman Tom Zikmund batted a robust .380; it would be a decade before a Bluefield player topped this mark. Catcher Frank Baldwin hit .312; he would be the only member of the team to make the majors. Pitcher Alfred Means won 17 games and led the league in shutouts.[4]

Bluefield's first big post-war star was outfielder Homer Moore. He was a battle-scarred World War II vet who had been awarded a Purple Heart and Bronze Star. In 1947 he slammed out 31 home runs. In addition, he hit the game-winning home run in the tenth inning to give the league all-stars the win over league champion Pulaski. Moore also batted .362 and drove in 117 runs. It was the most homers and the most RBIs ever by a Bluefield player. His 31 round-trippers shattered the Appy League record of 21 set by Leo "Muscle" Shoals the previous season. The only problem was that Shoals, playing for Kingsport, then hit 32 out of the park. Moore's 31 homers, however, still stands as the Bluefield record.

Muscle Shoals was the Appys' all-time star and the greatest West Virginia born home run hitter. Born Lloyd Cleveland Shoals, Jr., in 1916 in Camden, West Virginia, he went by Leo until he acquired the more descriptive nickname. He led his league seven times in home runs with a high of

55 in 1949. Shoals never made the major leagues, but he hammered 362 minor league home runs.[5]

Fans in both Bluefield and Welch loved their teams. Bluefield drew over 80,000 to its home games in 1947, by far the highest in the league. Welch fans had less to cheer about, as the Miners again finished last, but Blakely Field acquired a reputation as a tough place for opposing players and umpires. At one game the police had to be called in to escort the umpire to safety after he called a balk on a Welch pitcher.[6]

Welch made huge strides in 1948, both on the field and at the box office. The biggest plus was a working agreement with the Philadelphia Athletics, which allowed the Miners to jump from last the two previous years to second place in the league standings. The A's sent Elwood "Woodie" Wheaton to Welch as player-manager. He batted .357 as an outfielder and compiled a 14-6 record as a pitcher. His batting average would hold up as the highest in Welch's Appy League history. The Miners' top pitcher was Calvin Barnes, a holdover from 1947 when he had a 12-12 record. In 1948 Barnes emerged as Welch's first and only twenty-game winner with a 20-13 record. The workhorse led the league in innings pitched with 225. The excitement of a winning team brought 52,838 fans to the park, the all-time high for Welch.

Bluefield and its parent club, the Boston Braves, enjoyed a banner year in 1948. Before the season started, the Boston Braves acquired controlling interest in the Blue-Grays. The Braves' president, Louis R. Perini, became Bluefield's vice-president. The Braves won their first pennant since 1914 and drew a record number of fans. The BGs battled Pulaski and Welch to the wire before finishing third. Again, Bluefield led the league in attendance. First baseman Lawrence "Bud" Pennell established a league record by batting in 139 runs. The Blue-Grays ended Welch's season by winning three straight from the Miners in the playoffs, before themselves losing the championship to Pulaski.

Bluefield hit the jackpot in 1949. That season represents the high water mark for Bluefield baseball. The Blue-Grays captured their first Appalachian League pennant. Their 88-34 record was the league's best ever, with the most wins and the highest winning percentage. Home fans always expected a victory and the Blue-Grays accommodated their followers by reeling off 34 consecutive wins at Bowen Field. The team drew 116,572 fans at home, the all-time high for Bluefield and for the Appalachian League. For the last home game, 4,604 turned out, also a Bluefield high.

The club achieved its 1949 success without benefit of even one future major league player. Even so, manager Ernie White had all-stars at almost every position. There were .300 hitters galore: catcher Bob Pottenger hit

.386, first baseman Ed Heap .367, third baseman Joe Roddin .327, shortstop Nelson Cooper .307, outfielders John Karpenski .349, and centerfielder Bill Green .333. Outfielders Jack Zajac, who hit .323, and Ben Gregory, with a .445 average, did not appear in enough games to qualify for the batting title. Heap led the Appalachian League with 190 hits and set a new league mark with 44 doubles. Karpenski's 137 runs batted in and 20 home runs were the league's best.

After the regular season, the BGs took no prisoners in the playoffs. They topped Johnson City in two straight games with Heep and Gregory leading the way. They then swept Bristol three straight. Lefty Jim "Skip" Pope threw a three hitter in the first game as Gregory collected three hits. Then Bluefield resident Bob Bowman, a former major league pitcher, won game two behind Heep's home run. Finally, Willie Williams, a 14 game winner during the regular season, held Bristol to five hits and Karpenski drove in two runs, enough for the win and the championship.[7]

The 1949 season was not only a record-setting one in Bluefield; it marked a new beginning in Charleston. The capital city had been without a professional team since the Middle Atlantic League suspended operations in 1942. Kanawha Park had burned, leaving Charleston without a place for a team to play after the war. To make matters worse, the city's baseball leader since World War I, Walter "Watt" Powell, was in poor health. He did not live to see a new park, but shortly before his death city council did appropriate $300,000 for a baseball stadium. Built on the site of the Exhibition Park of 1916 on MacCorkle Avenue at 35th Street, the park was a steel and concrete structure seating 8,000 fans. The city named the facility Watt Powell Park after "the Father of Baseball" in Charleston. Bleachers down the foul lines could expand the seating capacity. The Chesapeake and Ohio Railroad ran behind the right field fence, giving the park a unique quality. A wooded hillside rose behind the railroad to provide a green backdrop.[8]

The construction of the new park allowed Charleston to shop for a league. The Class A Central League was pleased to admit a city with a new state-of-the-art park. A working agreement with the Cincinnati Reds gave Senators fans optimism, but Charleston's first post-war team finished a disappointing fourth in a six-team league. The Reds sent their former relief pitcher, Joe Beggs, to manage. He had little to work with except outfielder Bob Nieman and catcher Hobie Landrith, both of whom quickly moved to the majors.

Beggs' most challenging project was teaching control to a hard throwing, but wild, young left-handed pitcher named Joe Nuxhall. Back on June 10, 1944, Nuxhall had become the youngest player ever in the major leagues. The fifteen-year-old pitched in just one game before the Reds sent him to the low minors to learn to pitch. In 1949 Nuxhall was on his way back to the majors, but still learning his craft. Nuxhall credits Beggs, who taught school in the off-season, with teaching him the mechanics of pitching. Even so, Nuxhall posted a modest 8–11 record.[9]

Despite a mediocre record, Charleston could not get enough of its team. The new Watt Powell Park was an attraction itself; it was brand new with seats that had backs and armrests. After a seven-year absence from baseball, Charlestonians wanted to be at the park. The trek to the park began on Opening Day when a record crowd upwards of 10,000 turned out. The record pace continued for the whole summer. A Central League record 183,352 customers clicked the turnstiles. That 1949 attendance figure remains the largest in West Virginia baseball history. Charleston, like Bluefield, would never top its 1949 attendance mark.

The hot times continued in 1950. Bluefield romped to its second straight Appalachian League pennant. Bluefield and Charleston led their league in attendance. In Charleston, Joe Nuxhall showed potential for a return to the majors, winning a team high ten games. Otherwise the Senators gave their fans little to cheer about as the team finished next to the bottom of the Central League standings. Given their record, the team was delighted to draw nearly 113,000 fans.

Welch had high hopes before the 1950 season, but their dreams quickly crashed along with the Miners' pitching. The club reorganized as the McDowell County Baseball Corporation. The new leadership promised, "It can truly be said that this year the Baseball club belongs to the fans and the fans only." Unfortunately, the fans could not pitch. Despite the team leading the league in home runs, and Lewis Dolci having a league best 124 RBIs, the Miners finished 35 games out of first place. Not surprisingly, attendance dropped sharply from 41,000 to 34,000.[10]

The Boston Braves, again, sent a solid nucleus of young players to Bluefield. Only local favorite Bob Bowman was a holdover from the 1949 champs. Blue-Gray fans were sure their Italian double-play combo of Guido Pelosi (.336) and Julio Palazzini (.326) were headed for the majors. The team's best prospect, however, was left-handed pitcher Dick Kelly, who won 21 games and struck out a Bluefield record 202 batters. Despite winning both halves of the split season, manager Marion "Red" Adair's 1950 team lost the post season playoff to second place Bristol.

None of the pennant winning Blue-Grays made it to the majors, but then, few players from any Class D league of the late 1940s and early 1950s made the grade. The old Mountain State League, 1937–1942, sent more players to the majors than did the Appalachian League from 1946 to 1955. That did not matter to local fans, who always had their favorites and who loved to heckle opponents. Lots of chatter and a willingness to get dirty went a long way with fans. Welch fans, for example, voted catcher Bill "Yogi" Watts the most popular player despite his .217 batting average and the presence of six .300 hitters in the line-up. Both Bluefield and Welch fans were rabid, but Welch was downright dangerous. Umpires feared making calls against the home team. Once the Miners' business manager fought with an opposing manager in the clubhouse.

Baseball historians mark 1951 as the beginning of baseball's precipitous decline. From a peak of 448 minor league teams in 1949, the number dropped to 371 in 1951, to 292 by 1953, and continued to plummet throughout the decade. Attendance fell from 39,670,065 in 1949 to 26,115,291 in 1951, to 17,380,473 by mid-decade.

The decline began in West Virginia at the same time as it did nationally. Although Charleston again led the Central League in attendance in 1951, despite a decline in the number of paid admissions at Watt Powell Park, other league cities experienced more significant declines in their fan base. At season's end, the league quietly disbanded. In their three Central League years, Charleston never finished higher than fourth in the six-team circuit, but was always number one in attendance. Bluefield had led the Appy in attendance each season, but it fell to second in 1951. Welch was experiencing serious problems as it dropped to fifth in attendance.

Historians blame television and the broadcast of major league games into minor league territory as causes for the drop in minor league attendance. From the advent of commercial television in 1947 until 1951, there were no more than 100 television stations, and these were limited to major metropolitan areas. Then, the federal government took restrictions off, allowing an unlimited increase in stations.[11]

In Welch television most certainly could not be blamed for lower attendance; TV did not reach into McDowell County until 1955. Nor was McDowell County able to hear major league games on radio, except, of course, late at night on clear channel stations.

A contributing factor to the decline in the minors was the increasing difficulty local fans had in identifying with the players. As the farm system replaced independent teams, the development of prospects became the prime concern of teams. At the Class D level, development really meant identifying prospects and potential prospects from the rest. Prospects move up to a higher classification after one season. The others went home. The limitations imposed on "class players" (those with three or more years' experience) made it exceedingly difficult for independent teams to field a competitive club, and reduced the likelihood of marginal players hanging on. The Appy League in 1952 prohibited teams from having more than one veteran player. Thus, Appy rosters contrasted sharply with pre-war Mountain State League teams. Neither Bluefield nor Welch would have players like Eddie Guinter, Ed Hock, Vern Bickford or Red Martin who stayed in the league five, six, seven years. Only Welch's Frank Whitehead played three years in the Appy League.[12]

The class rule also made it exceedingly difficult for independent clubs to recruit players. Traditionally, the manager of independent teams used their contacts to find players. Veteran managers had an advantage, but they were best at bringing in minor league veterans. The one class player rule put a premium on signing first year professionals, making it more difficult even for managers with lots of contacts. Only major league teams possessed the contacts to scout, identify and sign youngsters coming out of high school.

The fortunes of Bluefield and Welch in 1952 illustrate the problems but also the possibilities for cities without an affiliation with a major league club. The Boston Braves club, facing mounting debt and on the verge of quitting Boston, divested itself of its Bluefield investment. N. D. Anderson headed up the local owners, who had no choice but to play as an independent. Welch faced the same dilemma when the Cincinnati Reds dropped the Miners. Bluefield hired well-known former major league pitcher and Charleston manager Joe Beggs to run the Blue-Grays. Welch was fortunate to hire veteran Appy manager Jack Crosswhite. Beggs had never had to recruit players and had little success. The Blue-Grays were so bad they had two no-hitters thrown at them in August. Not surprisingly, Bluefield attendance fell below 40,000 for the first time.

In Welch, Crosswhite, who had managed in the low minors since 1940, put together a strong team for 1952. After three last place finishes as a Reds farm team, the Miners jumped to third in the regular season. Jim Partin hit in 27 consecutive games and batted .336. Bob Ganung walked a record 121 times. Workhorse pitcher Paul Johnston, the "class man" of the team, won 15 games while logging in over 200 innings. The Miners then won the Shaughnessy playoffs to claim Welch's first professional title.

The Miners survived an early season embarrassment in one of baseball's most famous games. On May 13, 1952, Ron Neccici, a Pittsburgh farmhand pitching for Bristol, did not allow a hit and struck out 27 Welch batters. Never before or since has a pitcher accomplished such a feat. Neccici suddenly became the best-known minor league pitcher in the country. Pirate fans demanded the Bucs bring him to Pittsburgh. Unfortunately, he lasted only one season, finishing his major league career with a 1–6 record.

Welch's on-field success continued in 1953, making that two-year period, 1952–1953, the peak seasons in Welch baseball history. Business manager Henry Anderson arranged a working agreement with the Philadelphia Athletics, but kept Crosswhite as manager. The team retained three players from 1952, including Paul Johnston. Crosswhite's charges won the first half of the split season, but dropped a notch in the second half. The Miners took care of Johnson City in three straight games to capture their second Appy championship. Philadelphia farmhands captured the league batting titles. Third baseman Ernest Bousky compiled the highest batting average, while outfielder Ray Carr led in home runs with 21 and RBIs with 124. Johnston again topped the staff with 18 wins.

After the two triumphant seasons, things went downhill at Welch, but Bluefield enjoyed a championship year in 1954. Thanks to a working agreement with the Boston Red Sox, the Blue-Grays came alive after finishing last in 1953 and next to last in 1952. Manager Len Okrie directed the club to first place in the regular season. The BGs then ran the table with five straight wins in the playoffs. The club led the Appy League in batting with a resounding .291 average. Shortstop Jim Mahoney led the Blue-Grays at bat with a league high of 23 homers, and in the field where he topped the league in assists, put outs and double plays. He would spend four years in the Big Time. Another future major leaguer, pitcher Ken McBride, won 18 games. The pitching star, however, was Dick Morgan, who went 21–5 for a .808 winning percentage and worked 222 innings; all tops in the league.

While Welch and Bluefield were having their championship seasons, Charleston fans were not as fortunate, not by a long shot. With the collapse of the Central League following the 1951 season, Charleston was left without a place to play when the 1952 season opened. To the delight of Senator fans, in late June the American Association came calling. That Class AAA league, the minors' highest classification, had been as stable as the American and National leagues for fifty years. The Toledo franchise, one of the founding clubs of the league, had fallen on hard times after World War II. The team was bad and attendance fell off drastically. The 1952 team was horrible and in dire straits when *Charleston Gazette* managing editor Frank A. Knight put together a sweetheart deal that Toledo owner Danny Menendez could not refuse. On June 23, 1952, the Mud Hens became the Senators. Although Charleston's population was the smallest in the league, the metropolitan region compared with other league cities. Moreover, Charleston had established itself as a strong baseball town by leading the Central League in attendance despite having losing teams.[13]

Charleston was delighted to have a team in the American Association; it was big-time compared to previous leagues. Capital city boosters found themselves in company with other Class AAA cities including Milwaukee, Kansas City, Minneapolis, Los Angeles, San Francisco, San Diego, Seattle,

Oakland, and Baltimore. Teams at the AAA level not only had players on their way to the majors, but players whose names fans already knew. It was intoxicating to think of "big league" players in a Charleston uniform, even if big league was in the past tense. Fans responded to the new level by turning out in greater numbers than in 1950 and 1951. In the Senators' first full American Association season, 1953, attendance fell just 5,000 short of the 1949 record setting season. Charleston, however, would never draw that many again.

Fans quickly learned that the higher classification and recognizable names did not equate with a winning team. The Senators' roster always contained far more players on the way down than those on the way up to the majors. Such imbalance resulted in a string of bad teams. The team that came to Charleston from Toledo was mired in last place and the move did not improve its play. At season's end, it had lost 107 games, winning only 46, a pathetic .301 winning percentage, the worst in AAA leagues.

The fans' favorite, Herbert "Babe" Barna, exemplified the problem of Charleston American Association teams. The Clarksburg native had been a great athlete in his prime, a three-sport star at West Virginia University, from 1934 through 1937. He wore a major league uniform before the end of the 1937 season. Never a big league star, he hammered minor league pitching for over 300 home runs. Twice before, he had led the American Association in home runs. For the 1952 Senators he batted .287 with 14 home runs. Decent numbers, but it was obvious to Babe and his fans that 1952 should be his last year. He and Senators manager Rollie Hemsley opened a nightclub in Charleston that he operated for twenty years until his death.[14]

Year after year, Charleston's roster filled with "has-been" and "never-was" players. A working agreement with the Chicago White Sox in 1953–1954 did nothing to change the formula. The few players on their way to the majors did not remain on the roster for long. The White Sox sent Bob Boyd, a can't miss prospect, to Charleston. He batted .323, the only .300 hitter on the team, but the Sox recalled him in mid-season. That left Charleston with the likes of Dick Fowler, Hank Behrman, Tommy Byrne, Dick Young, Al Kozar, Angel Scull, and Frank Campos, all former major leaguers. The 1954 club was stocked with infielders Gordon Goldsberry and Don Kolloway, outfielder Cliff Mapes, catchers Sam Hariston and Aaron Robinson and pitchers Ross Grimsley, Dick Fowler, and Bill Voiselle. Miguel Fornieles, who had had two years in the majors before coming to Charleston, got his delivery sorted out, although he posted only a 7–7 record; he returned to the majors for nine productive seasons. He was an exception. That 1954 team had no .300 hitter, no one who hit ten homers or drove in

50 runs, and no pitcher who won even 10 games. The best that can be said for the team was that it did not lose 100 games, finishing with "only" 94 losses.

After two unhappy years as a White Sox affiliate, Charleston went the independent route in 1955. The Senators did some things right, but that did not prevent another last place finish. The team hired Danny Murtaugh as manager. A nine-year major league vet, he was coming off two highly successful seasons managing at New Orleans. In 1955, he was just two years away from assuming the helm of the Pittsburgh Pirates and three years from being selected National League manager of the year. Although he would become the most successful manager of his era, winning five National League pennants in fifteen years, Murtaugh could not squeeze out enough production from his Charleston players to get them out of the cellar. The team fired him in July and replaced him with back-up catcher Vern Rapp. Like Murtaugh, Rapp would manage in the majors. Interestingly enough, utility infielder Bobby Winkles would have a highly successful career as a college coach and would also manage in the majors.

The Senators also signed big Luke Easter, who had just finished a six-year major league career. Easter, who had been 35 when Cleveland signed him off the roster of the Homestead Grays, was 40 when his major league career ended in 1954. He would play another ten years of AAA ball. Wherever he played, fans loved him. The big guy (6'5", 240) moved slowly but his friendly, outgoing demeanor, not to mention his prodigious power, endeared him to the hometown crowd. Unlike most former major leaguers, Easter delivered for Charleston fans. He knocked 30 homers and drove in 102 runs.

Despite Luke Easter's bat and the managerial talent, the club finished deep in the cellar with 104 losses. Even more disturbing, Charleston finished last in attendance. After four straight last place teams, 1952–1955, and with attendance dropping, the future of Charleston baseball did not look bright.

The problems in Charleston were nothing compared to those in the Appalachian League cities. The Appy League expanded from six to eight teams in 1955, but attendance continued to drop to an average of 26,000 per team. That meant the league teams averaged fewer than 400 customers a game.

Bluefield fared better than Welch. In fact, the Blue Grays drew slightly better than the league average, but its season attendance of 29,914 was the lowest since the construction of Bowen Field in 1939. On the field, future Boston Red Sox outfielder Lu Clinton powered an otherwise feeble offense with a .361 average. Rookie Bill Monboquette showed little of the talent that led him to an eleven-year major league career; he won only two games for Bluefield. The team finished a distant sixth, but it did finish the season.

In Welch, life was rapidly becoming desperate both for the team and the city. By the mid-fifties, coal was no longer king in southern West Virginia. Coal production in West Virginia had fallen 35 percent between 1947 and 1955. Jobs in the coal industry dropped from 125,000 to 49,000 by decade's end. Unemployment in the state ran two to three times the national average and per capita income dropped to 75 percent of the national level. The great out-migration of West Virginians was underway. The union's seniority system assured that the young were the ones who left the state to seek jobs in Detroit, Cleveland, Cincinnati, and Pittsburgh. McDowell County suffered the most. It lost one-half of its population between 1950 and 1970. Coal companies began to close down whole towns in the county. The streets of Welch, once teeming on Saturdays with miners from outlying towns, now had young men returning home for the weekend from big city jobs. Baseball held little interest to those who stayed or who visited.[15]

Given the harsh economic reality, it was only a matter of time until professional baseball became too unprofitable to continue. To make matters worse, the 1955 Welch Miners were a bad team. Their resourceful manger of 1953 and 1954, Jack Crosswhite, moved to Salem, Virginia, where he, again, put together a pennant winning independent club. Welch's working agreement with Kansas City did little to help the Miners. Kansas City was not spending much money on a farm system and had no prospects for Welch. The team quickly sank into last place and stayed there.

By July the baseball situation in Welch reached crisis proportions. The club started the season in a financial hole with a $6,650 debt from 1954. Upkeep on the park cost the city another $2,000 per year. The first two months of the season, the team averaged 300 fans at best, and the debt was rising, another $4,500 in 1955. Club president H. E. Mauch announced that a four night home stand against Muscle Shoals' Kingsport team, July 11–14, would be a final test. If fans failed to turn out, the team would not be able to continue. After 405 turned out for the series opener and 460 for Fireworks Night, only 261 showed up at Blakely Field. Shoals remembered, rather unfairly, "Welch just couldn't hack it." Without waiting for the fourth game of the series, the board of directors called it quits. They returned the franchise to the league. Professional baseball had come to an end in Welch. On July 14, 1955, the Appalachian League transferred the Welch franchise to Marion, Virginia.[16]

At season's end, virtually all, if not all, Appalachian League cities reported financial losses and mounting debt. President Chauncey DeVault announced that the league itself would discontinue operations. In so doing, the Appy League joined a growing trend in minor league baseball. The number of minor leagues was down to 28 from a high of 52 and attendance was down over 50 percent and continuing to plummet. Where it would stop no one knew.

Although the low minor league teams had produced few major leaguers in the post-war years, the Mountain State sent a steady stream of native-born players to the majors. Andy Seminick, the veteran catcher of the 1950 Philadelphia Whiz Kids, had debuted in 1943. The Pierce native was the best catcher to come out of West Virginia. Seminick was followed to the majors by pitchers Arnold Carter of Rainelle, who made the majors in 1944, Steve Gerken of Grafton, who had a cup of coffee with the Athletics in 1945, Morgantown's Ray Flanigan in 1946, and left-handers Chuck Stobbs, a Wheeling native, and Harry Perkowski, a Beckley resident, in 1947. Shortstop John Bero and outfielder Hal Rice, both Coalfield players, came up in 1948. Lew Burdette from Nitro began his seventeen-year big-league career in 1950. He was the best right-handed pitcher the state ever produced. Following Burdette to the majors in the fifties were outfielders Mel Clark and Jim Fridley, infielders George Freese and Bill Mazeroski, pitchers Bob Milliken, John Kume, Bert Hamric, Walt Craddox, Earl Francis and catcher Dick Brown. Wheeling born Mazeroski is the only one of the group to make the Baseball Hall of Fame.

Special mention should be made of Larry Raines, who was the first West Virginia born African-American to make the majors. Born Lawrence Glen Hope Raines in St. Albans, Larry took a roundabout route to the majors. He played two years, 1951–1952, for the Chicago American Giants in the Negro leagues, then went to Japan for two more years. He returned to the U.S. to spend two years in the minor leagues. After he batted .309 at Indianapolis in 1956, the Cleveland Indians made him their regular shortstop as a 27-year-old rookie in 1957. With Cleveland, he hit only .253 in two seasons. He then went back to the minors and finally returned to Japan in 1962.

Most of the post-war major leaguers came out of the semi-professional leagues. In the boom years of the late-forties, semi-pro ball flourished. In southern West Virginia the coalfield leagues took up where they had left off before the war. Raleigh's A and B Leagues retained their eight-team lineup. The Omar Boosters from Logan County claimed the first post-war semi-pro championship. The Gary Miners and the Bishop Statesiders developed powerful teams in McDowell County. In the Charleston area the Kanawha Valley League included teams from Hurricane in the west to East Bank up river. The Charleston Industrial League had another six to eight teams. City Leagues also existed in Huntington and Parkersburg. In the Northern Panhandle the Wheeling Twilight League operated two divisions with teams from western Pennsylvania and eastern Ohio as well as from

West Virginia. A Northern Panhandle United Mine Workers League also had enough teams for two divisions. An Ohio Valley League, composed of small towns between Parkersburg and Huntington, was dominated by the Ripley Independents, who reeled off four consecutive state semi-pro titles. In North Central West Virginia, the Marion County League dated back before World War I. The Muntzing Jeeps and Swaney Coal of Clarksburg dominated the Central West Virginia League. The Mountain State League included teams from Belington in the mountains to Spencer in the west.[17]

As the state's coal economy began to slip after its peak in 1947 and dropped precipitously after 1950, the coalfield teams began to fall by the wayside. As young people left the region and coal companies sold off company towns, ball fields fell into disrepair and decay. By 1953 the McDowell Coalfield League was reduced from ten to four teams. The Raleigh County League declined from sixteen teams in 1946 to six by 1955. By the mid-fifties, few businessmen anywhere in the state showed any willingness to sponsor semi-pro teams. Retail merchants and small manufacturing businesses willingly put money behind Little League teams, but semi-pro teams found themselves high and dry.[18]

Economic decline aside, other attractions laid claim to people's time. Drive-in movies, bowling alleys, drive-in restaurants, softball, and Little League baseball pulled fans away from professional and semi-pro games. The largest cities had television stations by the early fifties. Communities no longer revolved around baseball. The most beloved of the coalfield players, John "Sheriff" Blake, lamented, "Nobody ain't got time for nothing anymore."[19]

As semi-pro ball became a thing of the past, college baseball staged something of a comeback, but it would remain a "minor" or "non-revenue" sport throughout the state's colleges. West Virginia University restarted its baseball program in 1946, with the Mountaineers playing a limited schedule with little success until Steve Harrick took over as coach in 1948. Harrick, who had graduated from WVU in 1924, came from West Virginia Tech, where he had coached baseball and wrestling for fourteen years. He would coach both sports at his alma mater for another twenty years. He built the baseball program into a Southern Conference power. Future major leaguers Jim Fridley, George Freese and Jim Heise appeared on WVU rosters in these years. In 1955, Harrick's Mountaineers enjoyed their first 20-win season since 1921. Heise led the NCAA in strikeouts. That team won the first of Harrick's six Southern Conference titles and advanced to the NCAA tournament, where it fell to Wake Forest.[20]

Baseball also showed renewed life at the small colleges in the state.

The West Virginia Intercollegiate Athletic Conference began crowning a baseball champion in 1947. Harrick's last West Virginia Tech team captured the initial title. Salem College won in 1948 and tied with Morris Harvey College in 1949. Morris Harvey, playing home games at Watt Powell Park, then reeled off undisputed titles in 1950, 1951, and 1952 without benefit of any great players. Players who reached the majors in the fifties dotted the rosters of other colleges: Bob Alexander pitched for Bethany College, Russ Kemmerer took the mound at Glenville State in 1949–1950, and Gene Freese played for West Liberty State.

The West Virginia Secondary School Activities Commission also commenced crowning a state high school champion after World War II. Beginning in 1949, the championship games were played at Watt Powell Park. Between 1946 and 1955, Wier High of Wierton, East Bank, and Parkersburg each won two state tournaments. East Bank had been a power even before the war, winning 51 consecutive games, 1939–1941, under coach Bill Calvert. They continued to be a power into the 1970s.

Both American Legion and Little League baseball reached their apex in the years after World War II. American Legion baseball had begun in the late twenties and continued even through the war. By 1950 over fifty teams competed throughout the state. The only post-war Legion team ever to advance to the American Legion World Series was the 1949 Post 1 team of Wheeling. Two fine pitchers, Dick Westfall and future WVU football star Carl Norman, led the club. After winning the state title, Wheeling captured the regional crown by defeating Baltimore and Bunker Hill of Washington, D.C. Next, in the sectional tournament, they beat Pittsfield, Massachusetts, twice to advance to the finals in Omaha, Nebraska. Losses to Cincinnati and eventual champion Oakland, California, doomed the Wheeling lads. However, a victory over Atlanta assured Wheeling of a third place finish.[21] The inability of Mountain State teams to reach the World Series after 1949 attests to the diminished quality of play at the Legion level.

Every community had its own Little League by the mid–1950s. Nothing was too good for the kids: uniforms, fences, manicured fields, dugouts, and a national, indeed international, organization. These teams drew fans from minor league and semi-pro ball and threatened to drive all other baseball off the sports pages; only the major leagues could compete. The only West Virginia Little League team ever to make the World Series in Williamsport, Pennsylvania, was the 1951 team from Fairmont. They just kept winning, beating Charleston West, Charleston East, and Morgantown to win the state crown. They took the regionals with wins over Hagerstown, Maryland, and Hamilton Township, New Jersey. At Williamsport,

Fairmont beat Pensacola, Florida, before losing to Stamford, Connecticut. They came back to take third place with a win over San Bernardino, California, as star pitcher Mike Hall won his fifteenth game of the season.[22] The post-war success of youth teams did not continue beyond 1951. The number of teams began to decline, not as rapidly as semi-pro clubs, but decline nonetheless. There would be far fewer West Virginia natives in the majors in the second half of the Twentieth Century than there had been in the first half. Mountain State baseball had seen its best days.

11

"Folks Don't Seem to Like Baseball Like They Used To"
The Nadir, 1955–1985

The decline of baseball, especially professional ball, which began in the early fifties continued for another twenty-five years. Attendance at major league and minor league games alike continued to drop for over a generation. Even at a time when the quality of play in the major leagues was at its all-time best, owners saw attendance drop. Major league owners, never a very foresighted lot, responded to decline with piecemeal, random expansion and by shifting franchises from one city to another.

Charleston sports writer and columnist A. L. Hardman, a keen observer of the game, cared deeply about his city and about baseball. He understood that minor league baseball suffered even more than the major leagues, and he knew that the major leagues' policies piled additional problems on the minors. The big leagues televised their games into minor league markets, robbing the local teams of their fans. Then they expanded into the most attractive cities, stealing the best markets from the minors and wreaking havoc on the rump leagues. "Baseball," Hardman once wrote, "was as restless as a Gypsy." But he was brutally honest in his analysis. When Charleston lost its AAA team in 1960, he opined: "Folks don't seem to like baseball like they used to like it."[1] Such words cut to the heart of fans, but they carried a hard truth. Football was surpassing baseball in attendance and among television viewers, and in West Virginia, high school and college basketball had become the favored sports.

With only Bluefield and Charleston fielding teams in Organized Baseball, and fewer and fewer semi-pro and amateur teams, kids were left without role models they could touch or see. Harry Perkowski, a major league player from 1947 to 1955, remembered that as a kid growing up in Beckley he played baseball from sunup to sundown. If the cover came off the ball they taped it up with electric tape. If they had no ball they wound string together and taped that up. By 1960 more and more boys played Little League ball in specially designed parks with manicured infields, using new balls and wearing uniforms modeled on those of the professionals. Fewer and fewer played sandlot ball on their own for the fun of it.[2]

By the mid-fifties, the major leagues could no longer ignore the plight of the minor leagues. Owners could not imagine how players would develop the skills necessary to play in the majors without the minor league teams. It seemed they had no choice but to keep the minor leagues afloat. So, in 1957 the major leagues agreed to a Stabilization Plan, key to which was a $500,000 fund to subsidize the low minor leagues.[3]

The infusion of major league money brought the Appalachian League back to life after it had lain dormant through 1956. In addition to providing money, a group of major league farm directors, led by Brooklyn's Fresco Thompson, concocted the idea of making the Appalachian a league for first year professionals. At an organizing meeting in Bluefield, the cities of Kingsport and Johnson City, Tennessee, and the Virginia towns of Salem, Pulaski, and Wytheville joined Bluefield in a reconstituted Appy League. The league would play a short season, operating between late June and Labor Day.[4]

Bluefield president Scott Litton then convinced Thompson to put a Brooklyn farm team in Bluefield. The Dodgers were America's favorite team, and since 1940 the winningest in the National League. The 1957 Blue-Grays produced the best record in Bluefield history, winning 47 and losing only 20 games. The .701 winning percentage matched the 1923 Martinsburg Blue Sox as the best in West Virginia history. Bluefield compiled that record with a team of overachievers and few stars. Pitcher Jim Duckworth led the league in victories, and mound mate Tom Donovan led in strikeouts, innings pitched and complete games. Outfielder Al Fantuzzi's .377 batting average was the league high. Despite the team's success and its Dodger star quality, Bluefield did not adopt the team. Only 17,264 paid their way into Bowen Field, leaving Bluefield fourth in attendance in the six-team league.[5]

Up the West Virginia Turnpike, Charleston operated at the top of the minor leagues in the Class AAA American Association. The fortunes of

Charleston baseball had begun to look up in 1956 when the Detroit Tigers purchased the team from Tony Menendez, who had moved the club there from Toledo. The 1956 club remained in the second division, but for a change the team had players on the way up to the majors. The Opening Day pitcher was future Hall of Famer and United States Senator Jim Bunning. With the improved play, attendance jumped nearly fifty percent to over 150,000. The club fell back a notch in 1957, but fans remained optimistic.[6]

Local fans were excited by the exploits of local product Lew Burdette. The Nitro native, who began pitching for Viscose in the Charleston Industrial League, was the hero of the 1957 World Series. He beat the New York Yankees three times, as his Milwaukee Braves won in an upset. He went on to win over 20 games in 1958 and 1959 and over 200 for his career.[7]

Fans hoped for a banner year when Detroit sent highly respected Bill Norman to lead Charleston in 1958. In fact, the Tigers liked Norman so much they called him back to Detroit on June 10 to take the helm of the parent club. Marion "Bill" Adair, former Bluefield manager, took Norman's place and guided the Senators to the American Association pennant. Pitcher Jerry Davie led the league with a 2.48 ERA and the Senators with 17 victories. The team was solid at every position with players on their way to the majors. First baseman Larry "Bobo" Osborne hit a team high 19 homers. Second baseman Wayne "Twig" Terwilliger led the league in runs and stolen bases. Third baseman Clarence "Buddy" Hicks topped the Senators with 98 RBIs, and shortstop Ron Samford was the club's only .300 hitter. Back-up infielders Ozzie Virgil and Milt Bolling were no slouches. Stan Plays, Jim Delsing, and Bill Taylor lined up in the outfield, while Wilmer Shantz and Charlie Lau shared the catching. Fans came to Watt Powell Park in large numbers; Charleston would never again top its attendance of 162, 914.

Charleston's 1959 team included many players from the pennant winners, but the team fell all the way to the basement of the American Association's Eastern Division. Key players produced far less than in 1958: Hicks' RBI total fell to 19; Davie's wins dropped from 17 to 4. The addition of promising left-handed pitchers Hank Aguirre and Ross Grimsley made no difference. Attendance fell by 60,000. Detroit, after just three years in Charleston, moved its AAA franchise to Denver. The economics were clear; Denver would draw over 200,000 while Watt Powell attracted less than 100,000.

Bluefield also hooked up with a new parent club, one that would hold on for over forty years. When the Dodgers moved to Los Angeles they pulled out of Bluefield. General Manager George Fanning arranged for the Baltimore Orioles to replace the Dodgers. It was not a popular move. The Dodgers had been highly successful while Baltimore was mired in the second division, seemingly going nowhere. Affiliation with losers carried little panache. Local fans were put off when Baltimore insisted that the team adopt the nickname of the parent Orioles, replacing the moniker "Blue-Grays" which Bluefield teams had used since 1924. When Bluefield failed to get even a single hit in the home opener, it supported the first impression. The 1958 club finished dead last with a dismal 21–51 record. Over the entire season, only 11,732 fans attended Bowen Field, the lowest figure since the park's construction in 1939.[8]

Things did begin to improve with the 1959 season. Baltimore was beginning to build a team from the bottom up, starting with Bluefield. The 1959 team moved up to the first division and had a few prospects. Shortstop Bob "Rabbit" Saverine led the Appy League with a .353 batting average; he was rushed into a Baltimore uniform before the end of the summer. Outfielder John "Boog" Powell was an even bigger crowd favorite. He batted .351 and led the team in home runs and runs batted in. Pitcher Wilmer Dean Chance won 10 while losing only 3 games and posting a 2.94 ERA. The following year, 1960, the team jumped to third place with its first winning record as an Oriole affiliate. Outfielder Sam Bowens and pitcher Tom Phoebus went up to Baltimore from the 1960 team. The 1961 club hit a robust .295 average, but finished fourth again, thanks mainly to dismal pitching. Outfielder Dick "Itch" Jones led the league in batting with a .380 average, the high point of his brief pro career. He turned to college coaching and had an enormously successful career at Southern Illinois University and the University of Illinois. He retired in 2005 with a record of 1240 wins and 752 losses.

In May 1959 the major leagues took another step to help save the minors, if the majors' public relations campaign was to be believed. The minors proposed that fifty percent of television revenue from games televised into minor league cities should go to the city affected. Instead the majors created a Player Development and Promotion Plan that created a $1,000,000 fund to help the minors. Under the arrangement Bluefield and other Class D teams received a $3,000 grant. Even at the lowest rung of the minors, that figure would not save a franchise from bankruptcy. Class AAA teams were eligible for $22,500, but teams owned outright by a major league club, including Charleston, were not eligible to receive anything.[9]

Charleston, however, was cut free by Detroit following the 1959 season. Sam Lopinski, himself a former West Virginia University player in the 1920s, took the lead in selling $75,000 in stock to back a new team. Not surprisingly, the new stockholders elected him president of the Senators.

Lopinski had no easy task. By the 1960s, the city of Charleston had passed the peak of its population growth. Unlike other areas of West

Virginia, Charleston's loss resembled that of other cities nationwide. Solid middle class families were moving to the suburbs. For the new suburbanites, a trip to Watt Powell Park became a family outing, an event to be planned and not done on impulse. The population shift also put new tax pressures on the city government. Mayors and city councils would be less likely to spend tax dollars on ballparks or to subsidize a baseball team than they had been even in the Depression.

Charleston needed a working arrangement with a major league team and Lopinski took what he could get, the Washington Senators. On the verge of moving to Minnesota, the Senators had a nucleus of promising young players, but they were several years from their prime. Charleston duplicated the parent club. Don Mincher, Zoilo Versalies, Sandy Valdespino, and Jim Kaat would help Minnesota capture an American League pennant, but in 1960 they were overmatched in the American Association. In August the team lost seventeen straight games to fall into the league cellar.

For the first time since baseball returned to Charleston in 1949, the 1960 team drew fewer than 100,000 fans. The lack of fan support assured that the team lost money; they finished $30,000 in debt. This time local investors were unwilling to risk losing more, as was the city government. Charleston had no choice but to return its franchise to the league. Charleston's nine-year membership in the American Association ended without a bang.

Despite losing its franchise for lack of fan interest in 1960, Charleston managed to return to AAA ball for a single year in 1961. The International League's Miami Marlins had moved to San Juan, Puerto Rico, for the 1961 season. It quickly became apparent that the team would lose money, and opposing teams would lose a great deal on their excursions to the island. League President Tommy Richardson explored moving the Marlins to Montreal or Miami before settling on Charleston. Marlin owner William P. "Bill" MacDonald and his general manager, Joe Ryan, agreed to the move after Charleston made a sweetheart deal. The Stadium Board of Charleston offered Watt Powell Park for a $1.00 rental fee and Mayor John Shanklin promised the city would handle the grounds and the maintenance on the park. A radio deal brought the club an additional $7,500.[10]

The Charleston Marlins would be a short-lived. Locals explained the incongruity of the nickname by noting that "Marlins" were a brand of hunting rifles popular among West Virginians. The Marlins finished second. Future St. Louis Cardinals regulars Julio Gotay, Dal Maxville and Tim McCarver played well and Ray Washburn topped the league with 16 victories. Despite the success, General Manager Joe Ryan pulled off a coup following the 1961 season. Ryan moved rapidly to get an International League franchise in the booming city of Atlanta when the venerable but lily-white Southern Association went out of existence rather than integrate. He then announced his decision to move the Marlins to the new mecca of the South. Charleston had again lost its AAA team. The city did not field another AAA team during the remainder of the sixties.

By the time Charleston was losing its team, the state's semi-pro tradition was coming to an end. Columnist Hardman's cutting comment about the decline of general interest in baseball certainly reflected reality in the semi-pro leagues. The gritty coalfield teams and community oriented town teams were a thing of the past by the early sixties. The strongest of the semi-pro leagues, the Raleigh County League, no longer existed. Beckley did have a team in the sprawling Kanawha Valley League along with Charleston, Hurricane, Kanawha City and Marmet. The United Mine Workers leagues were also gone. A few city leagues struggled along, but sponsoring businesses did no more than buy uniforms; they no longer paid players or gave them jobs. The decline of non-pro men's baseball was seen most vividly in Ripley. The Ripley Independents of the Jackson County League were a perennial in the State Semi-Pro Tournament, which Ripley won in 1959. The following June the team could not get off the ground. Little League had local baseball coverage all to itself.[11]

West Virginia's production of major league players nose-dived as the semi-pro teams died off. The pattern that had been established after World War II continued into the early sixties as a steady trickle of Mountain State natives entering the majors. Between 1955 and 1964 this group included Gene Freese, Walt Craddock, Bert Hamric, John Kume, Bill Mazeroski, Dick Brown, Larry Raines, Earl Francis, Doc Edwards, Jack Warner, Larry Brown, Corky Withrow, Dave Vineyard, and Paul Popovich. Then it was almost as if someone had turned off the faucet. An occasional drop came out—Joe Hague, Charley Manuel, and, the biggest drop, George Brett. Actually, neither Mazeroski nor Brett, the Hall of Fame players, grew up in West Virginia. Maz, born in Wheeling, spent his teen years across the river in Ohio. Brett was born just south of Wheeling in the town of Glen Dale, but moved with his family to California when he was two years old.

Professional ball continued, of course, in Bluefield, where the Baby Birds were reaping rich rewards from being a Baltimore farm team. Billy Hunter came to southern West Virginia to manage the Baby Birds and won back-to-back titles. The 1962 Bluefield Orioles featured the slickest fielding shortstop of his era in Mark Belanger. Never known for his hitting, Belanger batted a respectable .298 for Bluefield. He teamed with slick fielding Wayne Edwards, who led the Appalachian League with a .340 batting average. The 1963 team won the pennant in a romp without any future stars. Lefty Brian Holler never made the majors, but had the league's best ERA (2.41). Catcher George Shuford had a huge season. He led the league with a .364 batting average, in hits, and in total bases.

In 1963 the minors reached their nadir. Following the 1963 season, the Class AAA American Association, which had operated continuously since 1902, voted itself out of existence. The minors were reduced to a rock-bottom fifteen leagues. The majors forced a realignment of the minor leagues. The new arrangement conflated the old Class A, B, C and D leagues into a single Class A classification. The Appalachian League was an exception; it became a category of one, called the Rookie League.

After Charleston lost its International League team to Atlanta, team president Nate Dolin went shopping for a new league. He failed to interest Cincinnati in placing a team in Charleston, but the Class AA Eastern League jumped at the chance to take in Charleston. The Eastern League was a letdown for Charleston, as the fans there never really adopted it. The quality of AA baseball was not as good as the triple-A ball they had enjoyed. Few players had a major league resume. Dolin and general manager Dan Zerby did their best to market the team, but it was a hard sell. After averaging 128,117 fans between 1952–1961, the Senators averaged only 50,608 between 1961 and 1964.

The Cleveland Indians did its part, stocking Charleston with outstanding young prospects. The 1962 pitching staff included Luis Tiant, Tommy John, and Sonny Siebert. Behind the plate was Duane "Duke" Sims, who played eleven seasons in the big leagues. Still, the team finished a disappointing fifth.

In 1963 the Indians provided Charleston with a championship team. First baseman Bob Chance enjoyed a breakout season, one of the best ever seen in West Virginia. Chance's numbers rivaled those put up by Martinsburg's Reg Rawlings forty years earlier. Big Bob led the league in home runs (26), RBIs (114), batting average (.343), doubles (38), and total bases (285). Little wonder he donned a Cleveland uniform after the conclusion of the Eastern League season. In addition to Chance, the team included future major league outfielders Tommie Agee and Tony Curry, shortstop Jacinto Hernandez, catcher Duke Sims, and pitchers Tommy John (9-2-1.61), Steve Hargan (8-4-1.21), Steve Bailey (12-9-3.51), and Floyd Weaver (7-3-2.77).

The stars of 1963 moved up the ladder, leaving a club that struggled in 1964 to finish at .500. George Culver did win eleven games, and a youngster named Francis Smith pitched a no-hitter, but their efforts failed to compensate for woeful hitting. After the season, Cleveland decided to move its Class AA farm to Reading, Pennsylvania. For the third time in the 1960s Charleston found itself without a team. This time, no one seemed to care.

While professional ball struggled in the early 1960s, college baseball reached a level not seen since before World War I. West Virginia University enjoyed its most successful decade ever. Coach Steve Harrick had experienced a reasonable amount of success since taking over in 1948, guiding the Mountaineers to two NCAA tournaments. In the sixties, his teams became a major college power. The 1960 team featuring Flemington native Paul Popovich went 17–9. Popovich batted .426 before signing a $42,000 bonus with the Chicago Cubs. Then Harrick's boys ran off four straight Southern Conference titles followed by NCAA appearances, 1961–64. The 1963 team compiled the best record in school history with thirty wins against only three losses. It was the school's first thirty-win season, and it earned the school its highest national ranking. Pitching carried the team: John Radosevich (8-0-1.73) averaged striking out an NCAA high fifteen batters per game; Joe Jeran (7-1-1.15) won Southern Conference pitcher of the year honors; Dave Williams (7–1) and Wendell Backus (5–1) completed the rotation. The 1964 club had Bill Marovic, who became WVU's only All-American after batting .404 and stealing a school record 27 bases. To Harrick's credit, his 1961–64 teams achieved the NCAA tourneys without benefit of a single player who went on to the majors. His 1967 Mountaineers did have infielder Charles "Bucky" Guth, who had a cup of coffee with Minnesota.[12]

Coach Harrick retired following the 1967 trip to the NCAAs. He left WVU with a record of 334 victories against 160 losses. In 1975 the College Baseball Hall of Fame inducted Harrick into membership, and in 1978 he entered the West Virginia Sports Hall of Fame.

The small colleges of the state, members of the West Virginia Intercollegiate Athletic Conference (WVIAC), were also enjoying success. Fairmont State won three out of four WVIAC titles between 1957 and 1960. The 1958 Falcon team became the first West Virginia team to appear in the NAIA World Series. They beat Simpson (Iowa) College, but then lost their next two games in the double-elimination format. Shepherd College did not win a title, but sent pitcher Cecil Perkins (1959–63) to the majors.

The peak of small college baseball came with the success of West Liberty State College of 1963–1965. The Hilltoppers became the first team to capture the conference title in three consecutive years. In 1964 West Liberty gained the distinction of being the first and only West Virginia college to win a national baseball championship. The 'Toppers had all-conference players in first baseman Ray Prantil and shortstop Floyd Shuler, but it was great pitching that powered coach George Kovalich's team.[13]

The pitching tandem of Joe Niekro and Frank Ujcich overpowered college rivals. Niekro is the better known of the two. Joe and brother Phil combined to win 549 major league games, more than any other brother team. At West Liberty, Niekro became the first player to win all-conference honors three years. Only one year after the Chicago Cubs picked Joe in the third round of the 1966 draft, he made his major league debut. The knuckleball pitcher stayed twenty-two years, winning 221 games. At his peak, *The Sporting News* tabbed him as the best pitcher of 1979. The lesser-known pitcher Frank Ujcich was nearly as effective in college as Niekro. The New York Mets drafted Ujcich, who played briefly in the Mets' farm system before becoming a teacher and school administrator.

The 1964 Hilltoppers raced through the West Virginia conference and earned a spot in the NAIA World Series. They lost their first game to Wartburg College 2–1 in sixteen innings. Needing to win every game, they beat Western Washington 6–2. Then Niekro beat defending champion Sam Houston State 2–1 in ten innings. Ujcich shut out Georgia Southern 5–0. Niekro bested Grambling before little used Jerry Kraynick beat Grambling 3–2 for the title. Ujcich, Niekro, Shuler and third baseman Joe Doerr won all-tournament honors. Ujcich, who pitched 22 consecutive scoreless innings in the tournament, earned the NAIA Most Valuable Player trophy.

In the mid-sixties, when college teams enjoyed their greatest success, professional ball went further into the doldrums. Charleston lost its team in 1964. Bluefield had its Orioles, but they were bad. The 1964 O's finished at the bottom of the Appalachian League standings. Pitcher Albert "Sparky" Lyle would develop into a great relief pitcher in the seventies, but he contributed only three wins. The following season, the Baby Birds finished fifth in the six-team circuit. Then Joe Altobelli came to town as manager and things began to look up. His first team posted a winning record.

Altobelli's 1967 Orioles are remembered as one of the greatest Bluefield teams. In reality, the 1957, 1962, and 1963 teams won more games, but the 1967 team captured the city's imagination. That summer, 34,119 customers went through the turnstiles at Bowen Field, the highest attendance since 1954. The Orioles were Bluefield's version of San Francisco's Summer of Love. The Baltimore Orioles' 1966 World Series victory and Boog Powell's role in the winning generated excitement even before the season started. Fans could imagine they might see the next Boog playing in Bluefield. In fact they saw five future big-league players: catcher Johnny Oates, shortstop Bobby Grich, first baseman Larry Johnson and outfielders Lew Beasley and Don Baylor. The eighteen-year-old Grich batted only .254, but he would grow and improve enough to play seventeen major league seasons.

No one who saw the 1967 team doubted that Don Baylor would be the next Boog Powell. Baylor led the Appalachian League with a .346 batting average, and also topped the circuit in hits, total bases, walks, and stolen bases. In his 19 major league seasons he banged out 338 home runs, drove in 1276 runs, and stole 285 bases. His homer total was one less than Powell's, but he drove in 89 more runs. No Bluefield alum has stolen as many bases.

A hard throwing left handed pitcher on the 1967 team would contribute mightily to making the low minors romantic and popular. Ron Shelton struck out 44 batters in 41 innings and walked just 11 hitters. Despite that start, he did not make the majors. Instead he went into films. In 1988 he wrote and produced the blockbuster movie *Bull Durham*, a story of life in the low minors.

Following two down years 1968–69, the Orioles regained their domination of the league, winning the pennant again in 1970. The 1968 team had fallen to last place in spite of Javier Andino's leading the league in batting. The following year's team had improved slightly with first baseman Enos Cabell batting .374 and recording league bests in hits, runs and total bases. Then the 1970 club started fast and never looked back. The champions featured the double-play combo of shortstop Doug DeCinces and Bob Bailor, both of whom would have productive major league careers. Pitcher Herbert Hutson went 9-1 and got a late season call up to the parent Orioles. Manager Ray Malgradi earned Manager of the Year honors.

Bluefield repeated as league champions in 1971. That flag gave Bluefield five Appalachian League titles in a ten-year span. The Baby Birds turned out an outstanding shortstop in Alfonso "Kiko" Garcia, who fielded better than anyone since Belanger, and looked like a big-time prospect. The catcher, Ed Jordan, who led the club with a .323 average, and outfielder Gilberto Flores were all-stars. Bob Sekel's 1.59 ERA was the league best, and relief pitcher Leon Corbin topped the Appy in appearances and saves.

In West Virginia as well as across the nation, a malaise set in during the early 1970s. There were still energies to be spent in protest, against the Vietnam War and Kent State, for civil rights and the Equal Rights Amendment. Then Watergate, the energy crisis, trade deficits, austerity, and stagflation set in. Minor league baseball reflected the national temper. Attendance continued to drop. In Bluefield attendance stayed below 20,000 from 1970 until 1976. Even pennant winners could not move the fan base.

Charleston, at least, got back in the game in 1971 after a six-year absence. Bob Levine purchased the floundering Columbus franchise of the International League (IL) and moved it to Charleston. The city, according to A. L. Hardman, had gained a reputation as a "haven for distressed clubs." The new owner then named the team after his father, Charles Levine, an avid Charleston fan. The "Charlies" they would be.[14] The Pittsburgh Pirates were happy to have their top farm club just down Interstate 79. The Pirates were in the midst of their great "Lumber Company" teams with Willie Stargell and Roberto Clemente. They captured National League East titles in 1970, 1971, 1972, 1974 and 1975, winning the World Series in 1971.

Pittsburgh sent Joe Morgan to lead Charleston. The 1971 and 1972 clubs fell short. A New York team, the Rochester Red Wings, led by a group of ex–Bluefield Orioles, including International League MVP Bobby Grich, dominated the International League in 1971. Still, Charleston had things to cheer about. Richie Zisk had a breakout year, slamming out 29 homers and a league leading 109 RBIs. Outfielder John Jeter batted .324 and topped the IL in hits and stolen bases. Jeter and second baseman Rennie Stennett won all-star honors. Zisk again posted all-star numbers in 1972, including his league-leading 252 total bases. Gene Garber's IL best 2.26 earned run average earned him pitcher of the year honors.

Charleston's biggest year as a Pirate farm club came in 1973. Nineteen members of that team would go on to play major league ball. Big (6'5", 230 pound) Dave Parker starred until the Pirates called him up in mid–July. Parker left Charleston with a league leading .317 average but did not end up with enough at-bats to qualify for the batting crown. Samoan first baseman Tony Soliata produced big at the plate, and Frank Taveras had an all-star year at shortstop. That year the International League had no .300 hitter. Manager Joe Morgan got outstanding pitching from a group of eleven arms good enough to pitch in the majors, but, except for Bruce Kison (8–6 for Charleston), not good enough to stay long. For his role in the pennant-winning season, Joe Morgan was selected as manager of the year.

In the next three years, Charleston produced some future major leaguer players but garnered no pennants. Speedy outfielders Omar Moreno and Miguel Dilone gave the team a different look. Pitchers John Candeleria, Rick Langford and Kent Tekulve would have bright futures. Infielders Tony LaRussa, Willie Randolph, Bobby Valentine, Art Howe, and Ken Macha were ticketed to become major league managers. The fans, however, expressed dissatisfaction with their feet. Attendance continued to drop. And when general manager Carl Steinfeldt reported that the 1976 club had lost money, the Pirates left town.

The most intriguing members of the mid-seventies teams were Steve Blass and Bob Moose. Blass was one of the dominant pitchers in the game with a record of 100–67 when something went wrong. In 1973 he completely lost his effectiveness. No matter what he tried, he could not regain his form. Finally, in 1974, the Pirates sent him down to Charleston with the expectation that success in the minor leagues would restore his confidence. The opposite occurred. At Charleston he managed to win only two games while losing nine with an ERA of 9.74. Ever since, when a pitcher suddenly loses his effectiveness for no apparent reason he is diagnosed as having "Steve Blass disease."[15] Moose's problems were physical. In 1974 a blood clot required an operation that included removal of a rib. Then a thumb injury retarded his comeback, leading the Pirates to send him to Charleston to make the transition to being a relief pitcher. Although his 2-2 record did not show it, the plan worked and he became the Pirates' ace reliever in 1976. Shortly after the end of that season, however, he was killed in an automobile crash in Martin's Ferry, Ohio.

Bluefield baseball faced its own problems in the early- to mid-seventies. On May 23, 1973, disaster struck Bowen Field in the form of a devastating fire. The beautiful little park tucked in the woods burned to the ground; lights, grandstand, clubhouse, press box, and concession stand all went up in smoke. The park had survived spring floods of the Bluestone River and various lightning strikes, but never had it faced such devastation. The good news was that the fire demonstrated that the Orioles had become a Bluefield institution. Mayor Edwin Elliott, team president Allen Coppinger, and general manager George Fanning moved quickly to prepare a makeshift facility. By opening day they had bleachers for 500 fans and a new clubhouse. Fans turned out. They brought their own lawn chairs or sat on the ground, but they came. By season's end the club had drawn more than the year before.[16]

The team that survived the fire had one big drawing card, Eddie Murray. In 2003 Murray would became the first Bluefield Oriole elected to the National Baseball Hall of Fame. Baltimore drafted Murray out of Los Angles in the third round of the 1973 draft, and he headed to Bluefield. Only seventeen, he was a big (6'2", 200 pounds) but graceful first baseman. He would gain fame as one of the great switch-hitters of all time, but that came two years later; at Bluefield he just hit from the right side. Murray did not duplicate Don Baylor's 1967 season, but he made people take notice. He hammered 14 home runs and was chosen the league's all-star first baseman. Murray went on to become a better hitter than either Boog Powell or Don Baylor. When he retired in 1998 he had collected over 3,000 major league hits and 504 home runs.

Bluefield baseball reached a new plateau in 1976. The newfound patriotism of the bicentennial called for celebrating America and that carried over to the National Game. In 1976 attendance shot up to 28,487. The malaise was over. For the next decade attendance stayed above 20,000 regardless of how the team performed. Fans were coming to the park to have a good time, enjoy inexpensive family entertainment, and root for the home team win or lose.

Fans of 1976 did enjoy Mark Corey's banner season. He posted numbers

Eddie Murray began his Hall of Fame career at Bluefield, as did Cal Ripken, Jr. As a seventeen-year-old, Murray won Appalachian League all-star honors for the 1973 Baby Birds (National Baseball Hall of Fame, Cooperstown, N.Y.).

even more impressive than those of Powell, Baylor or Murray. Corey became the first Bluefield pro player to hit .400, finishing with that magic number. He led the Appy League in home runs, runs batted in, hits, triples, and total bases. Unfortunately, 1976 was the high point of his career. Corey did get to the majors, but stayed just long enough to demonstrate that he could not hit major league pitchers.

Charleston was unable to develop the loyal fan base that Bluefield enjoyed, but the 1977 and 1978 teams treated fans to championship seasons. The Houston Astros took over from Pittsburgh, and the 1977 Charlies won the post-season playoffs for the first time. Terry Puhl, J. J. Cannon, Dennis Walling and Craig Cacek batted over .300. Pitcher Tom Dixon led the league with a 2.25 ERA while Ron Selak won 15 games. Catcher Rick Cerone did not hit much but handled the pitching staff with skill. Although the Charlies finished two games short of a regular season pennant, they dominated the playoffs. Charleston beat Tidewater three games to one before sweeping regular season champ Pawtucket in four straight games to win the Governor's Cup.

The Charlies followed their 1977 playoff sweep with a regular season championship in 1978. Jim Beauchamp deserved the manager of the year award he received. No one on the club had much power, but second baseman Keith Dumright (.311) and designated hitter Jim Obradovich (.306) hit over .300. Pitchers Gary Wilson and Dan Larson each won 14 games. Frank Riccelli led the International League with a 2.78 ERA, and Oscar Zamora saved 10 games.

Charleston fans clearly preferred a winner. After drawing over 130,000 in 1977 and 1978, attendance fell to 72,609 for a second division team in 1979. The decline did not bode well. By comparison, Columbus drew just under 600,000. Not surprisingly, Houston pulled out of Charleston for Tucson, which would draw over 200,000 in the Astros' first year there.

Unlike Charleston, Bluefield's attendance continued to stay level even with a bad team. General Manager George Fanning gained recognition around the league for teaching Bluefield to enjoy the Baby Birds, win or lose. Even with bad teams in 1978, 1979, 1980, and a mediocre club in 1981, the team drew between 20,000 and 30,000, the best in the league. The Bird watchers saw some future big-league stars, including Cal Ripken, Jr., John "T-Bone" Shelby, Larry Sheets and George "Storm" Davis, and a number of journeymen players. Still, the atmosphere at the park seemed to matter more.

The 1978 Birds lineup that included Ripken, Jr., Sheets, and Shelby had the league's highest team batting average, but still managed to finish last. Ripken retained fond memories of Bluefield even though his first year performance gave little indication of future greatness. Third baseman Bob Boyce, Sheets and pitcher Ed Hook, all teammates at Bluefield, went higher than Ripken in the 1978 draft. In Bluefield, Ripken roomed with pitcher Brooks Carey in a boarding house that included Sheets, Mike Boddiker, and Tim Norris. With rent only $25 a month, Ripken managed to save a little of his $400 a month paycheck. On the field, young Cal committed a league high 33 errors, batted only .264 and hit no home runs. To no one's surprise, Boyce, not Ripken, was picked as the league's top prospect.[17]

Championships in Bluefield were less frequent than in Charleston, but manager John Hart's Baby Birds did roll to the league title in 1982. First baseman Jim Taber led the Appy with 63 RBIs in 61 games. Tandy Charley, who posted an 8–1 record, was picked as the best left-handed pitcher in the league. The best right-hander was Kingsport Met Dwight Gooden. Hart nailed down the manager of the year honor.

By the early 1980s, it was clear that a new day was dawning in minor league baseball. In the late 1970s the city of Columbus, Ohio, had pumped over $5,000,000 into renovating the city stadium, ushering in a willingness of municipalities to spend money on minor league facilities. A resurgence of fans followed. The year its renovated stadium opened, Columbus drew the unheard of attendance of 457,000. In 1979 minor league attendance jumped above ten million for the first time in twenty years.

In 1982 the Appalachian League retooled its way of operating in order to assure greater stability by centralizing the league operation. Members would be called on to tighten their financial belts. Teams now paid a franchise fee of $10,000 to the league, the hope being that the price would stop the revolving door of franchise changes. The league expanded from six to eight teams, and it maintained that level for the remainder of the decade. Home teams were allowed to keep all revenues from Opening Day and three other dates, but fifty percent of all other gate receipts went to the league. For its part, the league office, in addition to paying umpires, would negotiate and pay for transportation and lodging for visiting teams. Savings, not player comfort, was the priority in transportation and housing. On short hauls, teams would travel in yellow school buses. When teams visited the Tennessee cities—Bristol, Johnson City, Kingsport, and Elizabethton—they would be lodged in the dormitories of East Tennessee State University. The league office would also dish out meal money, $11.00 per day for teams on the road.[18]

Charleston did not keep pace with the changes just beginning. The Texas Rangers replaced Houston for one year in 1980. Then Cleveland arrived. The Indian farm hands finished fifth in 1981, then dropped to the basement in 1982. The cellar dwelling club drew 145,337 fans, which actually was an increase, but, even so, it was the lowest in the International League. To put Charleston's attendance in perspective, Louisville of the American Association, with a new 33,000 seat stadium, drew 868,418 in 1982, the most ever for a minor league team.[19]

In fact, Charleston's experience with Triple-A baseball was coming to an end. International League owners did not object when general manager Carl Steinfeldt arranged for a Maine lawyer, Jordan Kobritz, to buy the Charleston franchise. Doc Edwards from Red Jacket, West Virginia, managed the 1983 team to third place, but attendance continued to be the lowest in the league. At the end of the season, Kobritz moved the team to Old Orchard Beach, Maine, where they were known as the Maine Guides. It was not a good idea. By 1989 the Guides could not be found. Charleston, however, did not benefit from Maine's failure. The common wisdom was that the city was too small for a Class AAA team.[20]

In college baseball, 1982 saw the West Virginia State College Yellowjackets become the first team ever to go undefeated in the conference. State had overtaken West Liberty as the dominant team in the WVIAC in 1979, after the Hilltoppers had dominated the conference in the seventies. Ray Searage, who made the majors in 1981, was a big factor in WLSC's 1975 and 1976 title runs. Phil MacLaine, who succeeded Searage as the ace of the pitching staff, was even more dominating; his 1978 ERA of 0.90 was awe-inspiring. Then State won four times in the next eight years. Coach Calvin Bailey, himself an all-conference first baseman at State in 1966, built a powerhouse at his alma mater. In capturing the 1979 crown, Perry Estep hit a conference record .480. Pitcher Mark Grimmest allowed only 0.88 runs per game; no one since has come near that record. Over the next two years, State had the best record in the Southern Division, but Davis and Elkins College posted even more wins. In 1982, however, Bailey's team put it all together, going 15-0 in the WVIAC. Vernon Holstein was conference pitcher of the year. Chuck Carr set a conference record of 18 home runs, and catcher Jimmy Treble won hitter of the year honors with a .460 batting average. Bailey won his third coach of the year honor.[21]

At the University of West Virginia, Dale Ramsberg succeeded Harrick as coach. He enjoyed only modest success until the eighties. Then his 1982 and 1985 teams reached the NCAA tournaments.[22]

Also in 1982, Wheeling's American Legion team began a run unlike any in West Virginia baseball history. Back in 1949 Wheeling had had the only post-war West Virginia team to make it into the American Legion World Series. More recently, they had won state titles in 1963, 1964, 1966, 1975, and 1980. The 1982 championship was a surprise by a team with a losing record. After that, Wheeling just kept winning, running off a string of seven straight state championships, an unprecedented accomplishment.[23]

High school baseball did not experience anything like Wheeling's American Legion success. The West Virginia Secondary Schools Activities Commission ushered in two classifications, Class AAA and AA, in 1976. Huntington East was the only school to win three straight titles. The big name in high school baseball was Dave Merriman, who played for Magnolia High of New Martinsburg from 1980 through 1983. When he graduated, Merriman had national high school records for runs in a high school career

(159) and walks (133). He also stole 156 bases, the best ever in the state, and in the top five nationally.[24]

By the 1980s Baltimore was letting its farm system slip. Bluefield fans would not see future major league greats as they had done in the 1960s and 1970s. A couple of future journeymen big leaguers each year was all the fans could expect to see for the eighties. Of course there were prospects who did not pan out as expected. Greg Talamanez, the team's best pitcher of 1984, was picked by *Baseball America* as a better prospect than Greg Maddox; of course Maddox became a Hall of Fame shoo-in, and Talamanez failed to make the majors.

By the mid–1980s minor league baseball was clearly coming out of its thirty-year slough of despair. Bluefield had found its niche. The Baby Birds and their fans could look back on eight league titles since the Appalachian League reorganized in 1957, five of them between 1962 and 1971. The city had had a twenty-eight-year marriage with the Baltimore Orioles and had seen the best players that organization developed. Charleston had enjoyed a long run as a Triple-A team, but the population of the Kanawha Valley and the fickleness of Charleston's fandom were not able to sustain that level of baseball in the expansive period of the eighties. Other West Virginia cities demonstrated no interest in returning to organized baseball. The old coalfield teams, city leagues, and town teams were things of a distant past. College, American Legion, high school ball, and youth leagues continued, but at a level of quality that no longer turned out many professional players. Still, hope for the future existed in the quickening pace of minor league baseball.

12

"There's Nothing Like Baseball to Keep Your Mind Off Your Troubles"

A Minor Miracle, 1985–2000

Having reached its low point in the 1960s and early 1970s, professional baseball began to experience an upswing after 1976. By 1980, it was clear that the renaissance extended to, perhaps even favored, the minors. Attendance at minor league baseball games, which had bottomed out at fewer than seven million in 1967, soared over the twenty million mark in the late eighties for the first time in thirty-five years.[1] Over the next decade, a series of baseball movies sparked even greater enthusiasm. *The Natural* (1984) evoked a mystical quality about the game. *Long Gone* (1987) offered a raucous and gritty version of the game at the Class D level. In 1988, the blockbuster *Bull Durham*, with a better-known cast and more publicity, extended the spirit and fun of the lower minors to a larger audience. *A Field of Dreams* (1989) identified the bond between fathers and sons with baseball, bringing grown men to tears. *Eight Men Out* (1988) and *The Sandlot* (1993) evoked the romance of baseball past. The fans suddenly seemed to find in minor league parks a magic that did not exist in the cookie cutter stadiums of the majors.

A new generation of owners moved into baseball in the eighties. Young, brash, energetic and imaginative, they were willing to spend money to make money. Dennis Bastien was one of the new breed. He brought baseball back to Charleston after a four-year absence. Bastien had started in baseball administration at Gastonia, North Carolina, in 1979, moved to Macon, Georgia, in 1982, and became general manager at Spartanburg, South Carolina, in 1983. In 1984, at age thirty-one, he purchased his own team in Winston-Salem, North Carolina. When the South Atlantic League decided to expand by two teams, Bastien's DRB Management, Inc. obtained a franchise for Charleston. Dennis and his wife Lisa, eleven years his junior, went to work. Dennis doubled as his own general manager; Lisa served as business manager. Unable to line up a working agreement with a major league team for 1987, they got eight different major league clubs to stock the Charleston team with players. The new team adopted the name "Wheelers" to denote the old paddle-wheel boats that once plied the waters of the Kanawha and Ohio Rivers.[2]

While Bastien could not put together a decent team, he did spiffy up venerable Watt Powell Park. The city had done little to the park since the Charlies left in 1983, and the park showed the deferred maintenance. The new management did not spare the paint. Soon the old ballpark was decked out in a blue, green, and white motif: the exterior stark white with blue and green stripes, the grandstand seats blue and green, the dugouts and fences a light blue. The upbeat colors on the old steel and wood folding grandstand seats and the gigantic overhanging roof gave the park the appearance of a grand dame in modern new clothes. By the start of the season, sponsors had purchased fifty-five fence signs.

In the eighties, the Bastiens, like others of the new generation owners, were transforming minor league baseball. They understood, as George Fanning had earlier discovered in Bluefield, that in the era of farm systems the minor league teams couldn't count on a winning team to draw fans. Because the local team did not control player movement, it was helpless in developing a winning ball club. The major league organization that supplied the players was interested in the development of its young players, not the wins and losses of the minor league team. That reality required successful minor league teams to find other ways to attract people to the park. For Bastien the answer was to promote and market, and make their park fun at a reasonable price.

The Wheelers began to build their relationship with Charleston with paint in 1987, but the next year the Bastiens really got rolling. They invested in a new $250,000 lighting system. When the Wheelers became a Chicago Cubs farm club, the owners brought back ivy from Wrigley Field's outfield wall to transplant at Watt Powell. They even wrote a fight song, "Roll Wheelers Roll." Before games, players made themselves available at tables inside the gate to sign autographs. The game program grew to over 100 pages. The new operators were clever, professional, fun, and on the move.

Fans not only came to the park, but also became engaged. Bastien encouraged fans to bring signs to the park and to invent cheers. The 1988 club finished 35 games below .500, a terrible record. Despite the abysmal record, 125,998 customers paid their way into the park. Charleston's attendance was the highest in the twelve team South Atlantic League. For his efforts, Bastien received *The Sporting News* award as minor league executive of the year.[3]

Southern West Virginia also gained a new team when Princeton joined the Appalachian League in 1988. Princeton had always taken a back seat to Bluefield, just twenty miles to the south, even though Princeton was the seat of Mercer County. Gary Christie, Princeton's mayor, and Jim Thompson, president of the Mercer County Bank, wanted to make a statement about their city being as good as its cross-county neighbor. Bluefield had a baseball team, a long established institution. Princeton did not. The civic leaders set out to change the equation. Christie attended the baseball winter meetings in Dallas and came back with both the promise of a franchise in the Appalachian League and an agreement with the Pittsburgh Pirates to become the parent team of the new club. Thompson became president of Princeton Baseball, Inc., the official owner of the Princeton Pirates.[4]

Unfortunately, the park in Princeton bore little resemblance to Watt Powell Park or even Bowen Field in Bluefield. In fact, H. P. Hunnicutt Field in the Princeton Recreation Complex was really a high school field. There was nothing recognizable as a grandstand, only uncovered bleachers. Plastic lawn chairs atop a wooden platform at the edge of the dugouts were sold as "box seats." There was not even a tarp to cover the infield, so the team was at the mercy of rain. The school board prohibited the sale of alcohol and advertisements on the outfield fences. If the number of ads on fences was a measure of prosperity for minor league teams, and it was, the Princeton franchise was in trouble from the beginning. The team listed the park capacity at 1,500, but to reach that figure required fans to crowd close together on the bleacher seats. The club estimated it needed to draw an average of 1,000 a game to break even.

One big plus Princeton had going for it was a giant of a man named Raymond "Lefty" Guard. Officially, Lefty was the groundskeeper; unofficially he was "Mr. Baseball" in town. The city had even named a street after him. Guard had pitched in the minors in the forties, including stops in Huntington and Bluefield. The Boston Braves, he claimed, gave him a $6,000 bonus to sign in 1939. "It's still in the bank, $29,000 now," he explained in 1990. After his pro career, he had worked as a machinist in Princeton and played semi-pro ball. When he retired from a machinist job, he took over responsibility for the grounds at the recreation complex. When the team arrived, Lefty doubled as greeter and baseball ambassador-at-large. He loved his job because it got him back into baseball. After surviving two cancer operations, he could wax philosophically about baseball and life: "There's nothing like baseball to keep your mind off your troubles. I love it."[5]

Somehow, Princeton managed to survive despite the problematic beginning. The Princeton Pirates, even with second division teams, outdrew Bluefield in the first two years of the Princeton franchise. Then Pittsburgh, citing the lack of adequate facilities, pulled out of Princeton. Without an arrangement with a major league team, Princeton had no players, no team. Jim Thompson quickly appointed Faye Robertson general manager. One of a handful of women general managers, Robertson did not come from a baseball background; she worked at Jim Thompson's bank. Lefty Guard, grizzled old pro that he was, would not be expected to take kindly to women in baseball, but he became an ardent supporter of Faye. "She works sixty hours a week at the bank, and sixty hours a week here," according to Lefty. She managed to get several major league teams, mainly the Philadelphia Phillies, to send players for a co-op team. The 1990 Patriots finished twenty games off the pace. Attendance became a concern in 1991 and 1992 after the Cincinnati Reds established its rookie farm team in Princeton. Still, somehow, Jim, Faye and Lefty kept the team afloat through the first lean years.

A fourth West Virginia city joined the ranks of professional baseball in 1990. Huntington's last team had been in the Mountain States League in 1942. The new team came by way of Dennis Bastien. The Charleston Wheelers' owner purchased the Appalachian League's struggling Wytheville franchise and obtained approval to move the team to Huntington. The largest city in West Virginia, Huntington made an attractive site for the league. Bastien hired Bud Bickel, a crusty West Virginian, as general manager. Bickel had been Bastien's assistant general manager at Charleston. Seven weeks before the season opened, Bastien sold the team, at a tidy profit, to a group of young New Yorkers. The new owners, with no experience in the game except as ardent fans, included three doctors, a stockbroker, and a bank executive. Ed Poppiti, a native of the Bronx and vice president of Long Island Savings Bank, headed the group.[6]

As had been the case in Princeton, the Huntington management had a problem finding a place to play before settling on St. Cloud Commons. The ethereal park name belied the condition of the place. It did have a wooden grandstand covered with a roof, albeit seventy years old, small and dilapidated. Access to the park by a narrow two-lane street assured there would be traffic jams after every game. The Chicago Cubs agreed to stock the team, but made it clear that a new park would be needed soon for them to continue in Huntington. The owners, optimistically, advertised their expectation of building a new park in conjunction with Marshall University in two years.

Despite the park's shortcomings, the team drew well, pulling in 66,000 in the first year of operation. Local sportswriter Tom Stephens gushed over the new team and the park, writing: "Huntington has the rare opportunity to see baseball played the way it's supposed to be — outdoors on a grass field in an old-time ballpark with the smell of roasted peanuts in the air."[7] The rosy optimism of the owners always seemed to contrast with the West Virginia cynicism of general manager Bud Bickel. On Opening Day, Dr. Jim American, one of the vice presidents, looked at the overflow crowd of 4,000 and opined: "It's like hosting a big party that everybody wants to come to." Bickel remembered the occasion differently: "We were nailing up the outfield wall at 4 o'clock."[8]

The early nineties were a marvelous time for minor league baseball. No doubt the major leagues had created dissatisfaction among its casual fans. Free agency, strikes, astronomical salaries, the arrogance of major league players, and the skyrocketing cost of attending games at big league parks had turned off many people. Huntington's Stephens did not mince words: "The big league version [of baseball] glorifies ultra-rich cry-babies and half-hearted jerks who simply go through the motions on those rare days they feel like playing."[9] Minor league ball by contrast harkened back to a more innocent time when men played the game with verve for the sheer enjoyment of it. The *Bull Durham* effect, the romances of the spate of baseball movies, made minor league parks seem the "in" place to be. The aggressiveness and imagination of the new breed of young owners, including Dennis Bastien and Ed Poppiti, made the minor league parks an exciting place for clean entertainment. Maybe Lefty Guard had it right; people wanted to take their minds off their troubles. In 1992 the minors drew 27,180,170 fans, the highest attendance since 1950. The 212 teams that made up the minors that year were the most since 1955.[10]

The major league executives looking at this newfound prosperity in the minors saw an opportunity to reduce their costs at the expense of the minors. The majors basically forced the minor leagues to accept a new Professional Baseball Agreement, the document that defined the relationship between major and minor leagues. Under the agreement, some of the costs associated with running minor league teams were transferred from the parent to the farm club. In addition, a tax of at least five percent of gross revenues was imposed on each minor league team. Of greater consequence was the creation of a set of facility standards to which parks would be required to conform by 1994.[11]

12. *"There's Nothing Like Baseball to Keep Your Mind Off Your Troubles"*

The Charleston Wheelers made games fun for fans and players alike. The Dixieland band and picnic area were part of the fun that contributed to attendance records in the late 1980s and early 1990s.

In the short-run the new agreement hardly seemed to slow the growing prosperity of the minors. Bastien's Charleston Wheelers were packing fans into Watt Powell Park. On the field, Charleston had its best South Atlantic League years in 1990 and 1991. The Cincinnati Reds had replaced the Cubs as the parent team in 1989. The Bastiens continued to work at improving the atmosphere at the ballpark. A picnic area appeared down the right-field line, a Dixieland band preformed before games, and the game program grew to 150 pages. Hardly a night went by without a promotion. There were giveaways that allowed people to take something home from the park—caps, seat cushions, fanny packs, balls, collectable cards. The fans became more inventive. They began shouting "toast" at a visiting batter when he struck out. Some fans then brought "You are Toast" signs to hold up following a strikeout. That led one ardent Wheeler supporter to bring to the park an electric toaster that he was able to plug into an electric outlet and actually make toast, which he then threw into the air to the delight of other spectators. No wonder attendance rose even with a last place team.

The Wheelers became a team of destiny in 1990. The club started slowly, finishing the first half of the split season with a losing record.

Manager Jim Lett's players turned things around, finishing in a blaze, winning 19 of their last 22 regular season games to take the second half title. According to Lett, pitching carried the team. Pitchers Tim Pugh and John Roper won 15 and 14 games respectively, and Roper led the league with 189 strikeouts. Jerry Spradlin set a team record for saves. Outfielder Scott Pose, with a .298 batting average, was the closest to a .300 hitter on the team. Pose did lead the South Atlantic League in runs scored, bases on balls and in on-base percentage. Shortstop Trevor Hoffman hit a weak .212 but his arm strength convinced Lett to make him a pitcher; Hoffman developed into one of the top relief pitchers of the nineties.

In the playoffs, the Wheelers came into their own. Outfielder Bernie Walker exuded the team's confidence when he opined, "We can't be beaten." First, they swept Fayetteville in a best of three series, with Pugh and Bobby Ayala pitching shutouts. Then the Wheelers blanked Savannah three straight to take the league title. Pugh pitched another shutout in the final game. Charleston had its first pennant since 1977.[12]

The late season success of the 1990 team had caught the imagination of Charleston fans. So when the 1991 Wheelers got off to a fast start, Charlestonians flocked to the park in unprecedented numbers. Holdovers pitcher John Roper, who again won 14 games, topped the SAL with 189 strikeouts. Catcher Dan Wilson led the team with a .315 batting average. The real fan favorites were shortstop Rafael Bustamante, SAL all-star first baseman Tom Raffo, and the team's Most Valuable Player, outfielder Steve Gibralter. The Wheelers captured both halves of the split season, finishing with a combined 92–50 record. The Wheelers, however, managed to lose the playoffs to Columbia, South Carolina. When the tallies were in, Charleston had drawn 185,389 fans, an all-time record. Not even in the early post-war years had a Charleston team attracted so many spectators.

Bluefield also experienced an attendance boom in 1991. The Baby Birds had fielded mediocre to bad teams between 1985 and 1991. Fans came anyway. George Fanning was old school; he did not go for promotions and give-aways like the new breed of operators. He did pride himself on having the lowest prices in the league. Bluefield was the last team to have a $2.00 admission charge. The food was cheap and first rate. At Bowen Field, parking, admission, a hot dog, peanuts, and a soft drink cost $3.75. Many visitors believed Bluefield's hot dogs were the best in the league. Fanning usually greeted fans at the gate and his wife sold tickets. They set the tone for the friendliest park workers found anywhere. The park's beautiful, natural setting made Bowen Field a pleasant place to spend an evening. For whatever reason, people did come. The country music played between innings made it clear that Bluefield was in West Virginia, but the fans were not West Virginia stereotypes. A disproportionate number of college students and white-collar workers packed the stands. Over 55,000 fans moved the turnstiles in 1991, more than at any time since 1950.[13]

After a ten-year wait, a pennant came to Bluefield in 1992. The Orioles had the best hitting team in the league. The Baby Birds won nine straight in August and won the North Division going away. Future major league star Eric Chavez and catcher Marco Manrique earned all-star status. Relief pitcher Armando Benitez was often un-hittable, and often wild, traits that went with him to the majors. In the playoff series, the Orioles beat South Division winner Elizabethton with ease. Chavez batted .500, and pitchers Scott Emerson and Brian Sackinsky got the wins with Garrett Stephenson picking up a save. The final game, which brought the championship to Bluefield, was a birthday present of sorts to general manager George Fanning, who celebrated his eighty-third birthday on that day.[14]

Princeton was slow to share in the prosperity enjoyed by Bluefield, Charleston, and even Huntington. The 1992 season proved to be the low point. The club's administration turned over. Jim Thompson left as president, replaced by Dewey Russell, another banker. The Cincinnati Reds brought in Jim Holland as general manager. Holland was energetic and bright, but he needed time to find his way. The club did have the best player in the league in third baseman Dan Frey, who led the Appalachian League in home runs, RBIs, runs, hits, and total bases. Fans, however, stayed away in droves. Attendance tumbled to a precarious 18,642.

After the 1992 season, Princeton was at a crossroads. With attendance down and the club facing the absolute necessity of upgrading its facilities if the team was to continue, disbanding the franchise would have been a reasonable option. Fortunately, the Cincinnati Reds agreed to stay in Princeton for two more years. The city put money into the park, doubling the field lights and constructing a new clubhouse. The school board got a new leader who allowed signs on the fence for the first time. Holland sold out the outfield fence and began to promote, giving fans entertainment every inning. The mascot, Roscoe the Rooster, became a fan favorite, especially when an umpire kicked him out of a game.[15]

Princeton fans finally got something to cheer about in 1994. In the first six years of its existence, the Princeton team had never finished higher than fourth. Holland arranged radio coverage of the Reds games, helping people discover the new park. The Reds had a banner year. With outstanding pitching, good defense and timely hitting, the Reds nosed out Bluefield for the North Division title, much to the delight of Princeton residents. The double-play combination of Johnny Carvajal and Luis Ordaz won all-star honors. Outfielder Decombra Conner, fresh out of Greenville (S.C.) Junior

College, won the league's Most Valuable Player award. Pitcher Damon Callahan went 7–0, while workhorse Brian Lott led the Appalachian League in innings pitched. Emiliano Giron became an effective closer out of the bullpen. Princeton also won the playoffs, beating Johnson City two games to one; Giron saved two games and Conner's homer won the deciding contest.

The 1994 season was not as happy for Charleston and Huntington as it was for Princeton. Attendance in Charleston had already peaked in 1991, and in Huntington in 1990, as it had in Bluefield during the 1991 season. In the Capital City, Dennis Bastien sold the franchise he had worked so hard and so successfully to build. A conglomerate of investors headed by Mike Paterno, under the corporate name of Wheelers Baseball Limited Partnership, purchased the team. Attendance continued to drop, but it remained over 100,000 through 1995.

Huntington was a different story. The park remained the insurmountable problem. The owners' early optimism about a partnership with Marshall University to build a new facility proved to be misplaced. Nor could the team owners convince the city to build a new park, even though Huntington continued to draw more spectators than Princeton and Bluefield. The Chicago Cubs lost patience and pulled out of Huntington after the 1994 season. Efforts to find another major league sponsor failed because of the park's limitations. The Appalachian League allowed Huntington to function one more season as a co-op team called the River City Rumblers. The operation was woefully inadequate. A trailer was brought in as clubhouse for the home team, but visitors had to change in the local Econo Lodge. The team lost two-thirds of its games, including the final eleven. The abysmal play of the Rumblers eased somewhat Huntington's loss of its team. In its six year history the team finished in the first division just once, its first year. Huntington fans did get to see ten future big league players, but none became household names.[16]

Huntington general manager Bud Bickel saw the writing on the wall and struck out on his own. In 1993, in a daring move, he formed his own league that he named the Frontier League. The concept of "independent" leagues, functioning outside the structure of Organized Baseball, was just emerging. Bickel's idea was for his league to be an independent rookie league with limited salaries operating in small cities in West Virginia, Ohio and Kentucky. As Bickel conceived it, the league would be a throwback to the days when minor leagues operated without help from the majors. He organized a three-day tryout for prospective players before the season. Teams then drafted players from the camp. In theory, this arrangement and a salary cap would assure rough parity and fiscal sanity. He found backers for teams in

Portsmouth, Zanesville, Chillicothe, and Lancaster, Ohio; Richmond, Kentucky; and Parkersburg, West Virginia.[17]

Bickel kept franchises in Wayne, West Virginia, a town with a population of 1128, and nearby Ashland, Kentucky, for himself. The Wayne team he named the Coal Sox. Wayne High School's successful coach George Brumfield became the manager. Pitcher Rob Jackson, the team's top draft choice, won the Coal Sox's first game and followed that with a second win in the first week of the season. After that, it was all downhill for the Coal Sox; they won only one more game in the first month. To Bickel's dismay, Wayne averaged only 117 paying fans to the bleachers of tiny Pioneer Field. By the end of July the team could not pay the players and had to fold. The players, who had been housed in a Marshall University fraternity house, had not been paid since the season started. Needless to say they were not happy. Pitcher Dave Dorish, the winning pitcher in the team's final game, summed up the players' attitude: "We were living like dogs.... We all know that this is the minor league, but this is ridiculous."[18]

Like the Coal Sox, Bickel did not survive the season. His other franchise in Kentucky disbanded at the same time as Wayne. Then at midseason, the other team owners ousted Bickel as league commissioner. Because he had copyrighted the league name, it took a protracted court battle before Bickel and the league reached an agreement that allowed it to continue using the name Frontier League.[19]

Parkersburg's experience with independent baseball was better than expected given its failure to support teams in the past. The team, called the Ohio Valley Redcoats, lasted six years, as long as Huntington had been in the Appalachian League. The Redcoats started in a hole, playing their first fourteen games on the road while tiny Bennett Stump Field, a high school facility, was readied for the season. General manager Sam Riggs had done a good job of putting a team together. After firing their manager for allegedly stealing baseballs, the Redcoats finished strong in the second half of the 1993 season to make the playoffs. Under new manager Greg Lemasters, they then ran away with the pennant in 1994. That team posted a 50–17 record, an astounding .746 winning percentage. The Frontier League's Most Valuable Player, Corey Morris, led the league in home runs and runs batted in. A pitcher, Brendon Donnelley, would somehow make his way to the majors. Not surprisingly, he was the only Redcoat to do so. Following the 1994 season, Lemasters departed, the team floundered and attendance dropped. Four losing seasons followed. By fall of 1998, owner Jim Nelson was ready to unload the team. He sold to a group from Huntingburg, Indiana, bringing to an end professional baseball in Parkersburg.[20]

Minor league attendance declined everywhere in the late-nineties, but nowhere more drastically than in Charleston. Mike Paterno was unable to recreate the success of Dennis Bastien's Wheelers. The change of the team's name from Wheelers to Alley Cats in 1996 may not have been a cause for the team's decline, but it symbolized a change in fortune. The name Wheelers, at least, had some connection to the city; Alley Cats were a bad marketing gimmick, an effort to sell more team hats and other licensed products. Contributing to the decline, also, was the policy of the parent Reds to run a farm system on the cheap; that meant bad teams for Charleston. A shift to the equally frugal Kansas City Royals in 1999 made little difference in Charleston's fortunes. From 1995 to 2000 the Alley Cats finished last three times and next to last once.[21]

The exception to Charleston's run of bad teams came in 1997. The Alley Cats actually won the Northern Division of the South Atlantic League. Catcher Jason LaRue was that team's top hitter, and an all-star along with first baseman Jason Parsons. Pitcher Buddy Carlyle won fourteen games. Charleston, however, did lose the playoffs to Delmarva.

The Appalachian League teams had more on-field success to brag about than did Charleston. In Bluefield, the Baltimore farm hands created a minidynasty between 1995 and 1997. In fact, the 1995 Bluefield Orioles finished the season with the best record of any professional team in West Virginia history. Manager Andy Etchebarren's crew rolled to a record of 49 victories with only 16 losses. That record translated into a .754 winning percentage, higher even than the Martinsburg Blue Sox of the 1920s. Pitching coach Charlie Puleo worked with two great prospects, both of whom would reach the Big Leagues. Chris Fussell had a 9–1 record with a 2.19 ERA. *Baseball America* selected Fussell as the top prospect in the Appy League. Aruba native Sidney Ponson proved the better pitcher in the long run. Outfielders Eugene Kingsale (.316), Miguel Mejia (.298), and Dave Dellucci (.333) would make the majors. Appalachian all-stars Johnny Isom (.344) and shortstop Eddy Martinez (.308) would not be so successful.

The success of the 1995 team was a tribute to George Fanning in his last year as general manager. Longtime team president George McGonagle would assume Fanning's duties in 1996. A former high school chemistry teacher and baseball coach, Fanning had started working for the Bluefield team back when they were called the Blue Grays. Beginning as groundskeeper in 1948, he worked his way up to business and general manager in 1954. No baseball executive could match him for longevity. Late in his career, Fanning picked his all-time Bluefield Orioles team. It consisted of Steve Lake, catcher; Eddie Murray, first base; Mark Belanger, second base (even though he played shortstop at Bluefield and in the majors); Billy Ripken, third base; Cal Ripken, Jr., shortstop, John Shelby, Don Baylor, and

Mark Corey in the outfield, and pitchers Eric Bell, Storm Davis, John Habyan, and Dean Chance. His selections, with the exceptions of Lake and Corey, seemed to have been based more on their subsequent careers than their Bluefield accomplishments, but who can argue with a minor league legend.[22]

The Orioles continued their run in 1996 when they finished first in the East Division and continued their winning ways to capture the playoffs as well. Huge first baseman Calvin Pickering and tall third basemen Ryan Minor powered the team. Big Cal, whose weight was conservatively listed as 283 pounds, slammed league highs in home runs, RBIs, and total bases while batting .325. Minor, a former Oklahoma State basketball star, started slowly but came on at the end of the season. The hero in the playoffs against Kingsport, his two run homer cinched the decisive third game. Gabe Molina proved a dominant relief pitcher.

In 1997 the Orioles captured their third straight title. That team lacked the sluggers of the previous two seasons. Tight fielding and solid pitching allowed the Orioles to nose out Princeton by the slimmest of margins, one game, for the Northern Division title. The Baby Birds then beat Pulaski in two straight games to win the playoffs. Shortstop Jerry Hariston provided the glue to the infield defense and hit a robust .330. Outfielders Luis Matos and Tom Martin showed the promise that helped them reach the majors. Rick Bauer led the pitching staff that included John Stephens and Jay Spurgeon. Relief specialist Dave Mastrolonardo topped the league in saves and gained all-star status with a 1.08 ERA. His subsequent career proved disappointing. After winning three in a row, 1995–1997, the Orioles finished the decade on a down note with three losing seasons. The 2000 club did boast the Appalachian League player of the year in Octavio Martinez. Otherwise there was little to cheer, except Bowen Field.

Princeton closed out the century on a brighter note than did Bluefield. When the Cincinnati Reds pulled out of Princeton in 1996, it was a break for the local club. In their six-year stay, in only one year did the Reds win more games than they lost, the pennant year of 1994. When the Reds left, the local ownership, with Dewey Russell as president and Jim Holland as general manager, lined up an agreement with the expansion Tampa Bay Devil Rays.

To Princeton's good fortune, its new parent club was building from the bottom up. The Devil Rays sent a string of high quality players to West Virginia. The 1997 club just missed catching Bluefield. Second baseman Jared Sandberg was Appalachian League player of the year. Relief pitcher Victor Zambrano turned a lot of eyes with a blazing fastball and a 1.82 ERA. In 1998 it was Princeton's turn to best Bluefield. The Devil Rays captured the East Division crown but lost the playoff to Bristol. League sportswriters selected pitcher Jeremy Robinson as pitcher of the year. Battery mate Humberto Cota supplied the team's power. The double play partners, second baseman Derk Mann and shortstop Nestor Perez, were the best in the league at their positions. Pitchers James Lira, who led the league in saves, and Joe Kennedy looked to have promising futures.

The 1998 flag was Princeton's last, but Tampa Bay kept sending the prospects. The number one choice in the 1999 draft, Josh Hamilton, came to Princeton with a big reputation. He lived up to the lofty expectations. After he batted .347, the managers around the league selected him as the league's top prospect. They could have picked fellow outfielder Carl Crawford, who batted .319, and was on a faster track to the majors than Hamilton. Crawford would lead the American League in stolen bases in both 2003 and 2004. Princeton's next outstanding outfield prospect was Rocco Baldelli, who played centerfield in 2000. He batted a weak .216, but the talent showed through and league managers correctly rated him one of the top prospects in the league.

At the close of the twentieth century, West Virginia baseball fans looked back on an exciting decade and a half. At one time the state could boast of six professional teams, had the counting been done during the two-week life of the Wayne Coal Sox. Even without Wayne, there were more teams than any time since the summer of '42. The game had gone through a remarkable resurgence at the professional level. At century's end Charleston, Bluefield and Princeton had fewer fans than just a few years earlier, but they had stable operations capable of continuing into an indefinite future. The players, of course, were from around the globe—the Dominican Republic, Venezuela, Panama, Mexico, Puerto Rico, Aruba, Canada and Australia—but in 2000 not one player hailed from West Virginia. That fact told the story of Mountain State baseball below the professional level.

Notes

Introduction

1. Stefan Fatsis, *Wild and Outside: How a Renegade Minor League Revived the Spirit of Baseball in America's Heartland* (New York: Walker and Company, 1995), 3,5.

2. Peter Morris, *Baseball Fever: Early Baseball in Michigan* (Ann Arbor: University of Michigan Press, 2003). Ross Bernstein, *Batter-Up: Celebrating a Century of Minnesota Baseball* (Minneapolis: Nodin Press, 2002 is a folio size book with lots of photographs. Bob Burke, Kenny A. Franks and Royse Parr, *Glory Days of Summer: The History of Baseball in Oklahoma* (Oklahoma City: Oklahoma Heritage Association, 1999) offers valuable information on minor league baseball in a western state.

Chapter 1

1. *Wheeling Register,* August 2, 1866.

2. Allen Guttman, *From Ritual to Record: The Nature of Modern Sports* (New York: Columbia University Press, 1978), 15–55, provides a conceptual framework for folk and modern sports. Also see George Kirsch, *The Creation of American Team Sports: Baseball and Cricket, 1838–72* (Urbana: University of Illinois Press, 1989); and Benjamin G. Rader, *Baseball: A History of America's Game,* 2nd ed. (Urbana: University of Illinois Press, 2002); Stephen Hardy, *How Boston Played: Sport, Recreation, and Community, 1865–1915* (Boston: Northeastern University Press, 1982), 14–20.

3. Peter Morris, *Baseball Fever: Early Baseball in Michigan* (Ann Arbor: University of Michigan Press, 2003), 62–73; Charles A. Peverelly, *The Book of American Pastimes* (New York: np, 1866), 15; William J. Ryczek, *When Johnny Came Sliding Home: The Post–Civil War Baseball Boom, 1865–1870* (Jefferson, N.C.: McFarland, 1998), 17–25.

4. *The* [Morgantown] *New Dominion,* April 20, 1878; *Wheeling Register,* November 27, 1865.

5. *Wheeling Register,* November 6, 14, 1865.

6. *Ibid.,* November 20, 24, 27, 1865.

7. *Ibid.,* May 17, 1866. For the broader context of this attitude see Steven A. Riess, "Sport and the Redefinition of American Masculinity," *International Journal of the History of Sport,* 8 (May 1991), 5–22.

8. *Wheeling Register,* July 2, 4, 6, August 21, 1866.

9. *Ibid.,* October 11, 1871; Peter Boyd, *History of Northern West Virginia Panhandle* (Topeka, Ks.: Historical Publishing Co., 1927), 340–342; U.S. Census Office, 8th Census, 1860, Ohio County, West Virginia (Washington, D.C.: U.S. Census Office, 1870).

10. For reports of baseball clubs in 1866 see *Wheeling Register,* July 2, 4, 6, August 2, 13, 24, 25, September 6, 10, October 26, 1866.

11. *Wheeling Register,* August 2, 1866; Marshall Wright, *The National Association of Base Ball Players, 1857–1870* (Jefferson, N.C.: McFarland, 2000), 183.

12. United States Census Office, *Compen-*

dium of the Ninth Census (New York: Arno Press, 1976), 404; *Parkersburg Daily Gazette,* October 26, 1866.

13. John Alexander Williams, *West Virginia* (New York: W.W. Norton & Co., 1976), 30–55.

14. [Charles Town] *Virginia Free Press,* July 26 and August 2, 1866.

15. *Shepherdstown Register,* September 13 and 20, 1866.

16. *Ibid.,* August 15, 1866; [Charles Town] *Virginia Free Press,* July 21, 1866, August 2, 1866, October 11, 1866; *Wheeling Register,* July 6, 1866.

17. *Shepherdstown Register,* September 22, 1866; [Charles Town] *Virginia Free Press,* September 20, 1866; *Wheeling Register,* August 2, 1866.

18. *Morgantown Weekly Post,* June 20, 1868.

19. For rules see Dean A. Sullivan (ed.), *Early Innings: A Documentary History of Baseball, 1825–1908* (Lincoln: University of Nebraska Press, 1995), 118–119; Ryczek, *When Johnny Came Sliding Home,* 44–47; and *Beadle's Dime Base Ball Player* (New York: Beadle and Co., 1860), 21–26. *Shepherdstown Register,* August 22, 1866.

20. [Charles Town] *Virginia Free Press,* May 9, 1866, June 6, 13, 1867, July 4, 1867, August 29, 1867, September 10, 1867.

21. *Ibid.,* July 4, 1868, July 8, 1869.

22. Allen Guttman argues that baseball served to reconcile modern with traditional societies, "a ludic symbol of our ambivalence about the unknown future" (*From Ritual to Record,* 114). Clearly, baseball did not serve this purpose for the young men of the Eastern Panhandle. It could be argued, however, that this region which clung to values of Old Virginia would not find a sport with emphasis on merit a socially unattractive diversion.

23. [Charles Town] *Spirit of Jefferson,* June 8, 1869, August 24, 1869, August 23, 1870; G. Harrison Orians, "The Origins of the Ring Tournament in the United States," *Maryland Historical Magazine,* 36 (September 1941), 263–77.

24. *Huntington Argus,* August 21, 1872, October 8, 1872, April 19, 1873, September 5, 1873; [Charleston] *Tri-County Courier,* August 22, 1874; *Charleston Daily Courier,* May 13, 1874, July 23, 1874; Edwin A. Cubby, "The Transformation of the Tug and Guyandot Valleys: Economic Development and Social Change in West Virginia, 1888–1921,"

unpublished Ph.D. dissertation, Syracuse University, 1962, 61–62; David Alan Corbin, *Life, Work and Rebellion in the Coal Fields: The Southern West Virginia Miners, 1880–1922* (Urbana: University of Illinois Press, 1981), 36–37.

25. Charles H. Ambler, *A History of Education in West Virginia: From Early Colonial Times to 1949* (Huntington, W.V.: Standard Publishing Co., 1950), 361–362; *Morgantown Weekly Post,* April 25, 1868.

26. For Fleming's career see John Alexander Williams, *West Virginia and the Captains of Industry* (Morgantown: West Virginia University Library Press, 1976).

27. *Morgantown Weekly Post,* June 20, 1868.

28. *Ibid.,* June 20, 1868, July 11, 1868, September 5, 1868.

29. Wright, *The National Association of Base Ball Players,* 277.

30. *Wheeling Register,* July 22, 27, 1867, August 5, 19, 26, 31, 1867, September 10, 16, 30, 1867, October 7, 29, 1867, August 10, 24, 1868, September 8, 1868; *Wheeling Intelligencer,* September 7, 21, 1868.

31. *Wheeling Register,* July 27, 1867, November 4, 1867.

32. *Ibid.,* August 26, 1867, September 10, 1867, October 4, 22, 29, 1867, August 7, 1868, September 8, 1868.

33. *Ibid.,* November 4, 1867; Wright, *The National Association of Base Ball Players,* 193.

34. Bert H. Swartz, "The West Virginia State Fair Association," in Boyd, *History of Northern West Virginia,* 280–288.

35. *Wheeling Register,* July 13, 1868, August 21, 31, 1868, September 7, 1868.

36. *Ibid.,* September 8, 1868.

37. *Morgantown Weekly Post,* July 31, 1869, September 3, 1869, October 3, 1869.

38. *Wheeling Register,* August 21, 1868, September 8, 1868.

39. *Wheeling Intelligencer,* September 8, 1868.

40. Tom Melville, *Early Baseball and the Rise of the National League* (Jefferson, N.C.: McFarland, 2001), Ch. 3; Greg Rhodes and John Erardi, *The First Boys of Summer* (Cincinnati: Road West Publishing Co., 1994).

41. *Wheeling Register,* July 1, 1869.

42. *Ibid.*

43. Wright, *The National Association of Base Ball Players,* 248, 281; *Wheeling Intelligencer,* July 31, 1869, August 31, 1869.

44. *Wheeling Intelligencer,* August, 6, 8, 1870.
45. *Parkersburg Daily Times,* July 22, 23, 1870.
46. Wright, *The National Association of Baseball Players,* 289; *Wheeling Intelligencer,* July 31, 1870, August 30, 31, 1870.
47. *Wheeling Register,* July 3, 1870; *Wheeling Intelligencer,* July 8, 1870.
48. *Wheeling Register,* August 8, 1870.
49. *Ibid.,* July 3, 20, 1871; September 10, 1872; *Parkersburg Daily Times,* May 22, 1871.
50. *Wheeling Register,* July 3, 7, 16, 19, 1871, October 30, 1871, June 10, 24, 1872, June 16, 1873.

Chapter 2

1. Charles A. Wingerter, *History of Greater Wheeling and Vicinity* (Chicago: Lewis Publishing Co., 1912), I, 236; U.S. Census Office, *Report of Manufacturers of the United States at the Tenth Census* (Washington, D.C.: Government Printing Office, 1883), 380, 444.
2. U.S. Census Office, *A Compendium of the Ninth Census* (New York: Arno Press, 1976), 362.
3. *Wheeling Daily Intelligencer* covered baseball in 1874, especially *Intelligencer,* May 31, June 15, August 17, 23, 24, September 7, 21, 28, 1874.
4. For coverage of the Standards see *Wheeling Daily Intelligencer,* October 14, 19, 26, 1874, September 24, November 1, 1875, April 16, 1877; and *Wheeling Register,* especially April 29, May 6, 19, July 1, 3, 10, 26, August 18, 29, 1876, April 23, 30, May 1, 2, 12, 25, 26, June 18, 23, 27–29, July 12–16, 1877; *Cumberland News,* September 22, 1875.
5. William E. Benswanger, "Professional Baseball in Pittsburgh," *Western Pennsylvania Historical Magazine,* 30 (March–June, 1947), 9–14; John J. Miller, "Edward Sylvester Nolan," in Frederick Ivor-Campbell, et al. (eds.), *Baseball's First Stars* (Cleveland: Society of American Baseball Research, 1996), 121; Joseph Overfield, "First Great Minor League Club," *Baseball Research Journal,* 6 (1977), 1–6.
6. *Wheeling Daily Intelligencer,* August 30, 31, 1877; Pricilla Astifan, "1877 — Rochester's First Year of Professional Baseball," *Rochester History,* 64 (Fall 2002), 13.
7. *Wheeling Register,* May 7, 12, June 27, August 2, 20, September 17, 1877.

8. [Morgantown] *New Dominion,* June 9, 23, July 14, 1877.
9. Bert H. Swartz, "The West Virginia State Fair," in Peter Boyd, *History of Northern West Virginia Panhandle* (Topeka, Kan.: Historical Publishing Co., 1927), 381.
10. *Wheeling Register,* May 21, 1871.
11. *Parkersburg Sentinel,* August 16, 1878; [Morgantown] *New Dominion,* April 20, September 14, 1878; *Martinsburg Independent,* April 27, August 31, 1878; *Wheeling Evening Standard,* June 5, 1878.
12. William E. Akin, "The King of the Shortstops," *The West Virginian,* 6 (August 1977), 24–27; Robert L. Tieman, "John Wesley Glasscock," in Robert L. Tieman and Mark Rucker (eds.), *Nineteenth Century Stars* (Cleveland: Society for American Baseball Research, 1989), 143.
13. David Nemec, *The Beer and Whisky League* (New York: Lyons and Burford Publishers, 1994), 19–42; *Wheeling Register,* August 1, 4, 11, 12, 13, 16, September 3, 8, 9, 10, 30, 1882 (quote from September 10, 1882).
14. *Wheeling Register,* September 3, 6, 1882. Also see David W. Zang, *Fleet Walker's Divided Heart: The Life of Baseball's First Black Major Leaguer* (Lincoln: University of Nebraska Press, 1995), 30–32.
15. *Wheeling Register,* April 13, 16, 23, 1883.
16. *Ibid.,* June 22, July 1, August 30, September 15, 19, 1885; Sol White, *Sol White's Official Baseball Guide* (original, Philadelphia: H. Walter Schlichter; reprint, Columbia, S.C.: Camden House, 1984), 7.
17. Zang, *Fleet Walter's Divided Heart,* 35–36; *Sporting Life,* November 14, 1883.
18. John Thorn, et al. (eds.), *Total Baseball,* sixth edition (New York: Total Sports, 1999), 684, 1022, 1103, 1108, 1338.
19. *Wheeling Daily Intelligencer,* August 21, 27, 28, 1886; *Wheeling Register,* February 6, October 13, 1887.
20. Coverage of the 1887 team is found in *Wheeling Register,* February 6, May 3, 7, 1887, July 1–4, 29, 1890; *Sporting Life,* July 27, 1887; *Reach's Official American Association Base Ball Guide, 1888* (Philadelphia: A.J. Reach Co., 1989) np.
21. G. B. McKinney, "Negro Professional Baseball Players in the Upper South in the Gilded Age," *Journal of Sports History,* 3 (Winter 1976), 273–80; *Zanesville* (Ohio) *News,* November 19, 1887 for league statistics.

22. *The Sporting News*, March 31, 1888; *Wheeling Daily Intelligencer*, April 19, 20, 1888; Jerry Malloy, "Sol White and the Origins of African American Baseball," in John E. Dreifort (ed.), *Baseball History from Outside the Lines* (Lincoln: University of Nebraska Press, 2001), 62–91.

23. Norman L. Macht, "Edward James Delahanty," in Frederick Ivor-Campbell, et al. (eds.), *Baseball's First Stars* (Cleveland: Society for American Baseball Research, 1996), 50.

24. *Wheeling Register*, May 4, August 31, 1888; *Reach's Official American Association Base Ball Guide, 1889* (Philadelphia: A.J. Reach Co., 1889), 78–85.

25. *Wheeling Register*, April 27, July 5, August 3, 1888.

26. For the 1889 season see: *Wheeling Register*, April 29–31, July 7, 8, 14–17, 20, 22, 31, 1889; *Reach's Guide, 1889*, 24, 31.

27. Jack Kavanagh, "William P. Kennedy," in Ivor-Campbell, et al., *Baseball's First Stars*, 91.

28. An excellent account of the 1890 conflict is found in Robert F. Burk, *Never Just a Game: Players, Owners, and American Baseball to 1920* (Chapel Hill, N.C.: University of North Carolina Press, 1994), 81–115.

29. *Wheeling Register*, April 6, 31, May 5, 1890; *Reach's Guide, 1890*, 22–23.

30. *The Sporting Life Official Base Ball Guide, 1891* (Philadelphia: The Sporting Life, 1891), 132–37.

31. *Spalding's Official Base Ball Guide, 1891* (New York: A.G. Spalding and Bros., 1891), 166.

32. *Wheeling Register*, August 3, 1890, July 31, August 3, 16, 1891.

33. For coverage of other sports see *Wheeling Register*, August 31, 1888, July 14, 17, 18, 23, 1889, August 3, 1890, January 1, February 19, 27, September 17, 20, December 19, 1893; *Wheeling Daily Intelligencer*, August 5, 8, 1888, September 4, 1890, March 2, 1893, January 2, February 19, 20, March 17, 26, 28, 1894.

34. William E. Akin, "The Interstate League, 1895–1900," *Minor League History Journal*, 3 (1994), 1–4.

35. Edward G. Barrow with James H. Kahn, "My Baseball Story," *Colliers*, 30 (May 20, 1950), 83–85.

36. Zane Grey, *The Short Stop* (New York: Grosset and Dunlop, 1909), 155.

37. *Wheeling Register*, July 15, 17, August 1, 27, 28, 1895.

38. Barrow, "My Baseball Story," 19; *Wheeling Daily Intelligencer*, November 7, 1895.

Chapter 3

1. Charles H. Ambler, *A History of Education in West Virginia* (Huntington: Standard Publishing Co., 1951), 364–67, 468, 592, is old but still contains the best summary of early college sports. William C. Meyer, "Early Athletics," *The* [West Virginia University] *Atheneum*, 30 (June 1908), 27–30; and *The* [West Virginia University] *Monticola*, 6 (1896), 126 offer more detail on the 1890s.

2. *Wheeling Daily Intelligencer* provided detailed coverage of the events of 1896; Barrow's account is in Edward G. Barrow with James H. Kahn, "My Baseball Story," *Colliers*, 30 (May 20, 1950), 83–85.

3. *Wheeling Daily Intelligencer*, July 18, 1896.

4. *Ibid.*, January 15, 26, 28, February 19, 20, September 24, 1897; *Wheeling Register*, August 1–11, 1897.

5. *Toledo Blade*, March 9, 16, 1898.

6. *Wheeling Register*, August 8, 10, 1898.

7. *Ibid.*, September 3, 1891; *Wheeling Daily Intelligencer*, May 31, 1894, July 20, 1896.

8. *Sporting Life*, May 25, 1895; *Martinsburg Independent*, July 6, 13, August 23, September 7, 1895.

9. *Parkersburg Daily State Journal*, May 7–14, June 4, 7, July 6, 1897.

10. Statistics in this chapter are drawn from *Reach's Official Base Ball Guide* (Philadelphia: A. J. Reach Co., 1900–1906) and Henry Chadwick (ed.), *Spalding's Official Base Ball Guide* (New York: American Sports Publishing Co., 1900–1906).

11. *Wheeling Daily Intelligencer*, April 30, May 7, 1900; *Wheeling Register*, April 30, May 15, 16, 21, 28, 1900.

12. *Wheeling Register*, June 3, 1900.

13. Charlie Bevis, *Sunday Baseball: The Major League's Struggle to Play Baseball on the Lord's Day, 1876–1934* (Jefferson, N.C.: McFarland, 2003), 8–9, 283–285.

14. *Wheeling Daily Intelligencer*, April 10, 23, 26, June 1–3, 1901.

15. *Wheeling Register*, June 5, 9, 30, July 2, August 9, 1901.

16. John Antonik, *100 Seasons: The History of West Virginia University Baseball, 1892–1994* (Morgantown, W.V.: West Virginia University Department of Athletics, 1994), 1, 4; quote from Chadwick (ed.), *Spalding's Official Base Ball Guide, 1901*, 96.
17. Ambler, *Education in West Virginia*, 473; Kenneth M. Plummer, *A History of West Virginia Wesleyan College, 1890–1965* (Buckhannon, W.V.: West Virginia Wesleyan College Press, 1965), 50–51.
18. Rose R. Marino, *Welch and Its People* (Marceline, Mo.: Wadsworth Press, 1985), 335; Stuart McGehee, "Bluefield Baseball: The Tradition of a Century," *Goldenseal* 16 (Spring 1990), 50–51.
19. *Huntington Advertiser*, July 27, August 3, 1895; *Charleston Gazette*, July 4, 6, 20–26, 1899.
20. Early Twentieth Century baseball in Fairmont is covered in George W. Ramsey, Jr., "The Brief History of Organized Baseball in Fairmont," unpublished manuscript in Clarksburg Public Library, 1–3.
21. *Clarksburg Telegram*, May 23, July 16, 1903, March 24, 1904; *Clarksburg News*, March 15, 1904; *The Harrison County Herald*, October 11, 1905.
22. *Clarksburg Telegram*, June 1, 1900, July 23, August 3, 1908.
23. Arthur C. Prichard, *An Appalachian Legacy: Mannington Life and Spirit* (Parsons, W.V.: McClain Publishing Co., 1983), 182–84.
24. *Wheeling Register*, May 6, 8, 1901, April 18, May 2, 1903.
25. *The Sporting News*, February 14, 1903.
26. *The Sporting News*, December 5, 12, 1903.
27. *Sporting Life*, October 7, 1905.

Chapter 4

1. Dorothy Davis, *History of Harrison County, West Virginia* (Clarksburg: American Association of University Women, 1970), 278, 728–729, 749, 754–757.
2. George W. Ramsey, "The Brief History of Organized Baseball in Fairmont," unpublished manuscript in Clarksburg Public Library, 2–3; Davis, *Harrison County*, 479, 814–816; Steven A. Riess, *Touching Base: Professional Baseball and American Culture in the Progressive Era* (Westport, Conn.: Greenwood Press, 1980), 50–53, was the first to discuss the role of traction companies to minor league baseball.
3. *Fairmont Times*, March 2, 1907; *Clarksburg Telegram*, April 5, 13, 1907; Robert B. Van Atta, "The History of the Western Pennsylvania Class D Minor League of 1907," *Minor League History Journal*, 2 (1993), 17–20.
4. Statistics and records are from *Spalding's Official Baseball Guide* from 1908 through 1915 and Lloyd Johnson and Miles Wolff (eds.), *The Encyclopedia of Minor League Baseball* (Durham, N.C.: Baseball America, Inc., 1993).
5. Henry Lewis Gates, *Colored People: A Memoir* (New York: Alfred A. Knopf, 1994), 6–7, paints a compelling picture of his home town; *Piedmont Herald*, July 11, 1906.
6. *Clarksburg Telegram*, May 7, August 5, 17, 1907.
7. William E. Akin, "Hoblitzel, Richard Carleton," in David L. Porter (ed.), *Biographical Dictionary of American Sports: Baseball*, vol. 2 (Westport, Conn.: Greenwood Press, 2000), 679–681; Tom Simon, "Richard Carleton Hoblitzel," in Tom Simon (ed.), *Deadball Stars of the National League* (Washington, D.C.: Society for American Baseball Research, 2004), 249–250.
8. Prichard, *Mannington*, p. 184; *Clarksburg Daily Telegram*, April 2, 1917.
9. *The Sporting News*, January 23, 1908; *Fairmont Times*, March 28, May 9, 1908.
10. *Clarksburg Telegram*, April 10, 13, September 8–15, 1908.
11. Ibid., September 12, 15, 1908.
12. Taylor County Genealogical Society, *A History of Taylor County, West Virginia* (Grafton, W.V.: Taylor County Genealogical Society, 1986), 304–305; *Clarksburg Telegram*, July 27, 30, 1908; *Fairmont Times*, August 19, 1908.
13. Ramsey, "Fairmont," 6; *Clarksburg Telegram*, April 6, 1910; *Sporting Life*, September 18, 1909.
14. Peter J. Cava, "Scott, Lewis Everett," in David L. Porter (ed.), *Biographical Dictionary of American Sport: Baseball, 1374–1375*.
15. Ramsey, "Fairmont," 6–7; *Fairmont Times*, July 13, August 8, 1910.
16. *Clarksburg Telegram*, May 11, 31, July 10–27, August 5–28, 1911.
17. *Fairmont Times*, July 10, 29, September 5, 1912.

18. *Clarksburg Telegram,* May 28, June 1, 1914.
19. *Ibid.,* June 2, 9, 11, 1914; *100 Seasons,* 5–6; Lester G. McAllister, *Bethany: The First 150 Years* (Bethany, W.V.: Bethany College, 1990), 220.
20. Antonik, *100 Seasons* omits mention of the final WVU-WVWC game of 1914; *New York Times,* November 4, 1973, for obituary of Neale.
21. Ambler, *Education in West Virginia,* p. 592; *100 Seasons,* 6–7.
22. Prichard, *Mannington,* 185–186; *Clarksburg Telegram,* July 5–30, 1917, May 5, 1918.

Chapter 5

1. Statistics and records are from *Spalding's Official Baseball Guide* from 1906 through 1916 and Lloyd Johnson and Miles Wolff (eds.), *The Encyclopedia of Minor League Baseball* (Durham, N.C.: Baseball America, Inc., 1993).
2. *Sporting Life,* March 28, April 4, 1908, March 20, 1909.
3. *Ibid.,* December 11, 1909, February 19, 1910.
4. *Charleston Gazette,* July 13, 1909, April 3, 19, June 2, 1910.
5. *Ibid.,* June 6, 13, 1909.
6. *Sporting Life,* September 5, 1908; *Huntington Advertiser,* April 5, 1910.
7. *Sporting Life,* April 2, May 7, 1910; *The Mason [County] Republican,* April 8, 1910.
8. *Charleston Gazette,* April 9, May 5, 17, 1910; *Huntington Advertiser,* April 5, May 5, 1910; *The Mason [County] Republican,* April 15, 1910; *The [Parkersburg] State Journal,* July 12, 1910.
9. *Sporting Life,* September 17, 1910.
10. C. P. Stock, "George Baumgardner," *Baseball Magazine,* 10 (April 1913), 77–78.
11. David Jones, "Benjamin Michael Kauff," *Deadball Stars* (Cleveland: Society for American Baseball Research, 2004), 83–86; Bob Lemke, "The Benny Kauff Story," *Sports Collectors Digest,* April 2, 9, 16, 23, 1993; Johnson and Wolff (eds.), *The Encyclopedia of Minor League Baseball,* 125.
12. *The Montgomery News,* February 17, 1911.
13. *Ibid.*
14. *Point Pleasant Register,* July 5, 19, 1911; *The Mason [County] Republican,* June 23, 1911; *Spalding's Official Baseball Guide, 1912*

(New York: American Sports Library, 1912), 269.
15. *Huntington Advertiser,* September 15, 17, 1911.
16. *Ibid.,* July 3, 4, 10, 1912; *Charleston Gazette,* May 4, 18, July 2, 1912; *The Sporting News,* May 2, 1912.
17. Stuart McGehee, "Bluefield Baseball, The Tradition of a Century," *Goldenseal,* 16 (Spring 1990), 52.
18. *Sporting Life,* September 17, 1910.
19. *Ibid.,* December 16, 1911, September 14, December 14, 1912; *The Sporting News,* November 14, 1912.
20. *Wheeling Intelligencer,* April 9–July 20, 1913; *Sporting Life,* August 2, 1913.
21. *Wheeling Intelligencer,* May 7, July 23, 1913.
22. *Ibid.,* April 2, May 25, June 15, July 6, 1914.
23. *Charleston Gazette,* May 9, 1913.
24. *Ibid.,* May 10, 1913.
25. *Ibid.,* September 21, 23, 1913.
26. *Ibid.,* September 25, 1913; *Sporting Life,* September 21, November 23, 1913.
27. *Charleston Gazette,* September 5, 1914.
28. *Ibid.,* September 14, 1914.
29. McGehee, "Bluefield Baseball," 52.
30. *Huntington Advertiser,* July 11, 13, 1916.
31. Stan Cohen, *Kanawha County Images: A Bicentennial History, 1788–1988* (Charleston, W.V.: Kanawha County Bicentennial, Inc., 1987), 382; *Charleston Gazette,* March 17, 1916.
32. *Charleston Gazette,* July 8, 9, 1916.
33. *Huntington Advertiser,* July 13, 1916.
34. *Sporting Life,* February 2, March 13, 30, April 10, 17, 1915; *Wheeling Intelligencer,* February 23, 27, 1915.
35. *Wheeling Intelligencer,* March 11, April 6, 21, 1915.
36. *Huntington Advertiser,* July 10, 15, 1916; *Charleston Gazette,* May 6, 7, 1917, July 20, August 4, October 11, 1918.
37. *Wheeling Intelligencer,* April 26, 27, 28, 1916; February 6, 1917.

Chapter 6

1. William T. Doherty, *Berkeley County, U.S.A.* (Parsons, W.V.: McClain Publishing Co., 1972), 208–10.
2. *Martinsburg Independent,* July-August 1895.

3. *The* [Martinsburg] *World*, May 28–September 1, 1914.
4. *Martinsburg World*, May 30, 1914.
5. Mark Zeigler, "Class D Blue Ridge League," http//:www.blueridgeleague.org/history, provides an excellent summary of the league from its beginnings in 1915 through 1922. Zeigler's work is forthcoming in book form. Much of this chapter relies on his groundbreaking work. Also see Rebecca S. Kraus, *Minor League Baseball: Community Building Through Hometown Sports* (New York: Haworth Press, 2003), 119–20.
6. Rawlings' statistics are found in Lloyd Johnson (ed.), *The Minor League Register* (Durham, N.C.: Baseball America, Inc., 1993), 264.
7. League standings and leaders for each season can be found in Lloyd Johnson and Miles Wolff (eds.), *The Encyclopedia of Minor League Baseball* (Durham, N.C.: Baseball America, Inc., 1993).
8. Statistics for this chapter rely on *Spalding's Official Baseball Guide* (New York: American Sports Library, 1915–1930).
9. Mark Zeigler, "Lefty Clarke," bioproj.sabr.org. The Baseball Biography Project, 2005.
10. Bill McGowan, "The Umpire Talks Back," *Liberty Magazine* (September 11, 1937), 41–43; Cort Vitty, "Lu Blue," bioproj.sabr.org. The Baseball Biography Project, 2005.
11. *Martinsburg World*, April 24, 1918; *Piedmont Herald*, May 17, 1918.
12. William Louden file, National Baseball Library, Cooperstown, N.Y.
13. Jim Kaplan, *Lefty Grove: American Original* (Cleveland: Society for American Baseball Research, 2000), 39–46; Jim Kaplan, "The Best Pitcher Ever," *Baseball Research Journal*, 27 (1998), 62–65.
14. Joe Ward, who managed the Blue Sox in 1921, claimed Brooklyn and the New York Giants offered $5,000 for Grove but their offers arrived after the club agreed to Dunn's offer. His story cannot be verified. Kaplan, *Lefty Grove*, 47.
15. Robert Boone and Gerald Grunska, *Hack* (Highland Park, Ill.: Highland Press, 1978), 20–30; *The Sporting News*, March 24, 1921.
16. Clifford Blue Parker, *Fouled Away: Baseball Tragedy of Hack Wilson* (Jefferson, N.C.: McFarland, 2000), 19–22.

17. William W. Mowbray, *The Eastern Shore Baseball League* (Centerville, Md.: Tidewater Publishers, 1989), 10–17.
18. Parker, *Fouled Away*, 20–24.
19. Boone and Grunska, *Hack*, 26.
20. *Martinsburg Journal*, September 6, 1923.
21. *Ibid.*, February 28, March 2, April 1, 6, 7, 30, May 5, 9, 14, 15, 1927.
22. Donald Honig, *Baseball When the Grass was Real* (New York: Coward, McCann and Geoghegan, Inc., 1975), 194–195.
23. *Hagerstown Daily Mail*, January 5, 14, 22, 24, 30, February 14, March 26, 30, April 7, 16, 21, 23, 29, 1930; *The Sporting News*, February 30, April 17, May 1, 15, 1930.
24. *Martinsburg Evening Journal*, May 2, 1935; May 31, 1936.
25. Boone and Grunska, *Hack*, 147–149; Parker, *Fouled Away*, 194–195.

Chapter 7

1. Ronald D. Eller, *Miners, Millhands, and Mountaineers: Industrialization of the Appalachian South, 1880–1930* (Knoxville: University of Tennessee Press, 1982); Crandall A. Shifflett, *Coal Towns: Life, Work, and Culture in Company Towns of Southern Appalachia, 1880–1960* (Knoxville: University of Tennessee Press, 1991); and John Alexander Williams, *West Virginia* (New York: W.W. Norton Co., 1976) provide background on the southern West Virginia coalfields.
2. David Alan Corbin, *Life, Work, and Rebellion in the Coal Fields: The Southern West Virginia Miners, 1880–1922* (Urbana and Chicago: University of Illinois Press, 1981), 35–37.
3. John C. Hennen, *The Americanization of West Virginia: Creating a Modern Industrial State, 1916–1925* (Lexington, Ky.: University of Kentucky Press, 1996), 101.
4. *Ibid.*, 102; Eller, 220–21.
5. Stuart McGehee, "Bluefield Baseball: The Tradition of a Century," *Goldenseal*, 16 (Spring 1990), 50–51.
6. Williams, *West Virginia*, 146–47; Corbin, *Life, Work, and Rebellion*, 197–202; *Logan Banner*, July 19, 1929.
7. Bluefield baseball in 1924 is covered in McGehee, "Bluefield Baseball," 52; Stuart McGehee, "The Wedding of the Bluefields," *Goldenseal*, 29 (Summer 2003), 25–29; and *Bluefield Daily Telegram*, especially May 31,

June 1, June 29–July 21, August 1–September 15, 1924.

8. Stephanie Siegel, "Coal Camp Baseball," *Coal People Magazine,* 27 (December 2002), 25–26; Homer Hickham's trilogy— *October Sky, The Coalwood Way,* and *Sky of Stone*— paints a vivid picture of Coalwood in the 1950s. Unfortunately, baseball no longer dominated the social life of the town by the time of his boyhood.

9. Quote from Siegel, "Coal Camp Baseball," 25.

10. *Bluefield Daily Telegraph,* June 14, 1987; Rhonda Tanney Coleman, "Coal Miners and Their Communities in Southern Appalachia, 1925–1941," *West Virginia Historical Society Quarterly,* 15 (April 2001), 9; Paul J. Nyden, "Coal Town Baseball," *Goldenseal,* 6 (October–December 1980), 31–39.

11. Horace R. Givens, "Allen, Ethan Nathan," in David L. Porter (ed.), *Biographical Dictionary of American Sports: Baseball,* vol. I (Westport, Conn.: Greenwood Press, 2000), 13–14.

12. *Richlands News-Press,* September 21, 1988; *Welch Daily News,* October 7, 1924.

13. Charles C. Alexander, *John McGraw* (New York: Penguin Books, 1988), 242–43; *The Sporting News,* March 11, 1920.

14. Stuart McGehee, "Baseball in the Coalfields, 1900–1960," *Coal People Magazine,* 12 (October 1987), 11–13; Nyden, "Coal Town Baseball," 32–33; David S. Matz and John L. Evers, "Derringer, Samuel Paul" in Porter (ed.), *Biographical Dictionary,* vol. I, 377–78.

15. Jim Wood, *Raleigh County, West Virginia* (Beckley, W.V.: Raleigh County Historical Society, 1994), 647.

16. Jean Battlo, *Pictorial History of McDowell County, 1858–1958* (Parsons, W.V.: McClain Publishing Co., 2003), 245; *The Sporting News,* December 21, 1939.

17. Coleman, "Coal Miners and Their Communities," 1–11; Robert S. and Helen M. Lynd, *Middletown: A Study in American Culture* (New York: Harcourt, Brace and World, Inc., 1929), 225; Battlo, *Pictorial History of McDowell County,* 245.

18. Shifflett, *Coal Towns,* 162.

19. Walter R. Thurmond, *The Logan Coal Field of West Virginia* (Morgantown, W.V.: West Virginia University Library, 1964) 60; Eller, *Miners, Millhands, and Mountaineers,* 169; Darrell J. Howard, *"Sunday Coming":*

Black Baseball in Virginia (Jefferson, N.C.: McFarland, 2002), 37, 44, 194; *Raleigh Register,* May 26, 31, 1927.

20. Coverage of Raleigh County baseball in 1927–29 is found in *Raleigh Register,* especially April 7, 17, May 26, 31, 1927, April 1–September 16, 1929.

21. *Logan Banner,* June 21, July 19, 1929.

22. *Ibid.,* July 29, September 12, 16, 23, 1930.

23. *Huntington Herald-Dispatch,* March 9, 1931.

24. *Bluefield Daily Telegraph,* May 7, July 30, September 17, 19, 30, 1933.

25. *Ibid.,* August 12, 1934; *Richlands News-Press,* September 21, 1988.

26. *The Sporting News,* December 21, 1939.

27. Williams, *West Virginia,* 148; *Beckley Post-Herald,* April 19, 1932.

28. *Beckley Post-Herald,* April 19, May 10, 1932; *Raleigh Register,* July 15, August 27, September 3, 24, October 1, 1934; September 5, 9, 1935.

29. Coleman, "Coal Miners and Their Communities," 8–10; Nyden, "Coal Town Baseball," 31–42.

30. Nyden, "Coal Town Baseball," 31–32; *Logan Banner,* April 4, 1937; April 5, July 7, 16, 1938.

31. Howard, *"Sunday Coming,"* 37, 44, 194; Shifflet, *Coal Towns,* 164; Coleman, "Miners and Their Communities," 10.

32. *Logan Banner,* April 24, 1937; April 5, July 7, 16, 1938.

33. Nyden, "Coal Town Baseball," 38–42.

34. *Bluefield Daily Telegraph,* May 6, 1938; *Huntington Advertiser,* September 15, 1935, May 4, July 6, 1937.

Chapter 8

1. Robert Obojski, *Bush League: A History of Minor League Baseball* (New York: Macmillan Publishing Co., 1975), 269, for founding of the league. For quote see 269.

2. *Ibid.,* 270–74. The league published two official histories in the late 1940s. Russell Hockenbury, *A Short History of the Middle Atlantic League, 1925–47* (Scottdale, Pa.: Middle Atlantic League, 1947) is brief and of little help. Charles F. Kramer (ed.), *The Middle Atlantic League, 25th Anniversary, 1925–49* (Johnstown, Pa.: Middle Atlantic League, 1949) contains sketches of every

league team. Much of this chapter relies on Kramer. Also see *Spalding's Official Baseball Guide, 1940* (New York: American Sports Publishing, 1940), 298–99; James B. Holl, *The Canton Terriers: The Middle Atlantic Years, 1936–1942* (Canton, Ohio: Daring Books, 1990), 13, 42.

3. *Clarksburg Telegram,* April 9, 14, May 21, June 10, 1925.

4. George Ramsey, "A Brief History of Organized Baseball in Fairmont," unpublished manuscript, Clarksburg Public Library; Kramer, *The Middle Atlantic League,* 149.

5. Gus A. Bolden (ed.), *West Virginia, The State Beautiful* (Charleston, W.V.: The Tourist Publishing Co., 1929), 62; Works Projects Administration, *West Virginia: A Guide to the Mountain State* (New York: Oxford University Press, 1941), 280–92.

6. Statistics for the league are drawn from the *Spalding's Official Baseball Guide,* 1926–1943.

7. The [Fairmont] *West Virginian,* September 4–18, 1928; James P. Johnson, *The Politics of Soft Coal: The Bituminous Industry from World War I Through the New Deal* (Urbana, Ill.: University of Illinois Press, 1979), 95, 122–23.

8. *New York Times,* December 19, 1940, November 4, 1973.

9. *Clarksburg Telegram,* September 2, 1930; The [Fairmont] *West Virginian,* September 2, 1930.

10. *Beckley Post-Herald,* May 8, 1931; *Charleston Daily Mail,* March 5, 1931.

11. *Parkersburg Daily Sentinel,* June 19–July 11, 1931.

12. The [Fairmont] *West Virginian,* August 18, 1931.

13. Ibid.; *The Sporting News,* May 12, 1932.

14. Jerry Bruce Thomas, *An Appalachian New Deal: West Virginia in the Great Depression* (Lexington, Ky.: The University Press of Kentucky, 1998), 7, 23–25, 90, 207–9; *Charleston Daily Mail,* September 16, 20, 1931.

15. *Wheeling Intelligencer,* April 4–22, 1932.

16. Ken Brooks, *Last Rebel Yell* (Lynn Haven, Fla.: Seneca Park Publishing, 1986), 118; Lloyd Johnson (ed.), *The Minor League Register* (Durham, N.C.: Baseball America, Inc., 1994), 222–23.

17. Johnson, *The Minor League Register,* 42.

18. *Charleston Gazette,* September 8–15, 1932.

19. *Clarksburg Telegram,* January 31, February 14, 15, 22, 23, 24, 27, April 21, 23, 1933.

20. Robert S. and Helen Merrell Lynd, *Middletown: A Study in American Culture* (New York: Harcourt, Brace & World, 1929), 485.

21. *Clarksburg Telegram,* June 10, 1925.

22. *The Sporting News,* March 2, 1933.

23. Donald Honig, *Baseball Between the Lines* (New York: Coward, McCann and Geoghegan, Inc., 1976), 55; William E. Akin, "Jimmy Hitchcock," www.sabrbio-proj.com, 2003.

24. *Wheeling Intelligencer,* November 7, 12, 1934, January 22, 30, 1935.

25. Ibid., February 19, April 15, 1935.

26. Donald Honig, *Baseball When the Grass was Real* (New York: Coward, McCann and Geoghegan, Inc., 1975), 240–42.

27. *The Raleigh Register,* September 7, 1934.

28. Ibid., February 6, 10, 15, 1935; The [Beckley College] *Flight,* September 27, 1934.

29. *The Raleigh Register,* April 6, 25, September 9, 1935.

30. *Huntington Herald-Dispatch,* January 15–30, 1937.

31. Works Project Administration, *West Virginia: A Guide to the Mountain State* (New York: Oxford University Press, 1941), 177–95.

32. *The Sporting News,* February 25, 1943.

Chapter 9

1. Jerry Bruce Thomas, *An Appalachian New Deal: West Virginia in the Great Depression* (Lexington: University of Kentucky Press, 1998), Ch. 5.

2. *The Sporting News,* January 21, 1937; *Bluefield Daily Telegraph,* January 20, 1942.

3. Karl Winger, *The Appalachian League Black Book* (Bristol, Tenn.: The Appalachian League, 1949).

4. *Bluefield Daily Telegraph,* January 16, 1937 to May 13, 1937, provides the best reporting on the events leading to the formation of the Mountain State League.

5. Stuart McGehee, "The Wedding of the Bluefields," *Goldenseal,* 29 (Summer 2003), 25–29; and McGehee "Bluefield Baseball: The Tradition of a Century," *Goldenseal* (Spring 1990).

6. *Bluefield Daily News,* January 16, February 14, March 26, April 26, May 1, 1937.

7. Rose R. Marino, *Welch and Its People*

(Marceline, Mo.: Wadsworth Press, 1985), 8–9, 335, 355; Su Clauson Wicker, "Riding Route 52: The Old Coal Road," *Goldenseal*, 28 (Spring 2000), 10–19.
  8. *Mingo Republican*, May 6, 1937; *Williamson Daily News*, February–May, 1937.
  9. *Logan Banner*, February 20, 26, March 22–25, April 1–2, May 13, 1937.
  10. *Huntington Advertiser*, January–May, 1937.
  11. *The Sporting News*, April 8, 1937.
  12. *Beckley Post-Herald*, February 26, March 1, 20, 27, 31, April 2, 5, 9, 19, 26, May 3, 1937.
  13. *Huntington Advertiser*, May 4, July 23–27, August 2, 1937.
  14. Statistics for this chapter are from *Spalding's Official Baseball Guide* (New York: American Sports Publishing), 1938, 1939, 1940, 1941; *Official Baseball Record Book, 1942* (St. Louis: The Sporting News, 1942); and *1943 Baseball: Official Major and Minor League Records* (Chicago: Baseball Commissioner, 1943).
  15. *The Sporting News*, March 23, 1938; Logan *Banner*, February 3, March 14, April 5, 1938.
  16. James N. Giglio, *Musial: From Stash to Stan the Man* (Columbia: University of Missouri Press, 2001), 24–32.
  17. *Welch Daily News*, July 29, 1938.
  18. *Huntington Advertiser*, January 17, 1939.
  19. *The Sporting News*, January 26, 1939; *Williamson Daily News*, March 6, April 17, May 1, 1939.
  20. *Beckley Post-Herald*, January 9, 11, 1939; *The Sporting News*, January 26, 1939.
  21. *The Sporting News*, April 30, 1939; David F. Christman, *The History of the Virginia League* (Bend, Ore.: Maverick Publications, 1988), 68–72.
  22. *Bluefield Daily Telegram*, April 29, May 2, 14, 1939.
  23. Giglio, *Musial*, 32–33.
  24. *Bluefield Daily Telegram*, September 7–17, 1939.
  25. *The Sporting News*, January 22, 1942; *Beckley Post Herald*, July 24, 1940.
  26. *Bluefield Daily Telegram*, January 18, 20, 21, 1942; *The Sporting News*, January 22, February 5, 1942.
  27. *1943 Baseball: Official Major and Minor League Records* (Chicago: Office of the Commissioner, 1943), 604.
  28. *Williamson Daily News*, March 5, 6, 12, 1942.

Chapter 10

  1. *Bluefield Daily Telegram*, December 7–18, 1945.
  2. *Ibid.*, February 4–May 2, 1946.
  3. *Welch Daily News*, January 21, 25, February 4, 26, May 6, 1946.
  4. Statistics are from J. G. Taylor Spink (ed.), *Baseball Guide and Record Book* (St. Louis: Charles C. Spink and Son, 1947–1956).
  5. George Stone, *"Muscle:" A Minor League Legend* (Haverford, Pa.: Infinity Publishing Co., 2003), is an excellent biography of Muscle Shoals.
  6. *The Sporting News*, May 28, 1947.
  7. *Bluefield Daily Telegram*, September 3–10, 1949.
  8. *Charleston Gazette*, December 7, 1948, April 28, May 1, 1949.
  9. Gregg Howard, *Joe: Rounding Third and Heading for Home* (Wilmington, Ohio: Orange Frazer Press, 2004), 191–92.
  10. *Welch Daily News*, April 29–30, 1950.
  11. Rebecca Susan Kraus, *Minor League Baseball: Community Building Through Hometown Sports* (New York: Haworth Press, 2003), 137–39; Neil J. Sullivan, *The Minors* (New York: St. Martin's Press, 1990), 237–41.
  12. *Bluefield Daily Telegram*, May 1, 1952; Robert L. Finch, *et al., The Story of Minor League Baseball* (Columbus, Ohio: Stoneman Press, 1952), 63. For a contemporary recognition of the problem fans had in identifying with players see: Gordon Cobbledick, "Cure for Minors, Hometown Stars," *Baseball Digest* (March 1959), 65–66.
  13. Bill O'Neal, *The American Association: A Baseball History, 1902–1991* (Austin, Texas: Eakin Press, 1991), 341–43; *Charleston Gazette*, June 22–28, 1952.
  14. www.wvu.edu/~sports/hall_fame/babe_barna.htm; Lloyd Johnson (ed.), *The Minor League Register* (Durham, N.C.: Baseball America, Inc., 1994), 22.
  15. John Alexander Williams, *West Virginia* (New York: W.W. Norton & Co., 1976), 178–81.
  16. *Welch Daily News*, July 9–16, 1955; Rose R. Marino, *Welch and Its People* (Marceline, Mo.: Wadsworth Press, 1985), 335; Stone, *"Muscle,"* 295.
  17. *Welch Daily News*, May 25, 1946, September 6–7, 1952, August 23, September 3, 1953; *Raleigh Register*, August 10, 1946, Sep-

tember 11, 15, 22, 1947, September 20, 23, 1948, October 3, 10, 1949; *Parkersburg Sentinel,* July 1, 1948, July 5, 11, 1955; *Jackson [County] Herald,* July 22, August 5, 1953; *Charleston Gazette,* May 27, June 4, 1949; *Wheeling Intelligencer,* August 10, 15, 1949.

18. Rhonda Janney Coleman, "Coal Miners and Their Communities in Southern Appalachia, 1925–1941," *West Virginia Historical Society Quarterly,* 15 (April 2001), 9–11; Jim Wood, *Raleigh County, West Virginia* (Beckley, W.V.: Raleigh County Historical Society, 1994), 48; *Raleigh Register,* August 9, 1955; *Welch Daily News,* August 23, 1953; *Bluefield Daily Telegraph,* August 29, 1955.

19. Paul J. Nyden, "Coal Town Baseball," *Goldenseal,* 6 (October–December 1980), 38.

20. *100 Seasons,* 15–16.

21. *Wheeling Intelligencer,* August 13, 19, 23; September 2–5, 1949.

22. *Fairmont Times,* August 17, 20–25, 1951.

Chapter 11

1. *Charleston Daily Mail,* September 11, 1960.

2. Stuart McGehee, "Baseball in the Coalfields, 1900–1960," *Coal People Magazine,* 12 (October 1987), 11–13.

3. Rebecca Susan Kraus, *Minor League Baseball: Community Building Through Hometown Sports* (New York: Haworth Press, 2003), 92.

4. The formation of the league is covered in *Bluefield Daily Telegraph,* May 23, 27, June 8, 19, 20, 22, 1957.

5. Statistics and attendance figures are from *The Official Baseball Guide* (St. Louis: Charles C. Spink and Son, 1956–1986; Lloyd Johnson and Miles Wolff (eds.), *The Encyclopedia of Minor League Baseball* (Durham, N.C.: Baseball America, Inc., 1993); and Appalachian League, *Appalachian League, 1990 Record Book* (Bristol, Va.: Appalachian League, 1990).

6. *Charleston Gazette,* October 12, November 3, 6, 1955, April 23, 15, 1956; Bill O'Neal, *The American Association: A Baseball History, 1902–1991* (Austin, Texas: Eakin Press, 1991), 116, 127–35.

7. Gene Schoor, *Lew Burdett of the Braves* (New York: G.P. Putnam's Sons, 1960).

8. Mike Judge, "George Fanning, 82, Starting 39th Season as Bluefield G. M.," *Orioles Gazette* (June 19, 1992); *Bluefield Daily Telegraph,* June 29, 30, July 16, 1958.

9. J. G. Taylor Spink, et al. (eds.), *Baseball Guide and Record Book, 1960* (St. Louis: Charles C. Spink and Son, 1960), 108–11.

10. *The Sporting News,* May 10, 24, 31, November 22, December 6, 1961; Bill O'Neal, *The International League: A Baseball History, 1884–1991* (Austin, Texas: Eakin Press, 1992), 259.

11. *Jackson [County] Herald,* July 25, August 8, 1958, July 17, August 7, 1959, June 24, 1960; *Beckley Post-Herald,* August 13, 14, 1960; *Huntington Advertiser,* August 2, 10, 1960.

12. John Antonik, *100 Seasons* (Morgantown, W.V.: University of West Virginia Athletic Department, 1992), 19, 22–23.

13. For West Liberty's success see: Phil and Joe Niekro, *The Niekro File* (Chicago: Contemporary Books, 1988); *Wheeling Intelligencer,* June 9–15, 1964.

14. *Charleston Gazette,* April 13, 16, 17, 1971; O'Neal, *International League,* 258–60.

15. Luther W. Spoehr, "Blass, Stephen Robert 'Steve,'" in David L. Porter (ed.), *Biographical Dictionary of American Sports: Baseball Revised and Expanded Edition* (Westport, Conn.: Greenwood Press, 2000), 108–09.

16. *Bluefield Daily Telegraph,* May 24, June 8, 13, 14, 21, 1973.

17. Cal Ripken, Jr., and Mike Bryan, *The Only Way I Know* (New York: Penguin Putnam, Inc., 1997), 43–50.

18. Judge, "Fanning," 92.

19. Johnson and Wolff, *The Encyclopedia of Minor League Baseball,* 355, 368.

20. *Charleston Gazette,* April 3, 12, 13, September 7, 1983.

21. The West Virginia Intercollegiate Athletic Conference web site, wviac.org, contains detailed information for the 1970s and 1980s.

22. Antonick, *100 Seasons.*

23. *Wheeling Intelligencer,* August 9, 26–28, 1982.

24. Fred Mares (ed.), *National High School Sports Record Book* (Kansas City: National Federation of High School Associations, 1991).

Chapter 12

1. Rebecca Susan Kraus, *Minor League Baseball: Community Building Through*

Hometown Sports (New York: Haworth Press, 2003), 137–39.

2. *Baseball America,* May 10, 1987.

3. *Ibid.,* May 10, 1988, August 15, 1989; *1990 Charleston Wheelers Souvenir Game Program,* 12.

4. *Appalachian League 1989 Record Book* (Bristol, Tenn.: Appalachian League, 1989).

5. Interview with Raymond "Lefty" Guard, July 14, 1990; *Princeton Times,* July 12, 1990.

6. Allan Simpson (ed.), *Baseball America's 1990 Directory* (Durham, N.C.: Sports Publishing, 1990), 130, 132; *1990 Huntington Cubs Souvenir Program,* 5, 8.

7. *Huntington Herald-Dispatch,* June 21, 1993.

8. *Baseball America,* July 25, 1990.

9. *Huntington Herald-Dispatch,* June 21, 1993.

10. Kraus, *Minor League Baseball,* 139.

11. Allan Simpson (ed.), *Baseball America 1992 Almanac* (Durham, N.C.: Baseball America, 1992), 181–83. Statistics for this chapter are drawn from this annual publication.

12. *Charleston Gazette,* September 3–10, 1990.

13. David Lamb, *Stolen Seasons: A Journey Through America and Baseball's Minor Leagues* (New York: Random House, 1991), 157–60; Mike Judge, "George Fanning, 82, Starting 39th Season as Bluefield GM," [Baltimore] *Oriole Gazette* (June 19, 1992).

14. *Bluefield Daily Telegraph,* August 26–31, September 1–2, 1992.

15. Hank Davis, *Small-Town Heroes: Images of Minor League Baseball* (Lincoln, Neb.: University of Nebraska Press, 2003), 149–56; *Princeton Times,* March 25, June 24, 1993; *Bluefield Daily Telegraph,* August 15, 1992.

16. *Huntington Herald-Dispatch,* May 2, June 14, 17, August 29, 1995.

17. Jon C. Stott, *Leagues of Their Own: Independent Professional Baseball, 1993–2000* (Jefferson, N.C.: McFarland, 2001), 31, 34–35.

18. *Wayne County News,* June 9, July 21, 31, 1993.

19. David Pietrusza, *Minor Miracles: The Legend and Lure of Minor League Baseball* (South Bend, Ind.: Diamond Communications, Inc., 1995), 203–04.

20. *Parkersburg News,* July 1, 16–19, August 2, 1993.

21. Judith Blahnik and Phillip Stephen Schulz, *Mud Hens and Mavericks* (New York: Viking Studie Books, 1995), 252–53.

22. *Appalachian League 1990 Record Book* (Bristol, Tenn.: Appalachian League, 1990); Stuart McGehee, "Bluefield Baseball: The Tradition of a Century," *Goldenseal,* 16 (Spring 1990), 50, 55

Bibliography

Books

Ambler, Charles H. *A History of Education in West Virginia.* Huntington: Standard Publishing Co., 1951.
Antonik, John. *100 Seasons: The History of West Virginia University Baseball, 1892–1994.* Morgantown: West Virginia University, 1994.
Battlo, Jean. *Pictorial History of McDowell County, 1858–1958.* Parsons, W.V.: McClain Publishing Co., 2003.
Bernstein, Ross. *Batter-Up: Celebrating a Century of Minnesota Baseball.* Minneapolis, Minn.: Nodin Press, 2002.
Bevis, Charles. *Sunday Baseball: The Major League's Struggle to Play Baseball on the Lord's Day, 1876–1934.* Jefferson, N.C.: McFarland, 2003.
Boone, Robert, and Gerald Grunska. *Hack.* Highland Park, Ill.: Highland Press, 1978.
Boyd, Peter. *History of Northern West Virginia Panhandle.* Topeka, Kan.: Historical Publishing Co., 1927.
Burke, Bob, Kenny A. Franks, and Royse Parr. *Glory Days of Summer: The History of Baseball in Oklahoma.* Oklahoma City: Oklahoma Heritage Association, 1999.
Burt, Richard. *The Pittsburgh Pirates.* Virginia Beach, Va: Jordan and Co., 1977.
Christman, David F. *The History of the Virginia League.* Bend: Ore: Maverick Publications, 1988.
Cohen, Stan. *Kanawha County Images: A Bicentennial History, 1788–1988.* Charleston, W.V.: Kanawha County Bicentennial, Inc., 1987.
Corbin, David. *Life, Work and Rebellion in the Coal Fields: The Southern West Virginia Miners, 1880–1922.* Urbana: University of Illinois Press, 1981.
Davis, Dorothy. *History of Harrison County, West Virginia.* Clarksburg: American Association of University Women, 1970.
Davis, Hank. *Small-Town Heroes: Images of Minor League Baseball.* Lincoln: University of Nebraska Press, 2003.
Doherty, William T. *Berkeley County, U.S.A.* Parsons, W.V.: McClain Publishing Co., 1972.
Eller, Ronald D. *Miners, Millhands, and Mountaineers: Industrialization of the Appalachian South, 1880–1930.* Knoxville: University of Tennessee Press, 1982.
Finch, Robert L., et al. *The Story of Minor League Baseball.* Columbus, Ohio: Stoneman Press, 1952.

Bibliography

Gates, Henry Lewis. *Colored People: A Memoir*. New York: Alfred A. Knopf, 1994.
Giglio, James N. *Musial: From Stash to Stan the Man*. Columbia, Mo.: University of Missouri Press, 2001.
Grey, Zane. *The Short Stop*. New York: Grosset and Dunlop, 1909.
Guttman, Allen. *From Ritual to Record: The Nature of Modern Sports*. New York: Columbia University Press, 1978.
Hennen, John C. *The Americanization of West Virginia: Creating a Modern Industrial State, 1916–1925*. Lexington: University of Kentucky Press, 1996.
Hockenbury, Russell. *A Short History of the Middle Atlantic League, 1925–47*. Scottdale, Pa.: Middle Atlantic League, 1947.
Holl, James B. *The Canton Terriers: The Middle Atlantic Years, 1936–1942*. Canton, Ohio: Daring Books, 1990.
Howard, Darrell J. *"Sunday Coming": Black Baseball in Virginia*. Jefferson, N.C.: McFarland, 2002.
Howard, Greg. *Joe: Rounding Third and Heading for Home*. Wilmington, Ohio: Orange Frazer Press, 2004.
Ivor-Campbell, Frederick, et al. (eds.), *Baseball's First Stars*. Cleveland: Society for American Baseball Research, 1996.
Johnson, James P. *The Politics of Soft Coal: The Bituminous Industry from World War I Through the New Deal*. Urbana, Ill.: University of Illinois Press, 1979.
Johnson, Lloyd (ed.). *The Minor League Register*. Durham, N.C.: Baseball America, Inc., 1993.
_____, and Miles Wolff (eds.). *The Encyclopedia of Minor League Baseball*. Durham, N.C.: Baseball America, Inc., 1993.
Kaplan, Jim. *Lefty Grove: American Original*. Cleveland: Society for American Baseball Research, 2000.
Kirsch, George. *The Creation of American Team Sports: Baseball and Cricket, 1838–72*. Urbana: University of Illinois Press, 1989.
Kramer, Charles F. *The Middle Atlantic League, 25th Anniversary, 1925–49*. Johnstown, Pa.: Middle Atlantic League, 1949.
Kraus, Rebecca Susan. *Minor League Baseball: Community Building Through Hometown Sports*. New York: Haworth Press, 2003.
Lamb, David. *Stolen Season: A Journey Through America and Baseball's Minor Leagues*. New York: Random House, 1991.
Mares, Fred (ed.). *National High School Record Book*. Kansas City: National Federation of High School Associations, 1991.
Marino, Rose R. *Welch and Its People*. Marceline, Mo.: Wadsworth Press, 1985.
McAllister, Lester G. *Bethany: The First 150 Years*. Bethany, W.V.: Bethany College, 1990.
Melville, Tom. *Early Baseball and the Rise of the National League*. Jefferson, N.C.: McFarland, 2001.
Morris, Peter. *Baseball Fever: Early Baseball in Michigan*. Ann Arbor: University of Michigan Press, 2003.
Mowbray, William W. *The Eastern Shore League*. Centerville, Md.: Tidewater Publishers, 1989.
Nemec, David. *The Beer and Whiskey League*. New York: Lyons and Burford Publishers, 1994.
Niekro, Phil, and Joe Niekro. *The Niekro File*. Chicago: Contemporary Books, 1988.
Obojski, Robert. *Bush League: A History of Minor League Baseball*. New York: Macmillan Publishing Co., 1975.
O'Neal, Bill. *The American Association: A Baseball History, 1902–1991*. Austin, Texas: Eakin Press, 1991.

_____. *The International League: A Baseball History, 1884–1991.* Austin, Texas: Eakin Press, 1992.
Parker, Clifford Blue. *Fouled Away: The Baseball Tragedy of Hack Wilson.* Jefferson, N.C.: McFarland, 2000.
Pietrusza, David. *Minor Miracles: The Legend and Lure of Minor League Baseball.* South Bend, Ind.: Diamond Communications, Inc., 1995.
Porter, David L. (ed.). *Biographical Dictionary of American Sports: Baseball.* Westport, Conn.: Greenwood Press, 2000.
Prichard, Arthur C. *An Appalachian Legacy: Mannington Life and Spirit.* Parsons, W.V.: McClain Publishing Co., 1983.
Rader, Benjamin G. *Baseball: A History of America's Game.* Urbana: University of Illinois Press, 2002.
Riess, Steven A. *Touching Base: Professional Baseball and American Culture in the Progressive Era.* Westport, Conn.: Greenwood Press, 1980.
Ripken, Cal, Jr., and Mike Bryan. *The Only Way I Know.* New York: Penguin Putnam, Inc., 1997.
Ryczek, William J. *When Johnny Came Sliding Home: The Post-Civil War Baseball Boom, 1865–1870.* Jefferson, N.C.: McFarland, 1998.
Schoor, Gene. *Lew Burdette of the Braves.* New York: G.P. Putnam's Sons, 1960.
Shifflett, Crandall A. *Coal Towns: Life, Work, and Culture in Company Towns of Southern Appalachia, 1880–1960.* Knoxville: University of Tennessee Press, 1991.
Simon, Tom (ed.). *Deadball Stars of the National League.* Washington, D.C.: Society for American Baseball Research, 2004.
Stone, George. *"Muscle": A Minor League Legend.* Haverford, Pa.: Infinity Publishing Co., 2003.
Stott, Jon C. *Leagues of Their Own: Independent Professional Baseball, 1993–2000.* Jefferson, N.C.: McFarland, 2001.
Sullivan, Neil J. *The Minors.* New York: St. Martin's Press, 1990.
Taylor County Genealogical Society, *A History of Taylor County, West Virginia.* Grafton, W.V.: Taylor County Genealogical Society, 1986.
Thomas, Jerry Bruce. *An Appalachian New Deal: West Virginia in the Great Depression.* Lexington: University Press of Kentucky, 1998.
Thurmond, Walter R. *The Logan Coal Field of West Virginia.* Morgantown, W.V.: West Virginia University Library, 1964.
Tieman, Robert L., and Mark Rucker. *Nineteenth Century Stars.* Cleveland: Society for American Baseball Research, 1989.
White, Sol. *Sol White's Official Baseball Guide.* Columbia, S.C.: Camden House, 1984.
Williams, John Alexander. *West Virginia.* New York: W.W. Norton Co., 1976.
_____. *West Virginia and the Captains of Industry.* Morgantown: West Virginia University Press, 1976.
Winger, Karl. *The Appalachian League Black Book.* Bristol, Tenn: The Appalachian League, 1949.
Wingerter, Charles A. *History of Greater Wheeling and Vicinity.* Chicago: Lewis Publishing Co., 1912.
Wood, Jim. *Raleigh County, West Virginia.* Beckley, W.V.: Raleigh County Historical Society, 1994.
Works Projects Administration. *West Virginia: A Guide to the Mountain State.* New York: Oxford University Press, 1941.
Wright, Marshall. *The National Association of Base Ball Players, 1857–1870.* Jefferson, N.C.: McFarland Co., 2000.
Zang, David W. *Fleet Walker's Divided Heart: The Life of Baseball's First Black Major Leaguer.* Lincoln: University of Nebraska Press, 1995.

Articles

Akin, William E. "The Interstate League, 1895–1900," *Minor League History Journal*, 3 (1994), 1–4.

_____. "The King of the Shortstops," *The West Virginian*, 6 (August 1977), 24–27.

Astifan, Priscilla. "1877 — Rochester's First Year of Professional Baseball," *Rochester History*, 64 (Fall 2002), 2–23.

Barrow, Edward G. "My Baseball Story," *Colliers*, 30 (May 20, 1950), 83–85.

Benswanger, William E. "Professional Baseball in Pittsburgh," *The Western Pennsylvania Historical Magazine*, 30 (March–June 1947), 9–14.

Cobbledick, Gordon. "Cure for Minors, Hometown Stars," *Baseball Digest* (March 1959), 65–66.

Coleman, Rhonda Tanney. "Coal Miners and Their Communities in Southern Appalachia, 1925–1941," *West Virginia Historical Society Quarterly*, 15 (April 2001), 9–11.

Judge, Mike. "George Fanning, 82, Starting 39th Season as Bluefield GM," *Oriole Gazette* (June 19, 1992).

Kaplan, Jim. "The Best Pitcher Ever," *Baseball Research Journal*, 27 (1998), 62–65.

Lemke, Bob. "The Benny Kauff Story," *Sports Collectors Digest*, April 2, 9, 16, 23, 1993.

Malloy, Jerry. "Sol White and the Origins of African American Baseball." In John E. Dreifort (ed.), *Baseball History from Outside the Lines*. Lincoln: University of Nebraska Press, 2001, 62–91.

McGehee, Stuart. "Baseball in the Coalfields, 1900–1969," *Coal People Magazine*, 12 (October 1987), 11–13.

_____. "Bluefield Baseball: The Tradition of a Century," *Goldenseal*, 16 (Spring 1990), 50–52.

_____. "The Wedding of the Bluefields," *Goldenseal*, 29 (Summer 2003), 25–29.

McGowan, Bill. "The Umpire Talks Back," *Liberty Magazine* (September 11, 1937), 41–43.

McKinney, G. B. "Negro Professional Baseball Players in the Upper South in the Gilded Age," *Journal of Sports History*, 3 (Winter 1976), 273–80.

Meyer, William C. "Early Athletics," *The* [West Virginia University] *Atheneum*, 30 (June 1908), 27–30.

Nyden, Paul J. "Coal Town Baseball," *Goldenseal*, 6 (October–December 1980), 31–39.

Orians, G. Harrison, "The Origins of the Ring Tournament in the United States," *Maryland Historical Magazine*, 36 (September 1941), 263–77.

Ramsey, George. "A Brief History of Organized Baseball in Fairmont," unpublished manuscript, Clarksburg Public Library.

Riess, Stephen A. "Sport and the Redefinition of American Masculinity," *International Journal of the History of Sport*, 8 (May 1991), 5–22.

Siegel, Stephanie. "Coal Camp Baseball," *Coal People Magazine*, 27 (December 2002), 25–26.

Stock, C. P. "George Baumgardner," *Baseball Magazine*, 10 (April 1913), 77–78.

Van Atta, Robert B. "The History of the Western Pennsylvania Class D Minor League of 1907," *Minor League History Journal*, 2 (1993), 17–20.

Wicker, Clauson. "Riding Route 52: The Old Coal Road," *Goldenseal*, 28 (Spring 2000), 10–19.

Zeigler, Mark. "Lefty Clarke," bioproj.sabr.org, The Baseball Biography Project, 2005.

Newspapers

Baseball America [Durham, N.C.]
Beckley Post-Herald
Bluefield Daily Telegram
Charleston Courier
Charleston Daily Mail
Charleston Gazette

Charleston Tri County Courier
Charlestown Spirit of Jefferson
Charlestown Virginia Free Press
Clarksburg News
Clarksburg Telegram
Fairmont Times
Fairmont West Virginian
Hagerstown Daily Mail
Harrison County Herald
Huntington Advertiser
Huntington Argus
Huntington Herald-Dispatch
Jackson [County] *Sentinel*
Logan Banner
Martinsburg Independent
Martinsburg Journal
Martinsburg World
Mason [County] *Republican*
Mingo Republican
Montgomery News
Morgantown New Dominion
Morgantown Weekly Post
Parkersburg Daily Gazette
Parkersburg Daily Sentinel
Parkersburg Daily State Journal
Parkersburg News
Piedmont Herald
Point Pleasant Register
Princeton Times
Raleigh Register
Shepherdstown Register
Sporting Life [Philadelphia]
Sporting News [St. Louis]
Wayne County News
Welch Daily News
Wheeling Daily Intelligencer
Wheeling Register
Williamson Daily News
Zanesville [Ohio] *News*

Index

Adair, Marion "Red" 162, 175
Adams, Virgil 9
Adamston, WV 63
African-Americans 1, 23, 29, 32, 67, 76, 91, 115, 120–121, 169
Agee, Tommy 179
Aguirre, Hank 175
Alexander, Bob 171
Allen, Ethan 112–113
Alston, Walter 137
Altobelli, Joe 181
America, Jim 194
American Association 28, 30, 35, 51, 165–166, 174–177, 179, 187
American Legion 156–157, 171
Amigo, WV 114, 120, 122
Anderson, Henry 165
Anderson, John 82, 88
Anderson, N.D. 164
Andino, Javier 182
Andrews, Ed 102
Ansted, WV 105, 119
Appalachian League 141, 145, 158–163, 174–179, 181–186, 192–194, 196–202
Applegate, Able 85
Archer, Frank M. 113, 118, 150
Archer, R.M. 55
Archibold, Ray 124
Arnold, Walter 152
Ash, Ken 71–72
attendance 84–87, 93, 96, 102, 117, 121, 126, 128–130, 132, 135–136, 148, 156–157, 160, 162, 164, 166–169, 174–177, 179, 181–184, 186–187, 190, 192–199
Austin, Wayne 150
Ayala, Bobby 196

Bachman, Ed 155
Backus, Wendell 180
Bailey, Calvin 188
Bailey, Steve 179
Bailor, Bob 182
Baldelli, Rocco 202
Baldwin, Frank 159
Baldwin, R.M. 52
Ball, Art 38
Baltic Base Ball Club 15–17, 19
Baltimore and Ohio Railroad 6, 10, 22, 40–41, 57–58, 61, 66, 90, 97
Barboursville 51, 78, 118, 122
Barkley, Sam 25, 28, 30
Barlow, Fred 54
Barna, Herbert "Babe" 72, 166
Barnes, Calvin 160
Barrett, Clarence 86, 87
Barringer, Lon H. 80–81, 116
Barrone, Frank 70–71
Barrow, Ed 37–38, 44, 56
Bary, Quinto 159
Baseball Hall of Fame 46–47, 74, 76, 90, 95, 100, 105, 137, 169, 175, 178, 184
Bastien, Dennis 190–195, 198, 200
Bastien, Lisa 191
Batelle, William G. 8
Bateman, John L. 91

Batsch, Bill 70
Bauer, Rick 201
Baumgardner, George 78, 80, 85
Bayliss, Don 139
Baylor, Don 181–182, 184–185, 200
Bearsville, WV 74
Beasley, Lew 181
Beaver, WV 114, 116
Beckley, WV 109, 116–117, 119, 121, 130–137, 144, 148–149, 159, 169, 178
Beckley (Junior) College 136, 144, 145
Beckley Register 116, 119
Beers, Biddy 85, 89
Beggs, Joe 161, 164
Behrman, Hank 166
Belanger, Mark 178, 182, 200
Belington, WV 170
Bell, Eric 201
Bell, Frank 32
Benitez, Armondo 197
Berkeley Springs, WV 47
Bernard, Curt 65
Bero, Frank 89, 169
Berry, Joe 46
Berwind, WV 111, 113–115, 120
Bethany College 24, 26, 37, 42–43, 51, 68–71, 125, 171
Beverly, WV 41
Bickel, Bud 193–194, 198–199
Bickford, Vern 152, 155, 164
Binks, George 138
Birmingham Black Barons 121

Index

Bishop, WV 113, 115, 120, 169
Black, Dave 98–99, 102–103
Blake, John Frederick "Sheriff" 70–71, 195–106, 119–122, 170
Blakely, John W. 111, 116, 142
Blakely Field 116, 159, 168
Blatnick, John 138–139
Blennerhassett Base Ball Club 10, 28
Blottman, W.B. 81
Blue, Lu 94
Blue Ridge League 87, 92–107, 130
Blue Ridge League (semi-pro) 110–111, 118–120
Bluefield, WV 1, 52, 81, 85, 156–158
Bluefield Blue-Grays 109–114, 122, 141–154, 159–165, 167
Bluefield Daily Telegram 110
Bluefield Orioles 175–179, 181–189, 191–192, 196–202
Boddiker, Mike 186
Bolling, Milt 175
Bond, John C. 77, 80
Booe, Everitt 82
Boone, Danny 133
Booth, Washington I. 125
Borgman, Benny 136
Bousky, Ernest 165
Bowen, Harry 150
Bowen Field 150–151, 160, 167, 174, 176, 181, 184, 192, 196
Bowens, Sam 176
Bowles, Charles 144
Bowman, Billy 34, 36
Bowman, Bob 118, 145, 160, 162
Boyce, Bob 186
Boyd, Bob 166
Boyd, Jack 47, 90
Bradford, Gibson 127
Brainard, Asa 16, 18
Bramham, William G. 158–159
Bramwell, WV 81, 110–111, 113–114, 116, 118, 122, 143
Brandy, Bob 155
Breheney, Joe 99
Brett, George 46–47, 178
Bridgeport, WV 41, 53
Bridges, Tommy 128
Briggs, J.H. 9
Brillheart, Jim 120
Brinegar, Earl 147
Brittain, Gus 136

Brodie, Walter Scott "Steve" 33, 36
Brophy, Joe 98
Broskie, Sig 138, 145
Brown, Dick 169, 178
Brown, Larry 178
Brownlee, M.R. 9
Brumfield, George 199
Brush, John T. 50
Buckenberger, Al 33, 37–38
Buckhannon, WV 41, 63, 67, 58
Bull Durham 157, 182, 190, 194
Bumgardner, J. Lewis 136, 144, 149
Bunning, Jim 175
Burdette, Lew 169, 175
Burke, Frank 103–104
Burkett, Jesse 29, 37, 46–47
Bustamante, Rafael 196
Butcher, Max 120
Byers, Chuck 139
Byrne, Tommy 166

Cabell, Enos 182
Cacek, Craig 186
Cafego, Tom 120
Cain, Emmett A. 118
Cain, T.B. 125
Calbert, Ernie 85
Caldwell, Robert I. 149, 154
Callahan, Damon 198
Calvert, Bill 171
Cambria, Joe 130–132
Camden, WV 159
Campos, Frank 166
Candeleria, John 183
Cannon, J.J. 186
Capri, Pat 151
Carlisle, Ralph 64–65
Carlyle, Buddy 200
Carpenter, Paul 87
Carr, Chuck 188
Carr, Joe 83, 86–87, 141, 144, 158
Carr, Louis 63
Carr, Ray 165
Carter, Arnold 120, 169
Carvajal, Johnny 197
Cedro, WV 77, 81, 118
Central League 55–56, 75–76, 82, 87–88, 161–163, 165
Cerone, Rick 186
Chambers, Bill 66
Chance, Bob 179
Chance, Dean 176, 201
Charles Town, WV 10–12
Charleston, WV 1, 13, 23, 47, 52, 73, 76–89, 116–117

Charleston Alley Cats 200–202
Charleston Charlies 182–189
Charleston Gazette 84, 165
Charleston Industrial League 169, 175
Charleston Marlins 177–178
Charleston Senators 130–139, 144, 156–157, 161–171, 173–177, 179
Charleston Wheelers 190–196, 198, 200
Charleton, Oscar 121
Charley, Tandy 187
Chavez, Eric 197
Chiozza, Lou 133
Christie, Gary 192
Cincinnati Red Stockings 16, 17–18
Cirtsville, WV 114, 116
city leagues 46, 65, 67–68, 71–72, 77, 83, 89, 117, 169
Clark, Harley 133
Clark, Mel 169
Clarke, Alan 93–94
Clarksburg, WV 13, 27, 41, 52–53, 57–72, 124–130, 133, 135, 137, 159, 166
Clarksburg Telegram 62, 134
Clemans, W.M. 49
Clinton, Lu 167
Coalfield Association 116
Coalfield League 113
Coalwood, WV 111, 113, 115–116, 120
Cochran, Howard 80
Cogwelll, Charles 55
Colley, Frank 94, 99
Congalton, Bill 48
Conner, Decombra 197–198
Conoway, Bobby 64
Consolidation Coal Company 52, 58, 71, 109
Cook, Earl 136
Cooper, Nelson 160
Cooper, Wilber 74–75
Coppinger, Allen 184
Corbin, David 109
Corbin, Leon 182
Corey, Mark 184–185, 201
Cota, Humberto 202
Cousins, Art 127–128
Coyle, Burt 45
Coyle, W. Claude 45
Crab Orchard, WV 114
Craddock, Walt 178
Craddox, Walt 169
Cramer, Roger "Doc" 105
Cranberry, WV 114, 116
Crawford, C.D. 136
Crawford, Carl 202

Index

Crogan, John 32, 33
Cronin, Joe 126
Crosswhite, Jack 164–165, 168
Cuban Giants 33
Cullop, Henry "Nick" 118
Culver, George 179
Cumberland Valley League 47, 90
Currance, Stubby 154
Curry, Tony 179
Curtis, Gene 51, 55
Curtis, Pete 102

Dailey, Elmer 68, 70, 124–125, 130–132, 134, 137–139
Daniels, Doff D. 116–117, 130, 136
Danley, Earl 67–68
Dasher, Lee 79
Daubert, Harry 85, 87
Davis, Storm 186, 201
Davis and Elkins College 188
Dawson, Daniel Boone 138
Dawson, Fred 63–65
Dawson, John 63–64
Day, Worthington 152
Dean, Wayland 103, 117
Dearmond, John 86
DeCinces, Doug 182
Dehue, WV 117
Delahanty, Edward "Big Ed" 33, 35
Delaplaine, Louis S. 44–45
Dellucci, Dave 200
Delsing, Jim 175
Derringer, Paul 113, 116
DeVault, Chauncey 168
Devlin, Jim 26
Dickey, Bill 134
Dickey, George 134
Diehal, George 138
Dieters, Charles 55
Dilone, Miguel 183
Dixon, Tom 186
Doak, Bill 82
Dobbs, John 48
Doerr, Joe 181
Dolic, Lewis 162
Dolin, Nate 179
Doljack, Frank 128–129
Donald, Atley 135
Donnelley, Brendon 199
Donovan, Tom 174
Donovan, Willard 138
Doringer, Fred L. "Joe" 126, 131
Dorish, Dave 199
Douglas, Phil 113
Dresher, George 127

Duckworth, Jim 174
Dumright, Keith 186
Dunn, George 29, 32, 34
Dunn, Jack 97
Durham, A.L. 82
Dyer, Eddie 135

East Bank, WV 169, 171
East Gulf, WV 115
Easter, Luke 167
Eastern League 179
Eastern Panhandle 10–13, 21
Eccles, WV 116, 117, 120, 122
Edler, Shera 118
Edwards, Doc 178, 178
Edwards, Hank 138
Edwards, Wayne 178
Eight Men Out 190
Elkhorn, WV 111–112, 118
Elkins, Roy 117, 149, 154
Elkins, WV 67
Elliott, Charles 158
Elliott, Edwin 184
Emerson, Scott 197
English, W.T. 28–29, 35
Enterprise, WV 53, 63
Essler, Elmer 62
Etchebarren, Andy 200
Etchison, Clarence "Buck" 152
Evans, Angus 121
Evans, Louis "Steve" 61
Evans, Russell 136
Ewing, James M., Jr. 8

Fairmont, WV 13, 14–17, 27, 41, 52–53, 57–72, 109, 124–135, 137, 159, 171–172
Fairmont (Normal) State College 69, 125, 180
Fairmont Times 52, 60
Fannin, Cliff 155
Fanning, George 175, 184, 186, 191, 196–197, 200
Fantuzzi, Al 174
Farmington, WV 14, 17
Farnsworth, L.E. 118
Farrell, Red 101
Fatsis, Stefan 1
Fayette, WV 114
Fayetteville, WV 141
Ferry, Cy 127
Field of Dreams 190
Fireco, WV 114, 116
Fishbaugh, Harry 103
Fisher, Clarence 86
Fisher, Johnny 75
Fisher, Wilber 71
Flanagan, Pat 148
Flanagan, Ray 169

Fleming, Arch 52
Fleming, Aretus Brooke 14
Fleming, Brooks 126, 128
Fleming, Ralph 52
Flemington, WV 180
Flores, Gilberto 182
Follansbee, WV 67–68, 89
Fornieles, Miguel 166
Fowler, Dick 166
Fox, Ervin "Pete" 129
Fox, Fred 110
Frakenberry, Archie 62
Francis, Earl 169, 178
Frank, Harry 97
Franklin, Murray 145, 146, 147
Freese, Gene 171, 178
Freese, George 169–170
Frey, Dan 197
Fridley, Jim 169–170
Friel, Bill 75
Frontier League 198–199
Fussell, Chris 200

Gainer, Del 65–66
Gallagher, William 26
Galvin, George "Pud" 27
Ganung, Bob 164
Garber, Gene 183
Garcia, Kiko 182
Gardella, Al 145, 147
Gardella, Danny 147
Garner, Marvin 145
Gary, WV 52, 81, 86, 111–116, 120, 141, 169
Gates, Henry Louis 157
Gay, Harry S., Jr. 143
Gay, WV 110
Gaynor, Wells 154
George, Bill 29, 30, 35
Gerken, Steve 169
Gibralter, Steve 196
Gillenwater, Claude 127
Giron, Emiliano 198
Glasscock, Jack 18, 25, 27, 30, 38, 56, 66
Glen Dale, WV 178
Glen Falls, WV 63
Glen Jean, WV 81
Glen Morgan, WV 116
Glen Morrison, WV 114
Glen Rogers, WV 114, 120
Glen White, WV 114, 116, 119–122
Glenalvin, Bob 35, 36
Glenn, Eddie 48
Glenville State College 69, 171
Goldsberry, Gordon 166
Gomez, Jose 136
Gooden, Dwight 187

Index

Goodwin, Marvin 93
Gorsica (Gorczyca), John 120–121, 147
Gotay, Julio 177
Grafton, WV 13, 41, 54, 57–59, 61, 63–65, 127, 169
Gray, Carl 84
Gray, Sam 151
Great Depression 106–107, 118, 120, 129–134, 136, 138
Green, Bill 160
Gregory, Ben 160
Grey, Zane 37–38
Gribben, John 65
Grich, Bobby 181, 183
Griffith, Harry 105
Grimmest, Mark 188
Grimsley, Ross 166, 175
Grissom, Lee 136
Gronninger, James 63, 65
Grove, Robert "Lefty" 90, 96–97, 101, 103–104, 106
Guard, Raymond "Lefty" 192–194
Guinter, Edison 153, 164
Gumbert, Ab 42
Guth, Charles 180
Guy, Dick 124, 126–127, 135
Gwathmey, Bill 127–128
Gypsy, WV 53, 63

Haas, Bob 138
Habyan, John 201
Hagan, Deacon 25, 27
Hager, W.L. 77
Hague, Joe 178
Hague, Lucis 63
Haley, Fred 30
Hall, Ed 138
Hall, Mike 172
Hall of Fame *see* National Baseball Hall of Fame
Hamilton, E.S. "Lefty" 143, 149, 154
Hamilton, Josh 202
Hamric, Bert 169, 178
Hardman, A.L. 173, 178, 182
Hargen, Steve 179
Hariston, Sam 166
Harpers Ferry, WV 6, 10, 12
Harrick, Steve 170, 180
Harrington, William 63
Harris, A.N. 114
Harris, Eli 145, 149
Hart, John 187
Hartman, Bob 155
Harville, L.E. 154
Hassett, Buddy 134–135
Hastings, Charlie 48
Hatcher, Harry 149, 152

Haught, Elmer "Doggy" 61, 64
Hawley, Fred 110
Haymond, Thomas S. 59–69
Heep, Ed 160
Heise, Jim 170
Helen, WV 114
Helmick, William "Chick" 127–128
Hemphill, WV 120
Hemsley, Rollie 166
Henlawson, WV 117
Hennen, John 109
Henry, Hebar H. 80
Hernandez, Jacinto 179
Hershey, Robert 147
Hewitt, Charles "Jake" 42–43, 46
Hickey, Nat 147
Hickleville, WV 41
Hickman, Charles 43, 70
Hicks, Clarence "Buddy" 175
Highland, Virgil 125, 133
Higley, T.M. 118
Hinton, John 65
Hinton, WV 81
Hitchcock, Jimmy 134–135
Hoblitzel, Dick 62, 64, 66, 75, 131
Hock, Eddie 146, 147, 153, 164
Hodgin, Ralph 137
Hoffman, Trevor 196
Holden, WV 110, 114–115, 117, 120–121
Holland, Howard 127–128
Holland, Jim 197, 201
Holler, Brian 179
Holliday, Hugh 138
Holloway, Charles 129, 132
Holstein, Vernon 188
Homestead Grays 115, 120, 131, 167
Hook, Ed 186
Hopkins, Tom 132
Horkheimer, Meyer B. 34
Hornbrook, Jacob E. 5, 8, 9, 19
Hot Coal, WV 114
Hot Springs, WV 81
House of David 131, 148
Howe, Art 183
Howell, C.P. 104
Howell, David, Jr. 10
Howell, Millard 145
Howell, W.B. 34, 35, 48
Hubbard, C.R. 8, 9
Hulbert, William 25
Huling, Tom 62

Hulvey, Dwight 101
Hulvey, Hank 99
Hundred, WV 72
Hunkidori Base Ball Club 5, 8–10, 19
Hunnicutt Field 192
Hunt, Lou 64, 66–67
Huntington, WV 1, 13, 47–48, 52, 73, 76–89, 113, 116–118, 120, 122, 158–159, 169–170
Huntington Advertiser 41, 51, 75, 85, 87
Huntington Boosters (MSL) 130–138, 143–155
Huntington Cubs 193–194, 197–199
Hurricane, WV 169, 178
Hutson, Herbert 182
Hutton, Harry 137

Iaeger, WV 113, 118
International League 177–179, 182–187
Interstate League 37, 43, 45, 48–50, 82–83
Iron and Oil League 37, 43–44
Irwin, Clarence 8, 9
Irwin, William W. "Will" 36, 44, 50, 54, 75
Isom, Johnny 200

Jackey, Waldo 64, 66
Jacks, Phil C. 86
Jackson, Buck 61
Jackson, Rob 199
Jefferson Base Ball Club 10, 11
Jennings, Kelsey 117
Jeran, Joe 180
Jeter, John 183
John, Tommy 179
Johnson, Ban 50
Johnson, Larry 181
Johnson, Paul 164–165
Jones, Al 105
Jones, Carl A. 158
Jones, Dick 176
Jordan, Ed 182
June, Kester 71
Junkins, Joe 24, 27

Kaat, Jim 177
Kain, Frank 55
Kanawha City, WV 86, 178
Kanawha Park 161
Kanawha Valley League 169, 178
Karpenski, John 160
Kavanagh, Jack 34

Index

Keaton, Virgil 122
Keliher, Mickey 103
Keller, Orlando 66
Kelly, Dick 162
Kemmerer, Russ 171
Kenis, Joe 145
Kenna, Ed 50–51, 77, 81
Kennedy, Bill "Brickyard" 34, 36, 54–56
Kennedy, Joe 202
Kenova, WV 77, 118
Kermit, WV 114
Kerzit, John 122
Keystone, WV 113
Kimball, WV 113
Kimber, Sam 32
King, Chester 65
King, Lee 72
Kingsale, Eugene 200
Kirk, H.L. 87
Kison, Bruce 183
Klieman, Ed 138
Knauff, Benny 79
Knauss, Frank 33, 36
Knight, Frank A. 165
Knight, Jack 139
Knode, Kenneth "Mike" 91, 94
Kobritz, Jordan 187–188
Kohler, Vernon 147
Kolloway, Don 166
Koppers Coal Company 114, 119
Kovalich, George 180
Kozar, Al 166
Krajnik, Ed 148
Kume, John 169, 178
Kuzava, Bob 139
Kvadis, Tony 151
Kyle, WV 120–121

Lacy, George 159
Lake, Steve 200
LaMaster, Wayne 133, 135
Lambert, Walter 91
Landis, Judge Kenesaw M. 113
Landrith, Hobie 161
Lane, George "Cappy" 26, 27, 30
Langford, Rick 183
Larson, Dan 186
LaRue, Jason 200
LaRue, Judge J.R. 49
LaRussa, Tony 183
Lau, Charlie 175
Lawson, Alex "Al" 60
Layne, Herman 112
League of American Wheelmen (LAW) 36
Leetown, WV 101

Lemasters, Greg 199
Lester, WV 114, 116
Lett, Jim 196
Levine, Bob 182
Levine, Charles 182
Lewis, Grover 120–121
Lillybrook, WV 114, 116, 122
Lindberg, William S. "Gus" 143, 154
Linsly Institute 27
Lira, James 202
List, Harry 16, 17
Little League 157, 170–172, 178
Litton, Scott 174
Litwhiler, Danny 138
Livingstone, Pat 55
Locke, Frank 77
Logan County League 169
Logan, WV 110, 114, 117–118, 141–155, 157–159
Long, Henry 94
Long Civic Park 152, 154
Long Gone 190
Lopinski, Sam 176–177
Lorado, WV 117
Lost Creek, WV 53, 63
Lott, Brian 198
Louden, Bill 61, 95–97
Loup Creek, WV 114
Lower, Johnny 62–64
Lucas, Fred 101–102
Luciano, Joe 105
Lukins, A. 9
Lukins, Harry 25
Lukins, W. 9
Lumberport, WV 53, 63
Lyle, Sparky 181
Lyons, Denny 48
Lytle, Edward "Pop" 36, 48–49

Mabscott, WV 114, 116
MacDonald, William 177
Macha, Ken 183
Mack, Connie 100–101, 106, 145
Mack, Earle 100–102, 104–106
Mack, Joseph "Reddy" 61, 64, 79
MacLaine, Phil 188
Mahaffey, Lou 48
Mahoney, Jim 165
Maitland, William 98
Malgradi, Ray 182
Malichy, George 105
Mamaux, Albert 84–85
Man, WV 110
Mann, Derk 202
Mann, Earl 134

Mannington, WV 14, 17, 41, 54, 58–59, 62–68
Manno, Don 155
Manrique, Marco 197
Manuel, Charley 178
Mapes, Cliff 166
Maples, James G. 104–105
Marcus, Sigmund 48
Marietta College 28
Marion, Marty 137
Marks, Jack 125, 133
Marmet, WV 178
Marovic, Bill 180
Marshall (College) University 42, 51–52, 69, 77, 88, 98, 116, 144, 198–199
Martin, Earl "Red" 121, 145, 146, 147, 164
Martin, Tom 201
Martin, William M. 149
Martinez, Eddy 200
Martinsburg, WV 10–12, 41, 47, 90–107, 174
Martinsburg Journal 95, 104
Martinsburg World 91
Martynick, Mike 136–137
Mason City, WV 52
Mastrolonardo, Dave 201
Matewan, WV 114
Matos, Luis 201
Maxville, Dal 177
Maybeury, WV 111
Maynard, Beverly 118
Mazeroski, Bill 46–47, 169, 178
McAlpin, WV 114
McBride, Ken 165
McCarver, Tim 177
McClosky, Barney 137
McClure, Larry 70, 78–79
McCluskey, Virgil 49
McComas, WV 110, 122
McCombs, Billy 55, 67
McCord, Hugh 8, 9
McCormick, Frank 135–136
McDermith, W.H. 33
McGehee, Stuart 111
McGinty, James 65
McGonagle, George 200
McGowan, Bill 95
McGraner, Howard 79
McGraw, Gene 122
McGraw, John 122
McGraw, John J. 113
McGraw, John T. 64
McGraw, Willard 122
McGuire, J.W. 9
McIntire, Bob 103–104
McJunkin, R.K. 9
McKechnie, Bill 75, 82
McMillan, Charlie 112, 119

Index

McNichol, D.E. 125
McNichol, Ed 46
M'Conahay, G.G. 9
McQuade, Neddy 119
McQuinn, George 129
Mead, WV 114
Meadowbrook, WV 53
Means, Alfred 159
Meers, Russ 151
Mejia, Miguel 200
Melvin, Thayer 49
Memphis Red Sox 27
Menendez, Tony 175
Mercer, Win 46
Merrill, WV 117
Merrills, William O. 125
Merriman, Dave 188–189
Meyer, Henry 36
Middle Atlantic League 117, 124–139, 143, 144, 145, 161
Midkiff, Ezra 86, 149
Millek, Ed 104
Miller, Joe 28, 30, 63
Miller, Walt 55
Milliken, Bob 169
Milner, Holt "Cat" 117, 132–133
Mincher, Don 177
Minor, Ryan 201
Mitchell, E.C. 30
Mitchell, T.J. 9, 16, 17
Mlinsarik, Steve 138
M'Nulty, W.A. 9
Moffat, Joe 25, 28, 30
Moffat, Sam 25, 28, 30
Moffatt, James 9
Molina, Gabe 202
Momboquette, Bill 167
Monaville, WV 117
Monitor, WV 110, 114
Monongah, WV 53, 63, 67
Montana Mines, WV 54
Montezuma Park 150–151
Montgomery, WV 52, 73, 77–81, 84
Montrose, WV 65
Moore, Homer 159
Moore, Whitey 136
Moose, Bob 184
Moreland, George L. 37
Moreno, Omar 183
Morgan, Dick 165
Morgan, Joe 183
Morganette, WV 153
Morgantown, WV 13, 14–17, 27–28, 41, 57–58, 61, 169, 171
Morgantown Rough and Ready Club 28
Morison, Guy 112
Morris, Corey 199

Morris, Jim 138
Morris, Peter 1, 6
Morris, William "Country" 91–92, 94–96
Morris-Harvey College 51, 69, 156, 171
Morrisey, Jo-Jo 128
Morrison, Sam 32, 36
Moundsville, WV 89
Mt. Hope, WV 141
Mountain State(s) League 80–81, 116, 121, 140–155, 157–158, 162–163, 170, 193
Mounts, Terrance 153
Mullens, WV 114, 122, 141, 200
Murray, Eddie 184–185
Murtaugh, Danny 167
Musial, Stan 147–148, 151

National Association of Baseball Players (NABBP) 9, 12
National Baseball Hall of Fame 33, 35, 46–47, 74–76, 90, 95, 100, 105, 136, 147–148, 175, 178, 184
National League 21, 25, 35
The Natural 190
Nazel, Dutch 80
Neale, Earle 70, 74, 88, 127, 129
Neberger, Dick 110
Neccici, Ron 164
Needles, A.C. 52
Neiman, Bob 161
Nelson, Jim 199
Neun, Johnny 97–98
New River, WV 115, 120
Nichol, Sammy 29, 32, 33, 36
Nicholson, Frank 78, 80, 85
Nicholson, T.C. "Parson" 29, 36
Niekro, Joe 180–181
Niekro, Phil 180
night baseball 129, 132, 143, 146, 150, 191
Nitro, WV 169, 175
Nolan, Edward "The Only" 27
Nolley, Rufe 75
Nordscik, Charles 118
Norfolk and Western RR 63, 80, 108, 114, 120, 141, 143, 149–150, 158
Norman, Carl 171
Norris, Tim 186
Northfork, WV 111–113
Northwestern League 30
Nuxhall, Joe 161–162

Oak Hill, WV 116, 141, 144
Oates, Johnny 181
Obojski, Robert 124
Obradovich, Jim 186
Oceana, WV 114
Ohio-Pennsylvania League 67–68
Ohio State League 30, 32, 47, 82–88, 116–117
Ohio Valley League 47, 77, 118
Ohio Valley Redcoats 199
Ohio-West Virginia League 47
Okrie, Len 165
Old Dominion Base Ball Club 10
Olympic Base Ball Club 10, 19
Omar, WV 114, 117, 169
Ordaz, Luis 197
Orr, S.C. 9
Osborne, Fred 35, 36
Osborne, Larry "Bobo" 175
Otley, W.L. 81, 109
O'Toole, Edward 111, 113
Otterson, Billy 33, 36
Outlaw, Jimmy 136
Ozmer, Horace 10

Padden, Dick 87–88
Palazzini, Julio 162
Palica, Erv 138
Parker, Dave 183
Parkersburg, WV 6, 10, 19, 28, 48–49, 53, 65, 73, 77–79, 116–117, 130–131, 159, 170, 199
Parsons, Jason 200
Partin, Jim 164
Paterno, Mike 198, 200
Patten, N.N. 9
Patterson, John 151
Pax, WV 114
Peach Creek, WV 114
Pelosi, Guido 162
Pennell, Lawrence "Bud" 160
Pennington, Joe 152–153
Pennsboro, WV 53
Pennsylvania–Ohio–Maryland League 60–61, 124
Pennsylvania State League 125
Pennsylvania-West Virginia League 63
Pennywitt, Roy R. 83–85
Percy, Les 94
Perez, Nestor 202
Perini, Louis R. 160

Index

Perkins, B.F. 50, 54, 75, 83, 88
Perkins, Cecil 180
Perkowski, Harry 169
Peters, Ernest 151–152
Peterson, Bob 155
Phelps, Gordon "Babe" 130
Phillips, Bill 75–76, 82
Phillips, Joe 65, 127
Phoebus, Tom 176
Pickering, Calvin 201
Piedmont, WV 53, 60–62, 95–96, 157
Pierce, WV 169
Pineville, WV 114
Pioneer Field 199
Pittsburgh Browns 28
Pittsburgh Crawfords 121, 131
Pittsburgh Keystones 32
Players League 35
Plays, Stan 175
Pocahontas, WV 110, 113, 122
Poffenberger, Cletus 137
Point Pleasant, WV 73, 77–80
Pollard, Hugh 136
Ponson, Sidney 200
Pool, J.W. 87
Poole, Ed 48–49
Pope, Jim "Skip" 160
Popovich, Paul 180
Pose, Scott 196
Pottenger, Bob 160
Pottiti, Ed 193–194
Potts, Harry 152–153
Powell, John "Boog" 176, 181, 184–185
Powell, Mike 151
Powell, Walter "Watt" 96–87, 116–117, 130–131, 133, 138–139, 144, 150, 161
Powers, Charles B. 38, 43, 60
Powhatan, WV 111, 113
Prantil, Ray 180
Price, Edison "Ted" 55–56
Price, Ray 113
Price Hill, WV 114, 116, 120
Prichard, Bill 127–128
Prince, Ray 81, 85
Princeton, WV 1, 85, 110, 122, 192–193, 197–198, 202–203
Proctor, Dick "Red" 129–130
Prysock, Bob 67, 127
Pugh, Tim 196
Puhl, Terry 186
Puleo, Charlie 200

Quellich, George 101–102

Radosevich, John 180
Rainelle, WV 169
Raines, Larry 169, 178
Rainey, Dan 118
Raleigh, WV 109, 115–116, 120
Raleigh Coal and Coke Company 109
Raleigh County League 116–117, 119–121, 169–170, 178
Ramsberg, Dale 188
Randell, M.D. 14
Randolph, Jennings 134
Randolph, Willie 183
Raney, Bob 155
Rapp, Vern 167
Rawlings, George "Reg" 93, 95, 97–107, 179
Red Jacket, WV 114
Reed, D.J. 125
Reeder, Charles "Biggie" 67–68
Reilly, Arch 71, 88
Resolute Base Ball Club 15
Reynolds, J. Frank 20
Riccelli, Frank 186
Rice, Del 153
Rice, Hal 153, 169
Rice, Henry "Pete" 120, 122
Richmond, WV 103
Rickey, Branch 137
Ridgley, Duke 41, 75
Riggs, Sam 199
Ripken, Billy 200
Ripken, Cal, Jr. 186, 200
Ripley, WV 170
Ritter, Lou 48
River City, Rumblers 198
Riverside, WV 54
Roberts, Howard 127–128
Roberts, Ross 97, 99
Robertson, Bill 55–56, 75
Robertson, Faye 193
Robinson, Aaron 166
Robinson, Dick 25
Robinson, Jeremy 202
Roddin, Joe 160
Rodgers, Ira 70–71
Rodgers, L.E. 159
Rolland, Eugene 125
Rooney, Art 126
Rooney, Dan 126
Roper, John 196
Rosar, Warren "Buddy" 135
Rosemont Park 91–92, 96, 99, 103–104, 106
Rosemont, WV 63
Russell, Dewey 197, 201

Ryan, Joe 158, 177
Ryan, Ray 83, 140–146, 148–150, 154, 157–159
Ryczek, William J. 6

Sackinsky, Brian 197
St. Albans, WV 52, 169
St. Cloud Commons 193
St. Martins, WV 89
St. Mary's, WV 20
salaries 17, 26–29, 33, 37, 43, 48, 50, 61–64, 75, 80–82, 84, 92–93, 95, 98, 144, 154, 159
Salem College 69–70, 134, 171
Samford, Ron 175
Sampson, Tommy 120
Sandberg, Jared 201
The Sandlot 190
Saverine, Bob 176
Scarbro, WV 77, 119–120
Scarein, Art 155
Schaufele, Ben 96
Schmitt, Fred 68
Schmitt, Otto 68
Schull, Angel 166
Schumacher, Ed 145
Schumulbach, Harry 37, 44
Scott, Everitt 66
Scott, Thomas C. 142
Scott, Thomas H. 158
Seaman, Walter 99
Searage, Ray 188
Seeley, Oscar 30, 35
Selak, Ron 186
Seminick, Andy 169
Sessi, Walt 145, 150
Shanklin, John 177
Shannon, Hugh 69
Shantz, Wilmer 175
Sharp, Harold 151–152
Sheehan, Jack 134
Sheets, Larry 186
Shelby, John 186, 200
Shelton, Andrew Kemper 78–80, 114
Shelton, Ron 182
Shepherd College 101, 180
Shepherdstown, WV 10–12, 47
Sherling, Ed 101–102
Shetzline, John 32
Shewey, Bill 150–151
Shifflett, Crandall 115
Shinnston, WV 63
Shipley, H. Burton 91–92, 98–99
Shirley, W.A. 49
Shoals, Leo "Muscle" 159–160, 168

Index

Shott, Hugh "Ike" 110
Shriver, Harry 70–72, 87–88
Shuford, George 179
Shuler, Floyd 180–181
Siebert, Sonny 179
Siebert, William 77, 81
Sims, Duke 179
Singleton, Raleigh 147
Sington, Fred 132
Sistersville, WV 47
Skopec, John 48
Slab Fork, WV 120–121
Slabrock, WV 115, 120
Slaughter, Cecil 97, 129
Slone, Sherley 147
Slutz, Hol 118
Smith, Arthur 95
Smith, Don 153
Smith, Earl 52
Smith, Ed 158
Smith, Elmer 67
Smith, Howard 151
Smith, John "Chick" 112
Smith, Lewis "Bull" 51, 62, 66–68
Snodgrass, Walt 61, 64
Solita, Tony 183
Solters, Julius 127
Sorrell, Vic 112, 147, 151–152
South Atlantic League 192–198
South Side Park 60, 63, 67, 70–71, 126, 131
Southern, Dennis 102–103
Spalding, Albert G. 20
Speidel, Joe "Puggy" 32
Spencer, WV 170
Spradin, Jerry 196
Sprague, WV 114, 116, 120
Staley, Harry 38
Standish, Burt L. 41
Stansfield, WV 114
Stansford, WV 116
Stanwood, Earl 103
Stathers, William E. 125
Staunton, F.M. 86
Steinbeck, Lawrence 145
Steinfeldt, Carl 183, 187
Stennett, Rennie 183
Stenzel, Jake 32, 36
Stephens, Bryan 138
Stephens, Tom 194
Stephenson, Garrett 197
Steve Blass Disease 184
Stevens, Randall 154
Stewarttown, WV 17
Stobbs, Chuck 169
Stoehr, Henry 49
Stonecoal, WV 114–115, 120
Stoner, George W. 125
Stonewall Base Ball Club 10
Stotesbury, WV 114, 121–122
Stout, Sheriff Ross 69
Stover, Dewey 128
street car companies 44, 49, 52–53, 58–59
Streza, John 150
Stuart, Johnny 116–117, 130, 137, 143
Sullivan, WV 114, 116
Summerless, WV 121
Sunday baseball 34, 48–49, 68–69, 88, 115

Taber, Jim 187
Talamanez, Greg 189
Tams, WV 114–115, 120–121
Tams, Walter P. 114
Taylor, Bill 175
Taylortown, WV 27
Tekulve, Kent 183
Terwilliger, Wayne 175
Thomas, Clarence 112
Thompson, Jim 192–193, 197
Thompson, Lewis H. 94, 96–98, 100, 105–106
Thoner, Thomas 30
Thurmond, WV 81
Tiant, Luis 179
Tierney, Lawrence 111
Tighe, Jack 138
Tipton, Joe 139
Tobin, Jim 135
Tomas, Billy 127
Toney, Sebert, Jr. 111
Toothman, Vic 67
Torreyson, Frank 45
Totten, S. Garson 120
traction companies *see* street car companies
Treble, Jimmy 188
Trenchard, T.G. 43
Tri-City League 91–93, 96, 118
Triner, Tim 155
Tri-State League 35, 116–118, 122, 130
Tudor, Lefty 122
Turner, W.W. 89

Ujcich, Frank 180–181
uniforms 10, 11, 14, 24, 33, 35
Union Park 53, 59, 62, 64–65, 67, 69, 71
United Base Ball Club 15, 17, 19
United Mine Workers League 120, 170, 178

Valdespino, Sandy 177
Valentine, Bobby 183
Van Sant, Jim 147
Van Zant, Dick 33, 36
Vennum, Frank 24, 26
Versalies, Zoilo 177
Victory HS 133
Vineyard, Dave 178
Virgil, Ozzie 175
Virginia Valley League 77–78
Vitelli, Joe 135
Voiselle, Bill 166
Volcano, WV 28
Voltz, William 30
Von Schlegel, Max 91–96

Wagner, Al 44–45
Wagner, Honus 44
Walker, Bernie 196
Walker, Gerald 128
Walker, Moses Fleetwood 29, 30
Walker, Troy 147
Walker, Weldy 29
Walling, Dennis 186
Walsh, Jim 131
War, WV 113
Ward, Joe 97
Warner, Jack 178
Washer, William "Buck" 51
Washington-Irving HS 133–34
Watson, James E. 126
Watson, John 144
Watt Powell Park 139, 161, 171, 175, 177, 191–192, 195
Wayne, WV 77, 199, 202
Weaver, Floyd 179
Webb, Earl 119–120
Weber, Karl 127
Weigel, Ralph 139
Weiss, George 134–135
Welch, Frank 131
Welch, WV 52, 81, 111, 113, 114, 116, 141–168
Welch, Frank J. 60, 63
Wellsburg, WV 47
Wentzel, Stan 152–153
Werber, Bill 117
West, Milton "Buck" 33, 36
West Liberty State College 69, 171, 180–181, 188
West Union, WV 53
West Virginia Intercollegiate Athletic Conference 156, 171, 180, 188
West Virginia League 65–67
West Virginia-Pennsylvania League 135

Index

West Virginia Secondary School Activities Commission 156, 188
West Virginia Sports Hall of Fame 180
West Virginia State (College) University 188
West Virginia Tech 170–171
West Virginia University 13, 37, 42–43, 50–55, 62, 69–71, 74, 129, 156, 166, 170–171, 176, 180, 188
West Virginia Wesleyan College 51, 69–71, 88, 116, 119, 125, 129–130
Western Association 50
Western Pennsylvania League 60
Westfall, Dick 171
Westlake, Bob 29
Westlake, George 29
Weston, WV 58–59
Wetzel, Henry "Buzz" 83, 85
Whally, F. 9
Wheaton, Elwood 160
Wheeling, WV 5–10, 15–17, 22–39, 41–56, 75–76, 82–89, 124–135, 137, 141, 159, 169
Wheeling Daily Intelligencer 44, 132
Wheeling Light Infantry 36
Wheeling Red Lions 36
Wheeling Register 7, 37
Wheeling Turnverein Society 21

Wherle, John 77
White, Ernie 160
White, Sol 29, 32
White, Will 37
White Sulphur Springs, WV 120
Whitehead, Frank 164
Whitman, WV 143
Whittaker, H.C. 88
Wickel, Harrison 150–151, 153
Wicker, Kemp 135
Wilkinson, Sam 26
Williams, Dave 180
Williams, Willie 160
Williamson, WV 73, 77, 81, 113–114, 116, 141–155, 157–159
Willis, Charles 101, 103
Wilson, Bert 149
Wilson, Bill "Doc" 62–63, 65–66
Wilson, Dan 196
Wilson, Gary 186
Wilson, Lewis "Hack" 46–47, 90, 98–100, 102–103, 105–107
Wilson, Tom 25, 35
Wilsonburg, WV 41, 53, 63
Winding Gulf, WV 114, 120
Windsor, Buck 37
Winkles, Bobby 167
Winters, Jesse 72
Withrow, Corky 178
Wood, Ken 155
Woodburn Base Ball Club 14

Wooding, Art 105
Woodling, Gene 138
Woodruff, Charles 48
Workman, Harry 112
Works Projects Administration 122, 142
World War I 69–71, 767, 88–89, 95–96, 108
World War II 138–139, 153–155, 159
Worthington, WV 53
Wright, Harry 16
Wright, Samuel J. 81 84
Wright, W.S. 44–45, 49

Xajac, Jack 160

Yaik, Henry 33, 36
Yankovich, Frank 139
YMCA 36–37, 46, 76, 89
Yost, Harry 43
Young, Benjamin 29
Young, Dick 166
Young, Houston G. 77
Young, Nick 50

Zambrano, Victor 201
Zamora, Oscar 186
Zeigler, Mark C. 99, 101
Zerby, Dan 179
Ziegler, George 36
Zikmund, Tom 159
Zinn, Guy 65
Zisk, Richie 183